CARL HONORÉ

THE SLOW FIX

SOLVE PROBLEMS, WORK SMARTER AND LIVE BETTER IN A FAST WORLD

Collins

First published in 2013 by Collins

An imprint of HarperCollins*Publishers*
77–85 Fulham Palace Road
London W6 8JB

www.harpercollins.co.uk

1 3 5 7 9 10 8 6 4 2

. Text © Carl Honoré 2013

l Honoré asserts his moral right to
be identified as the author of this work

A ...e record for this book is
available from the British Library

HB ISBN: 978-0-00-750372-8
TPB ISBN: 978-0-00-742959-2

Printed and bound in Great Britain by
Clays Ltd, St Ives plc

Some names in this book have been changed
to protect people's privacy.

MIX
Paper from
responsible sources
FSC
www.fsc.org   FSC C007454

FSC™ is a non-profit international organisation established to promote
the responsible management of the world's forests. Products carrying the
FSC label are independently certified to assure consumers that they come
from forests that are managed to meet the social, economic and
ecological needs of present and future generations,
and other controlled sources.

Find out more about HarperCollins and the environment at
www.harpercollins.co.uk/green

THE SLOW FIX

Contents

To Miranda, Benjamin and Susannah

You cannot solve a problem from the same consciousness that created it. You must learn to see the world anew.
Albert Einstein

Pulling the Andon Rope

How poor are they who have not patience!
What wound did ever heal but by degrees?
William Shakespeare

In a small, windowless room, in a busy clinic in south London, a familiar ritual is about to begin. Let's call it Man with Back Pain Visits Specialist.

You may recognise the scene: the white walls are bare apart from an anatomical poster and a few smudged fingerprints. Fluorescent light falls from a bulb overhead. A faint whiff of disinfectant hangs in the air. On a trolley beside the treatment table, acupuncture needles are spread out like the tools of a medieval torturer.

Today, I am the man seeking relief from back pain. Face down on the treatment table, peering through a foam ring wrapped in tissue paper, I can see the hem of a white lab coat swishing above the floor. It belongs to Dr Woo, the acupuncturist. Though nearing retirement, he still moves with the liquid grace of a gazelle. To the hobbled masses in his waiting room, he is a poster boy for the benefits of Traditional Chinese Medicine.

Dr Woo is planting a small forest of needles along my spine. Each time he punctures the skin, he lets out a muffled grunt of triumph. And each time the sensation is the same: a prickling heat followed by an oddly pleasant contraction of the muscle. I lie still, like a butterfly yielding to a Victorian collector.

After inserting the final needle, Dr Woo dims the lights and leaves me alone in the half-darkness. Through the thin walls I can hear him chatting with another patient, a young woman, about her back trouble. Later, he returns to pull out my needles. My spirits are already lifting as we walk back to Reception. The pain has eased and my body is moving more freely, but Dr Woo remains cautious.

'Do not get carried away,' he says. 'Backs are complicated and they need time to heal properly, so you must be patient.' I nod, looking away as I hand over my credit card, knowing what is coming next. 'You should do at least five more sessions,' he tells me.

My response is the same as last time, the same as always: make a follow-up appointment while secretly planning to dodge it.

Two days later and, true to form, my back has improved enough that I cancel my return visit, feeling slightly smug about the time, hassle and money this will save. Who needs multiple rounds of acupuncture, anyway? One hit and I'm back in the game.

Or am I? Three months later I'm back on Dr Woo's treatment table and this time the pain is snaking down into my legs. Even lying in bed hurts.

Now it is Dr Woo's turn to be smug. While laying out his needles, he tells me that impatience is the enemy of good medicine, and then he gets personal. 'Someone like you will never get better,' he says, more in sorrow than in anger. 'Because you are a man who wants to fix his back quickly.'

Ouch.

Talk about a diagnosis that hits where it hurts. Not only am I guilty as charged – I have been in a hurry to fix my back for 20 years – but I really should know better. After all, I travel the world lecturing on how wonderful it is to slow down, take time, do things as well, rather than as fast, as possible. I have even sung the praises of slowness at medical conferences. But though my life has been transformed by deceleration, the virus of hurry still clearly lurks in my bloodstream. With surgical precision, Dr Woo has skewered an inconvenient truth that I have ducked for years: When it comes to healing my back, I remain addicted to the quick fix.

My medical history reads like a whistle-stop tour. Over the last two decades my back has been twisted, cracked and stretched by a procession of physiotherapists, masseurs, osteopaths and chiropractors. Aromatherapists have rubbed birch, blue chamomile and black pepper oils into my lower lumbar region. Reflexologists have worked the back-related pressure points on the soles of my feet. I have worn a brace, guzzled painkillers and muscle relaxants, and spent a small fortune on ergonomic chairs, orthotic insoles and orthopedic mattresses. Hot stones, hot cupping, electric currents, heat pads and ice packs, crystals, Reiki, ultrasound, yoga, Alexander Technique, Pilates – yup, been there, done all of that. I have even visited a Brazilian witch doctor.

Yet nothing has worked. Sure, there have been moments of relief along the way, but after two decades on the treatment treadmill my back still aches – and it's getting worse.

Perhaps I just haven't found the right cure for me. After all, others have conquered back pain using techniques from my treatment plan, and even that Brazilian witch doctor came with glowing references. Or maybe, and this seems far more likely, Dr Woo is right. In other words, I treat every single cure for back pain as a quick fix, targeting the symptoms without addressing the root cause, revelling in its temporary relief, chafing when progress slows or demands more effort before moving on to the next treatment at the drop of a hat, like a chronic weight-watcher flitting from one diet to the next. The other day I spotted a web link peddling 'Magnet Therapy' as a panacea for back pain. My first thought was not: 'Snake oil, anyone?' It was: 'Can I get that in London?'

This book is not a back pain memoir. Nothing is more tedious than listening to other people drone on about their aches and ailments. What makes my losing battle with my lumbar region worth exploring is that it points up a much bigger problem affecting every one of us. Let's be honest: when it comes to chasing instant results, I am not alone. In every walk of life, from medicine and relationships to business and politics, we are all hooked on the quick fix.

Looking for shortcuts is nothing new. Two thousand years ago Plutarch denounced the army of quacks hawking miracle cures to the gullible citizens of Ancient Rome. At the end of the eighteenth century infertile couples queued up in hope of conceiving in London's legendary Celestial Bed. The amorous contraption promised soft music, a ceiling-mounted mirror and a mattress stuffed with 'sweet new wheat or oat straw, mingled with balm, rose leaves, and lavender flowers', as well as tail hairs from the finest English stallions. An electric current allegedly generated a magnetic field 'calculated to give the necessary degree of strength and exertion to the nerves'. The promise: instant conception. The cost for one night of fertile fumbling: £3,000 in modern money.

Today, though, the quick fix has become the standard across the board in our fast-forward, on-demand, just-add-water culture. Who has the time or patience for Aristotelian deliberation and the long view any more? Politicians need results before the next election, or the next press conference. The markets panic if wobbly businesses or wavering governments fail to serve up an instant action plan. Websites are studded with ads promising fast solutions to every problem known to Google: a herbal remedy to reboot your sex life; a video to perfect your golf swing; an app to find Mr Right. In the old days, social protest entailed stuffing envelopes, going on marches or attending meetings in town halls. Now many of us just click 'Like' or fire off a sympathetic tweet. All over the world, doctors are under pressure to heal patients in a hurry, which often means reaching for a pill, the quick fix *par excellence*. Feeling blue? Try Prozac. Struggling to concentrate? Join Team Ritalin. In the never-ending quest for instant relief the average Briton now pops, according to one estimate, 40,000 pills in a lifetime. I am certainly not the only impatient patient in Dr Woo's waiting room. 'The easiest way to make money today is not to heal people,' he says. 'It is to sell them the promise of instant healing.'

Indeed, spending money has become a quick fix in itself, with hitting the mall touted as the fastest way to lift sagging spirits. We joke about 'retail therapy' as we show off that new pair of Louboutins or the latest iPad case. The diet industry has turned the quick fix into an art form. 'A bikini body by next week!' the ads scream. 'Lose 10 pounds ... in ONLY 3 days!'

You can even buy a quick fix for your social life. If you need a workout partner at the gym, a best man for your wedding or a kindly uncle to cheer your children at sports day, or if you just want a shoulder to cry on, you can now hire any of the above from rent-a-friend agencies. The going rate for a pal to hang out with in London is £6.50 per hour.

Every quick fix whispers the same seductive promise of maximum return for minimum effort. Trouble is, that equation doesn't add up. Think about it for a moment: is worshipping at the altar of the quick fix making us happier, healthier and more productive? Is it helping to tackle the epic challenges confronting humanity at the start of the 21st century? Is there really an app for everything? Of course not. Trying to solve problems in a hurry, sticking on a plaster when surgery is needed, might deliver temporary reprieve – but usually at the price of storing up worse trouble for later. The hard, unpalatable truth is that the quick fix never truly fixes anything at all. And sometimes it just makes things worse.

The evidence is all around us. Even as we drop billions of pounds on diet products promising Hollywood thighs and *Men's Health* abs in time for summer, waistlines are ballooning all over the world. Why? Because there is no such thing as One Tip to a Flat Stomach. Academic studies show that most people who lose weight on diets regain it all, and often more, within five years. Even liposuction, the nuclear option in the slimming arms race, can backfire. Fat sucked from a woman's thighs and abdomen usually resurfaces within a year elsewhere on her body, as bingo wings, say, or shoulder flab.

Sometimes, the quick fix can be worse than no fix at all. Look at 'retail therapy'. Buying the latest Louis Vuitton bag may lift your mood, but the effect is usually transient. Before long you're back online or in the mall hunting for the next thrill – while unopened bills pile up like snowdrifts by the front door.

Look at the damage wrought by our penchant for pills. Surveys suggest that nearly two million Americans now abuse prescription drugs, with more than a million hospitalised every year by the side effects of medication. Overdosing on legal pills is now a leading cause of accidental death in the US, where the black market in hard-to-get medication has fuelled a sharp rise in armed robberies at pharmacies. Even neonatal units are reporting a spike in the number of babies born to mothers with painkiller addictions. And it's not a pretty sight: newborns suffering from withdrawal scream, spasm and vomit, rub their noses raw and struggle to eat and breathe.

You certainly cannot solve hard problems by just throwing money at them. To mend its ailing public schools, New York City began linking teacher pay to pupil performance in 2008. After forking out more than $55 million over three years, officials scrapped the programme because it was making no difference to test scores or teaching methods. It turns out that fixing a floundering school, as we will see later in the book, is a lot more complicated than just doling out cash bonuses.

Even in business, where speed is usually an advantage, our fondness for the quick fix is backfiring badly. When firms hit choppy waters, or come under pressure to goose the bottom line or jack up a sagging stock price, the knee-jerk response is often to downsize. But shedding staff in a hurry seldom pays off. It can hollow out a company, demoralise the remaining workforce and spook customers and suppliers. Often it leaves deeper problems untouched. After sifting through 30 years' worth of longitudinal and cross-sectional studies, Franco Gandolfi, a professor of management, came to a stark conclusion: 'The overall picture of the financial effects of downsizing is negative.'

The rise and fall of Toyota is a cautionary tale. The Japanese car-maker conquered the world by obsessively tackling problems at their source. When something went wrong on the assembly line, even the lowliest worker could pull a cord, known as the Andon rope, which would cause a buzzer to ring and a light bulb to flash overhead ('andon' means 'paper lantern' in Japanese). Like a toddler, staff would ask 'Why, why, why?' over and over again, until they reached the root cause of the problem. If it turned out to be serious, they might stop the entire production line. In every case, they would devise a permanent solution.

But everything changed when Toyota embarked on a headlong dash to become the number one car-maker in the world. Management overreached, lost control of the supply chain and ignored warnings from the factory floor. They started putting out fires without asking why those fires were breaking out in the first place.

Result: a recall of more than 10 million faulty vehicles that shredded the firm's reputation, wiped out billions of dollars in revenue and unleashed a barrage of lawsuits. In 2010 Akio Toyoda, the company's chastened president, explained to the US Congress how Toyota fell from grace: 'We pursued growth over the speed at which we were able to develop our people and our organisation.' Translation: we stopped pulling the Andon rope and fell for the quick fix.

You see the same folly in professional sports. When a team hits a slump, and the clamour for a turnaround reaches fever pitch in the stands and the media, owners reach for the oldest fix in the playbook: fire the coach and hire a new one. As the world has grown more impatient, the scramble for results on the field has turned more frantic. Since 1992 the average tenure of a manager in professional football in England has fallen from 3.5 years to 1.5 years. In the lower leagues six months to a year is now the norm. Yet turning management into a revolving door is a bad way to run a team. Academic research shows that most new managers deliver no more than a short honeymoon period of better results. After a dozen games the team's performance is usually the same, or worse, than it was before the regime change. Just like a weight-watcher piling the pounds back on after a crash diet.

You see the same mistakes in war and diplomacy. The US-led coalition failed to back up the shock-and-awe invasion of Iraq in 2003 with proper long-term plans for rebuilding the country. As Western troops amassed on the border,

Donald Rumsfeld, then the US Secretary of Defense, put a modern spin on the old chestnut that the soldiers would be 'home for Christmas'. The war in Iraq, he declared, 'could last six days, six weeks. I doubt six months.' What followed was years of chaos, carnage and insurgency, capped by an ignoble retreat from a job half done. In the salty argot of the US military, the brass ignored the golden rule of the seven Ps: Prior Planning and Preparation Prevents Piss-Poor Performance.

Even the technology industry, that great engine of speed, is learning that you cannot solve every problem by simply crunching more data and writing better algorithms. A team of IT specialists recently rode into the World Health Organisation headquarters in Geneva on a mission to eradicate tropical diseases such as malaria and Guinea worm. A culture clash ensued. The Tropical Diseases department is a million miles from the hip working spaces of Silicon Valley. Grey filing cabinets and in-trays piled high with folders line a dimly lit corridor. A yellow, hand-written note saying 'Hors Service' (out of order) is taped to the coin slot of the drinks machine. Sandal-wearing academic types work quietly in offices with tropical fans on the ceiling. It feels like the sociology department of an underfunded university, or a bureaucratic outpost in the developing world. Like many of the experts here, Pierre Boucher was stunned and amused by the can-do swagger of the IT interlopers. 'These tech guys arrived with their laptops and said, "Give us the data and the maps and we'll fix this for you," and I just thought, "Will you now?"' he says, with a wry smile. 'Tropical diseases are an immensely complex problem that you can never just solve on a keyboard.'

'Did the uber-nerds make any inroads?' I ask.

'No, nothing at all,' says Boucher. 'Eventually they left and we never heard from them again.'

Bill Gates, the high priest of high-speed problem-solving, has learned the same lesson. In 2005 he challenged the world's scientists to come up with solutions to the biggest problems in global health in double-quick time. The Bill and Melinda Gates Foundation awarded $458 million in grants to 45 of the more than 1,500 proposals that flooded in. There was giddy talk of creating, for instance, vaccines that needed no refrigeration within five years. But five years later the mood was sober. Even the most promising projects were still a long way from delivering real solutions. 'We were naïve when we began,' Gates conceded.

The bottom line here is clear: the quick fix is the wrong horse to back. *On its own*, no algorithm has ever solved a global health problem. No impulse buy has ever turned around a life. No drug has ever cured a chronic illness. No box of chocolates has ever mended a broken relationship. No educational DVD has ever transformed a child into a baby Einstein. No TED Talk has ever changed the world. No drone strike has ever killed off a terrorist group. It's always more complicated than that.

Everywhere you look – health, politics, education, relationships, business, diplomacy, finance, the environment – the problems we face are more complex and more pressing than ever before. Piss-poor performance is no longer an option. The time has come to resist the siren call of half-baked solutions and short-term palliatives and start fixing things properly. We need to find a new and better way to tackle every kind of problem. We need to learn the art of the Slow Fix. Now is the moment to define our terms. Not all problems are created equal. Some can be fixed with a quick and simple solution. Inserting a single line of code can stop a misfiring webpage from inflicting mayhem on a company. When someone is choking on a morsel of food, the Heimlich manoeuvre can dislodge the offending object from the windpipe and save the victim's life. My focus in this book is on a very different kind of problem, where the parameters are unclear and shifting, where human behaviour comes into play, where there may not even be a *right* answer. Think climate change, the obesity epidemic, or a company grown too big for its own good.

When dealing with such problems, the quick fix addresses the symptoms rather than the root cause. It puts short-term relief before long-term cure. It makes no provision for unwelcome side effects. Every culture has a tradition of skin-deep fixes. The French call it a 'solution de fortune'. The Argentines 'tie it all up with wire'. In English we talk of 'band-aid cures' and 'duct-tape solutions'. The Finns joke about mending a puncture with chewing-gum. The Hindi word 'jugaad' means solving problems – from building cars to repairing water pumps – by throwing together whatever scraps are to hand. My favourite metaphor for the folly of the quick fix is the Korean expression 'peeing on a frozen leg': warm urine delivers instant relief, followed by worse misery as the liquid freezes solid on the skin.

So what is the Slow Fix? That is the question we will answer in the coming pages. But already it seems clear that it rests on a virtue that is in short supply nowadays: patience.

Sam Micklus knows that better than most. He is the founder of Odyssey of the Mind, the closest thing we have to an Olympics of problem-solving. Every year, pupils in 5,000 schools around the world set out to tackle one of six problems set by Micklus himself. They might have to build a weight-bearing structure from balsa wood, stage a play where a food defends itself in a mock court from charges of being unhealthy, or depict the discovery of archaeological treasures from the past and the future. Teams square off in regional and then national competitions to win a place at the annual World Finals. NASA is the chief sponsor of Odyssey of the Mind, and sends staff along to scout for talent.

I catch up with Micklus at the 2010 World Finals in East Lansing, Michigan. A retired professor of industrial design from New Jersey, he now lives in Florida, and looks every inch the American pensioner, with his comfortable shoes, silver hair and light tan. At the World Finals, however, surrounded by the hubbub of children pulling on costumes and fine-tuning their presentations for the judges, he is buzzing like a kid on Christmas morning. Everyone refers to him fondly as Dr Sam.

During 30 years at the helm of Odyssey of the Mind, Micklus has watched the cult of the quick fix tighten its grip on popular culture. 'The real trouble nowadays is that no one wants to wait for anything any more,' he says. 'When I ask people to think about a problem even for just a minute or two, they are already looking at their watches after ten seconds.'

He takes a sip of water from a plastic bottle and looks around the enormous gymnasium where we are chatting. It feels like backstage at a West End musical, with children scurrying to and fro, bellowing instructions, assembling stage props and testing surprisingly elaborate floats. Micklus's eyes come to rest on a clutch of 11-year-old girls struggling to fix a faulty chain on their homemade camper van.

'Even here at the World Finals, where you're talking about the best problem-solvers of the future, a lot of the kids still want to pounce on the first idea that comes along and make it work immediately,' he says. 'But your first idea is usually not your best, and it may take weeks or even longer to find the right solution to a problem and then make it come to fruition.'

No one, not even Micklus, believes we have to solve every problem slowly. There are times – patching up a soldier on the battlefield, for instance, or cooling a damaged nuclear reactor in Japan – when sitting back to stroke your chin and ponder the big picture and the long term is not an option. You have to channel MacGyver, reach for the duct tape and cobble together a solution that works right now. When the astronauts on the Apollo 13 radioed Houston about their 'problem' back in 1970, the boffins at NASA mission control did not launch a full inquiry into what caused the space craft's oxygen tanks to explode. Instead, they rolled up their sleeves and toiled round the clock to devise a quick-and-dirty workaround that would modify the carbon dioxide filters so the astronauts could use the lunar module as a life-boat. Inside 40 hours the crack problem-solvers in Houston came up with an ingenious solution using materials on board the ship: cardboard, suit hoses, plastic stowage bags, even duct tape. It was not a permanent fix, but it brought the Apollo 13 crew home safely. Afterwards NASA pulled the Andon rope, spending thousands of hours working out exactly what went wrong with those oxygen tanks and devising a Slow Fix to make sure they never exploded again.

Yet how many of us follow NASA's lead? When a quick fix eases the symptoms of a problem, as that acupuncture session did for my back, our appetite for pulling the Andon rope tends to fade. After a tidal wave of bad debt threatened to torpedo the world economy in 2008, governments around the world swiftly put together bail-outs totalling over $5 trillion dollars. That was the necessary quick fix. Once the threat of global meltdown receded, however, so too did the will to follow up with a deeper fix. Everywhere, politicians failed to push through the sort of root and branch reform that would guard against *Financial Armageddon 2: The Sequel.*

Too often, when a quick fix goes wrong, we wring our hands, promise to turn over a new leaf and then go back to making the same mistakes all over again. 'Even when a more fundamental change is required, people still go into quick-fix mode,' says Ranjay Gulati, a professor of business administration at Harvard Business School. 'They appear to make the right noises and take the right steps, but ultimately they fail to follow through, so that what starts out as a slow fix ends up being just another quick fix. This is a common problem.'

BP is a textbook example. In 2005 the company's refinery in Texas exploded, killing 15 workers and injuring 180 more. Less than a year later, oil was twice found to be leaking from a 25-kilometre stretch of corroded BP pipeline off the coast of Alaska. Coming so close together, these two incidents should have been a wake-up call, a warning that years of cutting corners had started to backfire. In 2006 John Browne, then BP's chief executive, seemed to agree the time for quick fixes was over. 'We have to get the priorities right,' he announced. 'And job one is to get to these things that have happened, get them fixed and get them sorted out. We don't just sort them out on the surface, we get them fixed deeply.'

Only that never happened. Instead, BP carried on much as before, earning a slew of official reprimands and a hefty fine for failing to live up to Browne's pledge. In April 2010 the company paid the price for its cavalier approach when an explosion ripped through its Deepwater Horizon rig, killing 11 workers, injuring 17 others and eventually spewing more than 200 million gallons of crude oil into the Gulf of Mexico, making it the worst environmental disaster in US history.

The BP fiasco is a reminder of just how perniciously addictive the quick fix can be. Even when lives and large sums of money are at stake, when everything from our health and relationships to our work and the environment is suffering, even when bombarded by evidence that the road to calamity is paved with band-aid solutions, we still gravitate towards the quick fix, like moths to a flame.

The good news is we can beat this addiction. In every walk of life, more and more of us are starting to accept that when tackling hard problems faster is not always better, that the best solutions take flight when we invest enough time, effort and resources. When we slow down, in other words.

There are many questions to answer in this book. What is the Slow Fix? Is it the same recipe for every problem? How do we know when a problem has been properly solved? Above all, how can we put the Slow Fix into practice in a world addicted to speed?

To answer those questions, I have been travelling the planet, meeting people who are taking a fresh approach to solving tough problems. We will visit the mayor who revolutionised public transport in Bogotá, Colombia; hang out with the warden and inmates at a state-of-the-art prison in Norway; explore how Icelanders are reinventing democracy. Some solutions we encounter may work in your own life, organisation or community, but my goal is to go much deeper. It is to draw some universal lessons about how to find the best solution when anything goes wrong. That means spotting the common ground between problems that on the surface seem completely unrelated. What lessons can peace negotiators in the Middle East, for instance, take from the organ donor system in Spain? How can a community regeneration programme in Vietnam help boost productivity in a company in Canada? What insights can French researchers trying to reinvent the water-bottle take from the rehabilitation of a failing school in Los Angeles? What can we all learn from the troubleshooters at NASA, the young problemsolvers in Odyssey of the Mind, or gamers who spend billions of hours tackling problems online?

This book is also a personal quest. After years of false dawns and half-measures, of shortcuts and red herrings, I want to work out what is wrong with my back. Is it my diet? My posture? My lifestyle? Is there an emotional or psychological root to all this spinal misery? I am finally ready to slow down and do the hard work needed to repair my back once and for all. No more duct tape, band-aid or chewing-gum cures. No more peeing on frozen legs.

The time has come for the Slow Fix.

CHAPTER ONE

Why the Quick Fix?

I want it all, and I want it now.
Queen, rock group

St Peter's Church seems untouched by the impatient swirl of downtown Vienna. It stands in a narrow square, tucked away from the noisy shopping streets that criss-cross the Austrian capital. Buildings lean in from all sides like soldiers closing ranks. Visitors often wander past without even noticing the church's delicious baroque façade and green domes.

Stepping through the immense wooden doors is like passing through a wormhole to a time when there were few reasons to rush. Gregorian chants whisper from hidden speakers. Candles cast flickering light on gilded altarpieces and paintings of the Virgin Mary. The smell of burning incense sweetens the air. A stone staircase, winding and weathered, leads down into a crypt dating back a thousand years. With thick walls blocking out mobile phone signals, the silence feels almost metaphysical.

I have come to St Peter's to discuss the virtues of slowing down. It is a soirée for business people, but some clergy are also present. At the end of the evening, when most of the guests have dispersed into the Viennese night, Monsignor Martin Schlag, resplendent in his purple cassock, comes up to me, a little sheepishly, to make a confession. 'As I was listening to you, I suddenly realised how easy it is for all of us to get infected by the impatience of the modern world,' he says. 'Lately, I must admit, I have been praying too fast.'

We both laugh at the irony of a man of the cloth behaving like a man in a suit, but his transgression underlines just how deep the quick-fix impulse runs. After all, prayer may be the oldest ritual for solving problems. Throughout history and across cultures, our ancestors have turned to gods and spirits in times of need, seeking help in tackling everything from floods and famine to drought and disease. Whether praying can actually solve problems is a matter of debate, but one thing is clear: no god has ever offered succour to those who pray faster. 'Prayer is not meant to be a shortcut,' says Monsignor Schlag. 'The whole point of praying is to slow down, listen, think deeply. If you hurry prayer, it loses its meaning and power. It becomes an empty quick fix.'

If we are going to start solving problems thoroughly, we must first understand our fatal attraction to speedy solutions. We need to know why even people like Monsignor Schlag, who devote their lives to serene contemplation in places like St Peter's, still fall for the quick fix. Are we somehow hardwired to reach for the duct-tape? Does modern society make it harder to resist peeing on frozen legs?

After my encounter with the monsignor, I turn to a secular expert on the workings of the human brain. Peter Whybrow is a psychiatrist and director of the Semel Institute for Neuroscience and Human Behavior at the University of California in Los Angeles. He is also the author of a book called *American Mania*, which explores how brain machinery that helped early man survive in a world of privation makes us prone to gorging in the modern age of plenty. Along with many in the field of neuroscience, he believes our addiction to the quick fix has physiological roots.

The human brain has two basic mechanisms for solving problems, which are commonly known as System 1 and System 2. The first is fast and intuitive, almost like thinking without thinking. When we see a lion eyeing us from across a watering hole, our brains instantly map out the best escape route and send us hurtling towards it. Quick fix. Problem solved. But System 1 is not just for life-or-death situations. It is the shortcut we use to navigate through daily life. Imagine if you had to reach every decision, from which sandwich to buy at lunch to whether to smile back at that fetching stranger on the subway, through deep analysis and anguished navel-gazing. Life would be unbearable. System 1 saves us the trouble.

By contrast, System 2 is slow and deliberate. It is the conscious thinking we do when asked to calculate 23 times 16 or analyse the possible side effects of a new social policy. It involves planning, critical analysis and rational thought, and is driven by parts of the brain that continue to develop after birth and into adolescence, which is why children are all about instant gratification. Not surprisingly, System 2 consumes more energy.

System 1 was a good match for life in the distant past. Our early ancestors had less need to ruminate deeply or take the long view. They ate when hungry, drank when thirsty and slept when tired. 'There was no tomorrow when living on the savannah, and survival depended on what you did each day,' says Whybrow. 'So the physiological systems that we inherited in the brain and body focused on finding short-term solutions and rewarding us for pursuing them.' After farming began to take hold 10,000 years ago, planning for the future became an asset. Now, in a complex, post-industrial world, System 2 should be king.

Only it is not. Why? One reason is that, inside our 21st-century heads, we are still roaming the savannah. System 1 holds sway because it takes a lot less time and effort. When it kicks in, the brain floods with reward chemicals like dopamine, which deliver the kind of feel-good jolt that keeps us coming back for more. That's why you get a little thrill every time you graduate to the next level in *Angry Birds* or cross an item off your To-Do list: job done, reward delivered, move on to the next thrill. In the cost–benefit calculus of neuroscience, System 1 offers maximum return for minimum effort. The rush it delivers can even become an end in itself. Like coffee addicts itching for a shot of caffeine, or smokers dashing outside for a cigarette, we get hooked on the quick fix of the quick fix. By comparison, System 2 can seem a dour taskmaster, demanding toil and sacrifice today in return for the promise of some vague pay-off in the future, like a personal trainer barking at us to eschew that chocolate éclair in favour of another 20 push-ups, or a parent nagging us to hit the books instead of running outside to play. Henry T.

Ford was referring to System 2 when he said, 'Thinking is the hardest work there is, which is the probable reason why so few engage in it.'

System 2 can also act like a spin doctor, rationalising our preference for short-term rewards. After yielding to temptation and wolfing down that éclair, we convince ourselves that we deserved a treat, needed the energy boost or will burn off the extra calories in the gym. 'The bottom line is that the primitive brain is wired for the quick fix; it always has been,' says Whybrow. 'The delayed gratification that comes with taking the long view is hard work. The quick fix comes more naturally to us. That's where we get our pleasure. We enjoy it and soon we want it quicker and quicker.'

That is why our ancestors warned against quick fixes long before Toyota invented the Andon rope. In the Bible, Peter urges Christians to be patient: 'The Lord is not slow to fulfil his promise as some count slowness, but is patient towards you, not wishing that any should perish, but that all should reach repentance.' Translation: God is not in the business of supplying real-time solutions. Nor was it just religious authorities that fretted over man's soft spot for the siren call of short-termism. John Locke, a leading thinker of the Enlightenment, warned that quick-fix merchants were on the road to ruin. 'He that has not mastery over his inclinations, he that knows not how to resist the importunity of present pleasure or pain, for the sake of what reason tells him is fit to be done, wants the true principle of virtue and industry, and is in danger never to be good at anything,' he wrote. A century later, Alexander Hamilton, one of the founding fathers of the United States of America, restated the danger:

'Momentary passions and immediate interests have a more active and imperious control over human conduct than general or remote considerations of policy, utility or justice.' A distrust of snap decisions lingers even in the modern era. In the face of a dire medical diagnosis, the conventional advice is to seek a second opinion. Governments, businesses and other organisations spend billions gathering the data, research and analysis to help them solve problems thoroughly.

So, why, despite all these warnings and exhortations, do we still fall for the quick fix? The lure of System 1 is only part of the explanation. Over hundreds of thousands of years, the human brain has evolved a whole array of quirks and mechanisms that distort our thinking and nudge us in the same direction.

Consider our natural penchant for optimism. Across cultures and ages, research has shown that most of us expect the future to be better than it ends up being. We significantly underestimate our chances of being laid off, divorced or diagnosed with a fatal illness. We expect to sire gifted children, outperform our peers and live longer than we actually do. To paraphrase Samuel Johnston, we let hope triumph over experience. This tendency may have an evolutionary purpose, spurring us to strive and push forward, rather than retreat to a dark corner to brood on the unfairness of it all. In *The Optimism Bias*, Tali Sharot argues that belief in a better future fosters healthier minds in healthier bodies. Yet she warns that too much optimism can backfire. After all, who needs regular health check-ups or a retirement savings plan if everything is going to pan out in the end? '"Smoking kills" messages don't work because people think their chances of cancer are low,' says Sharot. 'The divorce rate is 50 per cent, but people don't think it's the same for them. There is a very fundamental bias in the brain.' And that bias affects the way we tackle problems. When you slip on the rose-tinted spectacles, the easy quick fix suddenly looks a whole lot more plausible.

The human brain also has a natural fondness for familiar solutions. Instead of taking the time to understand a problem on its own merits, our habit is to reach for fixes that have worked on similar problems in the past, even when better options are staring us in the face. This bias, uncovered in study after study, is known as the Einstellung effect. It was useful back in the days when mankind faced a limited set of urgent and straightforward problems such as how to avoid being eaten by a lion; it is less helpful in a modern world of spiralling complexity. The Einstellung effect is one reason we often make the same mistakes over and over again in politics, relationships and careers.

Another is our aversion to change. Conservatives do not have a monopoly on wanting to keep things as they are. Even when confronted with compelling arguments for a fresh start, the human instinct is to stay put. That's why we can read a self-help book, nod in agreement all the way through, and then fail to put any of the advice into practice. Psychologists call this inertia the 'status-quo bias'. It explains why we always sit in the same place in a classroom when there is no seating plan or stick with the same bank, pension provider and utility company when rivals offer better deals. This resistance to change is woven into our vernacular. 'If it ain't broke, don't fix it,' we say, or, 'You can't teach an old dog new tricks.' Along with the Einstellung effect, the status-quo bias makes it harder for us to break out of a quick-fix rut.

Combine that with our reluctance to admit mistakes and you end up with another obstacle to the Slow Fix: the so-called 'legacy problem'. The more we invest in a solution – staff, technology, marketing, reputation – the less inclined we are to question it or search for something better. That means we would rather stand by a fix that is not working than start looking for one that does. Even the nimblest problem-solvers can fall into this trap. In the early 2000s a trio of software whizzes in Estonia wrote some code that made it easy to make telephone calls over the Internet. Result: the birth of one of the fastest-growing companies of the 21st century. A decade later the Skype headquarters in Tallinn, the capital of Estonia, remains a shrine to start-up chic, with bare brick walls, bean bags and funky art. Everywhere you look, multinational hipsters are sipping mineral water or fiddling with iPads. On a landing near the room where I meet Andres Kütt, Skype's young, goateed business evangelist, stands a whiteboard covered in squiggles from the last brainstorming session.

Even in this iconoclastic bear pit, the wrong fix can win stubborn defenders. At 36, Kütt is already a seasoned problem-solver. He helped pioneer Internet banking and spearheaded efforts to get Estonians to file their tax returns online. He worries that, by growing old enough and big enough to have vested interests, Skype has lost some of its problem-solving mojo. 'Legacy is now a big problem for us, too,' he says. 'You make a massive investment to solve a problem and suddenly the problem is surrounded by a huge number of people and systems that want to justify their existence. You end up with a scenario where the original source of the problem is hidden and hard to reach.' Rather than change tack, people in those circumstances usually plough on with the prevailing fix. 'It is scary to step back and deal with the idea that your old solutions may not even work, and to contemplate investing time, money and energy in finding better ones,' says Kütt. 'It's so much easier and safer to stay in your comfort zone.'

Clinging to a sinking ship may be irrational, but the truth is we are not as rational as we like to imagine. Study after study shows that we assume people with deeper voices (usually men) are cleverer and more trustworthy than those who speak in a higher register (usually women). We also tend to think good-looking folk are smarter and more competent than they really are. Or consider the Side Salad Illusion. In one study carried out at the Kellogg School of Management, people were asked to estimate the number of calories in unhealthy foods, such as bacon-and-cheese waffles. They then guessed the caloric content of those same foods when paired with a healthy side dish, such as a bowl of carrot and celery sticks. Time and again, people concluded that adding a virtuous accompaniment made the *whole* meal contain fewer calories, as if the healthy food could somehow make the unhealthy food less fattening. And this halo effect was three times more pronounced among avid dieters. The conclusion of Alexander Chernev, the lead researcher: 'People often behave in a way that is illogical and ultimately counterproductive to their goals.'

You can say that again. Our gift for tunnel vision can seem limitless. When confronted by awkward facts that challenge our favoured view – proof that our quick fix is not working, for instance – we tend to write them off as a rogue result, or as evidence that 'the exception proves the rule'. This is known as the confirmation bias. Sigmund Freud called it 'denial', and it goes hand in hand with the legacy problem and the status-quo bias. It can generate a powerful reality distortion field. When told by doctors they are going to die, many people block out the news entirely. Sometimes we cling to our beliefs even in the face of slam-dunk evidence to the contrary. Look at the cottage industry in Holocaust denial. Or how, in the late 1990s, Thabo Mbeki, then the president of South Africa, refused to accept the scientific consensus that AIDS was caused by the HIV virus, leading to the death of more than 330,000 people.

Even when we have no vested interest in distorting or filtering out information, we are still prone to tunnel vision. In an experiment repeated dozens of times on YouTube, test subjects are asked to count the number of passes made by one of two teams playing basketball together in a video. Because both sides have a ball, and the players are constantly weaving in and out around one another, this demands real concentration. Often, that sort of focus is useful, allowing us to block out the distractions that militate against deep thinking. But sometimes it can narrow the lens so we miss valuable bits of information and fail to see the forest for the trees. Halfway through the video a man dressed in a gorilla suit wanders into the middle of the basketball game, turns towards the camera, beats his chest, and walks out again.

Guess how many people fail to spot the gorilla? More than half.

What all this underlines is an alarming truth: the human brain is chronically unreliable. The optimism, status-quo and confirmation biases; the lure of System 1; the Einstellung effect, denial and the legacy problem – sometimes it seems as if embracing the quick fix is our biological destiny. Yet neurological wiring is only part of the story. We have also built a roadrunner culture that steers us into Quick Fix Avenue.

These days, hurry is our answer to every problem. We walk fast, talk fast, read fast, eat fast, make love fast, think fast. This is the age of speed yoga and one-minute bedtime stories, of 'just in time' this and 'on demand' that. Surrounded by gadgets that perform minor miracles at the click of a mouse or the tap of a screen, we come to expect everything to happen at the speed of software. Even our most sacred rituals are under pressure to streamline, accelerate, get up to speed. Churches in the United States have experimented with drive-thru funerals. Recently the Vatican was forced to warn Catholics they could not gain absolution by confessing their sins through a smartphone app. Even our recreational drugs of choice nudge us into quick fix mode: alcohol, amphetamines and cocaine all shift the brain into System 1 gear.

The economy ramps up the pressure for quick fixes. Capitalism has rewarded speed since long before high-frequency trading. The faster investors turn a profit, the faster they can reinvest to make even more money. Any fix that keeps the cash flowing, or the share price buoyant, stands a good chance of carrying the day – because there is money to be made right now and someone else can clean up the mess later. That mindset has sharpened over the last two decades. Many companies spend more time fretting over what their stock prices are doing today than over what will make them stronger a year from now. With so many of us working on short-term contracts, and hopping from job to job, the pressure to make an instant impact or tackle problems with little regard for the long term is immense. This is especially true in the boardroom, where the average tenure for a global CEO has fallen sharply in recent years. In 2011, Leo Apotheker was fired as the boss of Hewlett-Packard after less than 11 months in the post. Dominic Barton, the managing director of McKinsey and Company, a leading consulting firm, hears the same lament from chief executives around the world: we no longer have enough time or incentive to look beyond the next quick fix. His verdict: 'Capitalism has become too short-term.'

Modern office culture tends to reinforce that narrowing of horizons. When did you last have the time to take a long, hard look at a problem at work? Or even just to think deeply for a few minutes? Never mind tackling the big questions, such as where you want to be five years from now or how you might redesign your workplace from the bottom up. Most of us are too distracted by a never-ending blizzard of trivial tasks: a document to sign, a meeting to attend, a phone call to answer. Surveys suggest business professionals now spend half their working hours simply managing their email and social media inboxes. Day after day, week after week, the immediate trumps the important.

Politics is also steeped in the quick fix. Elected officials have every incentive to favour policies that will bear fruit in time for the next election. A cabinet minister may need results before the next reshuffle. Some analysts argue that each US administration enjoys only six months – that window between the Senate's confirming its staff and the start of electioneering for the mid-term elections – when it can look beyond the daily headlines and polling numbers to concentrate on strategic decisions over the long term. Nor does it help that we tend to favour decisive, shoot-from-the-hip leadership. We love the idea of a lone hero riding into town with a ready-made solution in his saddle bag. How many figures have ever won power by declaring 'It will take me a long time to work out how to solve our problems?' Slowing down to reflect, analyse or consult can seem indulgent or weak, especially in moments of crisis. Or as one critic of the more cerebral Barack Obama put it: 'We need a leader, not a reader.' Daniel Kahneman, author of *Thinking, Fast and Slow* and only the second psychologist ever to win the Nobel Prize for Economics, believes our natural preference for politicians who follow their gut turns democratic politics into a carousel of quick fixes. 'The public likes fast decisions,' he says, 'and that encourages leaders to go with their worst intuitions.'

Nowadays, though, it is no longer just politicians and business chiefs that believe they can wave a magic wand. We're all at it in this age of bullshit, bluster and blarney. Look at the parade of tone-deaf wannabes vowing to be the next Michael Jackson or Lady Gaga on *The X Factor*. With so much pressure to stand out, we embellish our CVs, post flattering photos on Facebook and holler for attention on blogs and Twitter. A recent study found that 86 percent of 11-year-olds use social media to build their 'personal brand' online. Some of this chest-thumping may win friends and influence people, but it can also drive us into the arms of the quick fix. Why? Because we end up lacking the humility to admit that we do not have all the answers, that we need time and a helping hand.

The self-help industry must take some of the blame for this. After years of reading and writing about personal development, Tom Butler-Bowdon fell out of love with his own field. Too many motivational gurus, he decided, hoodwink the public with short cuts and quick fixes that do not really work. As a riposte, he published *Never Too Late to Be Great*, which shows how the best solutions in every field, from the arts to business to science, usually have a long gestation period. 'By glossing over the fact that it takes time to produce anything of quality, the self-help industry has bred a generation of people that expect to fix everything tomorrow,' he says.

The media add fuel to that fire. When anything goes wrong – in politics, business, a celebrity relationship – journalists pounce, dissecting the crisis with glee and demanding an instant remedy. After the golfer Tiger Woods was outed as a serial philanderer, he vanished from the public eye for three months before finally breaking his silence to issue a *mea culpa* and announce he was in therapy for sex addiction. How did the media react to being made to wait that long? With fury and indignation. The worst sin for a public figure on the ropes is to fail to serve up an instant exit strategy.

That impatience fuels a tendency to overhype fixes that later turn out to be complete turkeys. An engineer by training, Marco Petruzzi worked as a globetrotting management consultant for 15 years before abandoning the corporate world to build better schools for the poor in the United States. We will meet him again later in the book, but for now consider his attack on our culture of hot air. 'In the past, hard-working entrepreneurs developed amazing stuff over time, and they *did* it, they didn't just *talk* about it, they *did* it,' he says. 'We live in a world now where talk is cheap and bold ideas can create massive wealth without ever having to deliver. There are multi-billionaires out there who never did anything but capture the investment cycle and the spin cycle at the right moment, which just reinforces a culture where people don't want to put in the time and effort to come up with real and lasting solutions to problems. Because if they play their cards right, and don't worry about the future, they can get instant financial returns.'

From most angles, then, the quick fix looks unassailable. Everything from the wiring of our brains to the ways of the world seems to favour band-aid solutions. Yet all is not lost. There is hope. Wherever you go in the world today, and in every walk of life, more people are turning away from the quick fix to find better ways to solve problems. Some are toiling below the radar, others are making headlines, but all share one thing in common: a hunger to forge solutions that actually work.

The good news is the world is full of Slow Fixes. You just have to take the time to find and learn from them.

CHAPTER TWO

CONFESS: The Magic of Mistakes and the *Mea Culpa*

*Success does not consist in never making mistakes but in
never making the same one a second time.*
George Bernard Shaw

On a crisp night in early September, four Typhoon fighter
jets roared across the sky above the freezing waters of the
North Sea. Locked in a two-on-two dogfight, they swooped,
banked and sliced through the darkness at up to 500 miles
per hour, searching for a kill-shot. It was a training exercise,
but to the pilots it all seemed very real. Strapped into his
cockpit, with 24,000 pounds of killing machine throbbing at
his fingertips, Wing Commander Dicky Patounas was feeling
the adrenaline. It was his first night-time tactical sortie in one
of the most powerful fighter jets ever built.

'We're in lights off because we're doing this for real, which
we don't do very often, so it's pitch black and I'm on goggles
and instruments only,' Patounas recalls. 'I'm working the

radar, putting it in the right mode by shortening the range, changing the elevation, all basic stuff. But the plane was new to me, so I'm maxed out.' And then something went wrong.

A few months later Patounas relives that night back on the ground. His air base, RAF Coningsby, is in Lincolnshire, an eastern county of England whose flat, featureless terrain is prized more by aviators than by tourists. Dressed in a green flight suit festooned with zippers, Patounas looks like a *Top Gun* pilot from central casting – square jaw, broad shoulders, ramrod posture and cropped hair. He whips out pen and paper to illustrate what happened next on that September night, speaking in the clipped tones of the British military.

Patounas was flying behind the two 'enemy' Typhoons when he decided to execute a manoeuvre known as the overshoot to a Phase 3 Visual Identification (VID). He would pull out to the left and then slingshot back onto his original course, popping up right behind the trailing enemy plane. But something unforeseen happened. Instead of holding their course, the two rival jets up ahead banked left to avoid a helicopter 20 miles away. Both pilots announced the change on the radio but Patounas failed to hear it because he was too distracted executing his manoeuvre. 'It's all quite technical,' he says. 'You've got to do 60 degrees angle of bank through 60 degrees and then roll out for 20 seconds, then put your scanner down by 4 degrees, then change your radar to 10-mile scale, and after 20 seconds you come right using 45 degrees angle of bank, you go through 120 degrees, you roll out and pick up the guy on your radar and he should be at about 4 miles. So I'm working all this out and I miss the radio call stating the new heading.'

When Patounas rolled back out of the manoeuvre, he spotted an enemy Typhoon in front of him just as expected. He was pumped. 'This aircraft now appears under my cross where I put it for the guy to appear, so I think I've done the perfect overshoot,' he says. 'I've set my radar up, pitched back in and the guy I'm looking for is under my cross in the pitch black. And I go, "I'm a genius, I'm good at this shit." I was literally thinking I've never flown one so perfectly.'

He shakes his head and laughs wryly at his own hubris: it turned out the wrong Typhoon was in his crosshairs. Instead of ending up behind the trailing jet, Patounas was following in the slipstream of the frontrunner – and he had no idea. 'It was my mistake: I basically lost awareness of two of the aircraft,' he says. 'I knew they were there but I didn't ensure I could see two tracks. What I should have done was bump the range scale up and have a look for the other guy, but I didn't because I said to myself, "This is perfect."'

The result was that Patounas passed within 3,000 feet of the rear Typhoon. 'It wasn't that close but the key is I had no awareness, because I didn't even know he was there,' he says. 'It could have been three feet, or I could have flown right into him.' Patouanas falls quiet for a moment, as if picturing the worst-case scenario. On that September night his wingman watched the whole fiasco unfold, knew there was no real danger of a collision and allowed the exercise to continue, but a similar mistake in real combat could have been catastrophic – and Patounas knew it.

The rule of thumb in civil aviation is that a typical air accident is the result of seven human errors. Each mistake on its own may be harmless, even trivial, but string them together and the net effect can be lethal. Flying modern fighter jets, with their fiendishly complex computer systems, is an especially risky business. While enforcing the no-fly zone over Libya in 2011, a US F-15E crashed outside Benghazi after a mechanical failure. A month earlier, two F-16s from the Royal Thai air force fell from the sky during a routine training exercise.

What was surprising about the Typhoon incident over the North Sea was not that it happened but how Patounas reacted: he told everyone about his mistake. In the macho world of the fighter pilot, *mea culpas* are thin on the ground. As a 22-year veteran of the RAF and commander of a squadron of 18 Typhoon pilots, Patounas had a lot to lose yet still gathered together his entire crew and owned up. 'I could have come away from this and not said anything, but the right thing to do was to raise it, put it into my report and get it in the system,' he says. 'I briefed the whole squadron on how I make mistakes and the mistake I made. That way people know I'm happy to put my hand up and say I messed up too, I'm human.'

This brings us to the first ingredient of the Slow Fix: admitting when we are wrong in order to learn from the error. That means taking the blame for serious blunders as well as the small mistakes and near misses, which are often warning signs of bigger trouble ahead.

Yet highlighting errors is much harder than it sounds. Why? Because there is nothing we like less than owning up to our mistakes. As social animals, we put a high premium on status. We like to *fare bella figura*, as the Italians say, or look good in front of our peers – and nothing ruins a nice *figura* more than screwing something up.

That is why passing the buck is an art form in the workplace. My first boss once gave me a piece of advice: 'Remember that success has many fathers but failure is an orphan.' Just look at your own CV – how many of your mistakes from previous jobs are listed there? On *The Apprentice*, most boardroom showdowns involve contestants pinning their own blunders on rivals. Even when big money is at stake, companies often choose to bury their heads in the sand rather than confront errors. Nearly half of financial services firms do not step in to rescue a floundering project until it has missed its deadline or run over budget. Another 15 per cent lack a formal mechanism to deal with a project's failure.

Nor does it help that society often punishes us for embracing the *mea culpa*. In a hyper-competitive world, rivals pounce on the smallest error, or the tiniest whiff of doubt, as a sign of weakness. Though Japanese business chiefs and politicians sometimes bow and beg for forgiveness, their counterparts elsewhere bend both language and credibility to avoid squarely owning up to a mistake. In English, the word 'problem' has been virtually excised from everyday speech in favour of anodyne euphemisms such as 'issue' and 'challenge'. Hardly a surprise when studies show that executives who conceal bad news from the boss tend to climb the corporate ladder more quickly.

In his retirement, Bill Clinton makes it a rule to say 'I was wrong' or 'I didn't know that' at least once a day. If such a moment fails to arise naturally, he goes out of his way to engineer one. He does this to short-circuit the Einstellung effect and all those other biases we encountered earlier.

Clinton knows the only way to solve problems in a complex, ever-changing world is to keep an open mind – and the only way to do that is to embrace your own fallibility. But can you imagine him uttering those phrases while he was President of the United States? Not a chance. We expect our leaders to radiate the conviction and certainty that come from having all the answers. Changing direction, or your mind, is never taken as proof of the ability to learn and adapt; it is derided as flip-flopping or wimping out. If President Clinton had confessed to making mistakes, or entertaining doubts about his own policies, his political enemies and the media would have ripped him to pieces.

The threat of litigation is another incentive to shy away from a proper *mea culpa*. Insurance companies advise clients never to admit blame at the scene of a traffic accident, even if the crash was clearly their fault. Remember how long it took BP to issue anything resembling an official apology for the Deepwater Horizon oil spill? Nearly two months. Behind the scenes, lawyers and PR gurus pored over legal precedents to fashion a statement that would appease public opinion without opening the door to an avalanche of lawsuits. Nor is it just companies that shrink from accepting blame. Even after they leave office and no longer need to woo the electorate, politicians find it hard to own up to their errors. Neither Tony Blair nor George W. Bush has properly apologised for invading Iraq in search of weapons of mass destruction that did not exist. Remove individual ego from the equation, and collectively we still shy away from *mea culpas*. Britain waited nearly four decades to issue a formal apology for the Bloody Sunday massacre in Northern Ireland in 1972.

Australia only apologised in 2008 for the horrors visited upon its aboriginal peoples, followed a year later by the US Senate apologising to African-Americans for the wrongs of slavery.

Even when there are no witnesses to our slip-ups, admitting we are wrong can be wrenching. 'Nothing is more intolerable,' Ludwig van Beethoven noted, 'than to have to admit to yourself your own errors.' Doing so forces you to confront your frailties and limitations, to rethink who you are and your place in the world. When you mess up, and admit it to yourself, there is nowhere to hide. 'This is the thing about fully experiencing wrongness,' wrote Kathryn Schulz in her book *Being Wrong*. 'It strips us of all our theories, including our theories about ourselves ... it leaves us feeling flayed, laid bare to the bone and the world.' Sorry really is the hardest word.

This is a shame, because mistakes are a useful part of life. To err is human, as the saying goes. Error can help us solve problems by showing us the world from fresh angles. In Mandarin, the word 'crisis' is rendered with two characters, one signifying 'danger', the other 'opportunity'. In other words, every screw-up holds within it the promise of something better – if only we take the time to acknowledge and learn from it. Artists have known this for centuries. 'Mistakes are almost always of a sacred nature,' observed Salvador Dalí. 'Never try to correct them. On the contrary: rationalise them, understand them thoroughly. After that, it will be possible for you to sublimate them.'

That same spirit reigns in the more rigorous world of science, where even a failed experiment can yield rich insights and open new paths of inquiry. Many world-changing inventions occurred when someone chose to explore – rather than cover up – an error. In 1928, before leaving to spend August with his family, Sir Alexander Fleming accidentally left a petri dish containing *staphylococcus* bacteria uncovered in his basement laboratory in London. When he returned a month later he found a fungus had contaminated the sample, killing off all the surrounding bacteria. Rather than toss the dish in the bin, he analysed the patch of mould and found it contained a powerful infection-fighting agent. He named it *Penicillium notatum*. Two decades later, penicillin, the world's first and still most widely used antibiotic, hit the market, revolutionising healthcare and earning Fleming a Nobel prize in Medicine. 'Anyone who has never made a mistake,' said Einstein, 'has never tried anything new.'

Military folk have always known that owning up to mistakes is an essential part of learning and solving problems. Errors cost lives in the air force, so flight safety has usually taken precedence over *fare bella figura*. In the RAF's long-running monthly magazine, *Air Clues*, pilots and engineers write columns about mistakes made and lessons learned. Crews are also fêted for solving problems. In a recent issue, a smiling corporal from air traffic control received a Flight Safety Award for overruling a pilot and aborting a flight after noticing a wingtip touch the ground during take-off.

In the RAF, as in most air forces around the world, fighter pilots conduct no-holds-barred debriefings after every sortie to examine what went right and wrong. But that never went far enough. RAF crews tended to share their mistakes only with mates rather than with their superiors or rival squadrons.

As one senior officer says: 'A lot of valuable experience that could have made flying safer for everyone was just seeping away through the cracks.'

To address this, the RAF hired Baines Simmons, a consulting firm with a track record in civil aviation, to devise a system to catch and learn from mistakes, just as the transportation, mining, food and drug safety industries have done.

Group Captain Simon Brailsford currently oversees the new regime. After joining the RAF as an 18-year-old, he went on to fly C130 Hercules transport planes as a navigator in Bosnia, Kosovo, northern Iraq and Afghanistan. Now 46, he combines the spit-and-polish briskness of the officers' mess with the easy charm of a man who spent three years as the Equerry to Her Majesty Queen Elizabeth II.

On the whiteboard in his office he uses a red felt-tip pen to sketch me a picture of a crashed jet, a dead pilot and a plume of smoke. 'Aviation is a dangerous business,' he says. 'What we're trying to do is stop picking up the deceased and the bits of the broken aeroplane on the ground and pull the whole story back to find out the errors and the near misses that can lead to the crash, so the crash never happens in the first place. We want to solve issues before they become problems.'

Every time crew members at RAF Coningsby catch themselves doing something that could jeopardise safety, they are now urged to submit a report online or fill in one of the special forms pinned up in work stations all over the base. Those reports are then funnelled to a central office, which decides whether to investigate further.

To make the system work, the RAF tries to create what it calls a 'just culture'. When someone makes a mistake, the automatic response is not blame and punishment; it is to explore what went wrong in order to fix and learn from it. 'People must feel that if they tell you something, they're not going to get into trouble, otherwise they won't tell you when things go wrong, and they might even try to cover them up,' says Brailsford. 'That doesn't mean they won't get told off or face administrative action or get sent for extra training, but it means they'll be treated in a just manner befitting what happened to them, taking into account the full context. If you make a genuine mistake and put up your hand, we will say thank you. The key is making sure everyone understands that we're after people sharing their errors rather than keeping it to themselves so that we're saving them and their buddies from serious accidents.'

RAF Coningsby rams home that message at every turn. All around the base, in hallways, canteens and even above the urinals, posters urge crew to flag even the tiniest safety concern. Toilet cubicles are stuffed with laminated brochures explaining how to stay safe and why even the smallest mishap is worth reporting. Hammered into the ground beside the main entrance is a poster bearing a photo of the Station Flight Safety Officer pointing his finger in the classic Lord Kitchener pose. Printed above his office telephone number is the question: 'So what did you think of today?' The need to admit mistakes is also baked into cadets at military academy. 'It's definitely drilled into us from the start that "we prefer you mess up and let us know",' says one young engineer at RAF Coningsby. 'Of course, you get a lot of stick and banter from your mates for making mistakes, but we all understand that owning up is the best way to solve problems now and in the future.'

The RAF ensures that crew see the fruits of their *mea culpas*. Safety investigators telephone all those who flag up problems within 24 hours, and later tell them how the case was concluded. They also conduct weekly workshops with engineers to explain the outcome of all investigations and why people were dealt with as they were. 'You can see their eyebrows go up when it's clear they won't be punished for making a mistake and they might actually get a pat on the back,' says one investigator.

Group Captain Stephanie Simpson, a 17-year veteran of the RAF, is in charge of safety in the engineering division at Coningsby. She has quick, watchful eyes and wears her hair scraped back in a tight bun. She tells me the new regime paid off recently when an engineer noticed that carrying out a routine test on a Typhoon had sheared off the end of a dowel in the canopy mechanism. A damaged canopy might not open, meaning a pilot trying to jettison from the cockpit would be mashed against the glass.

The engineer filed a report and Simpson's team swung into action. Within 24 hours they had figured out that an elementary mistake during the canopy test could damage the dowel. There was no requirement to go back and check afterwards. Flight crews immediately inspected the suspect part across the entire fleet of Typhoons in Europe and Saudi Arabia. The procedure was then changed to ensure that the dowel is no longer damaged during the test.

'Ten years ago this would probably never have been reported – the engineers would have just thought, "Oh, that's broken, we'll just quietly replace it," and then carried on,' says Simpson. 'Now we're creating a culture where everyone is thinking, "Gosh, there could be other aircraft on this station with the same problem that might not be spotted in future so I'd better tell someone right now." That way you stop a small problem becoming a big one.'

Thanks to Patounas's candour, an RAF investigation discovered that a series of errors led to the near miss above the North Sea. His own failure to hear the order to bank left was the first. The second was that the other pilots changed course even though he did not acknowledge the fresh heading. Then, after Patounas overshot, the whole team failed to switch on their lights. 'It turned out a whole set of factors were not followed and if anyone had done one of the things they should have, it wouldn't have happened,' says Patounas. 'The upside is this reminds everyone of the rules for doing a Phase 3 VID at night. So next time we won't have the same issue.'

Others in his squadron are already following his lead. Days before my visit, a young corporal pointed out that certain procedures were not being properly followed. 'What she said was not a particularly good read, but that's going in her report as a positive because she had the courage of her convictions to go against the grain when she could have been punished,' says Patounas. 'Twenty years ago, she wouldn't have raised the question or if she had she'd have been told, "Don't you say how rubbish my squadron is! I want my dirty laundry kept to me," whereas I'm saying thank you.'

The RAF is not a paragon of problem-solving. Not every mistake or near miss is reported. Similar cases are not always dealt with in the same manner, which can undermine talk of a 'just culture'. Some officers remain sceptical about persuading pilots and engineers to accept the virtues of airing all their dirty laundry. Many of the *mea culpa* columns in *Air Clues* magazine are still published anonymously. 'Sorry' remains a hard word to say in the RAF.

Yet the change is paying off. In the first three years of the new regime, 210 near misses or errors were reported at RAF Coningsby. Of these, 73 triggered an investigation. In each one, steps were taken to make sure the mistake never happened again. 'Given that we never reported near misses before, that's a quantum shift, a big leap of faith in people,' says Brailsford. 'Instead of putting a plaster over problems, we're now going deeper and dealing with them at their root. We're nipping problems in the bud by stopping them before they even happen.' Other air forces, from Israel to Australia, have taken notice.

Adding the *mea culpa* to your problem-solving toolbox pays off beyond the military. Take ExxonMobil. After the epic *Exxon Valdez* oil spill off the coast of Alaska in 1989, the company set out to catch and investigate every screw-up, however small. It walked away from a large drilling project in the Gulf of Mexico because, unlike BP, it decided drilling there was too risky. Safety is now such a part of the corporate DNA that every buffet laid out for company events comes with signs warning not to consume the food after two hours. In its cafeterias, kitchen staff monitor the temperature of their salad dressings.

Every time an error occurs at an ExxonMobil facility, the first instinct of the company is to learn from it, rather than punish those involved. Staff talk about the 'gift' of the near miss. Glenn Murray, an employee for nearly three decades, was part of the *Valdez* clean-up. Today, as head of safety at the company, he believes no blunder is too small to ignore. 'Every near miss,' he says, 'has something to teach us if we just take the time to investigate it.'

Like the RAF and Toyota, ExxonMobil encourages even the most junior employee to speak up when something goes wrong. Not long ago a young engineer new to the company was uneasy about a drilling project in West Africa – so he temporarily closed it down. 'He shut down a multi-million dollar project because he felt there were potential problems and we needed to pause and think it all through, and management backed him,' says Murray. 'We even had him stand up at an event and named him Employee of the Quarter.' By every yardstick, Exxon now has an enviable safety record in the oil industry.

Mistakes can also be a gift when dealing with consumers. Four out of every five products launched perish within the first year, and the best companies learn from their flops. The Newton MessagePad, the Pippin and the Macintosh Portable all bombed for Apple yet helped pave the way for winners like the iPad.

Even in the cut-throat world of brand management, where the slightest misstep can send customers stampeding for the exit and hobble the mightiest firm, owning up to mistakes can deliver a competitive edge. In 2009, with sales tanking in the United States, Domino's Pizza invited customers to deliver their verdict on its food. The feedback was stinging. 'Worst excuse for a pizza I've ever tasted,' said one member of the public. 'Totally devoid of flavour,' said another. Many customers compared the company's pizza crust to cardboard.

Rather than sulk, or sit on the results, Domino's issued a full-blown *mea culpa*. In documentary-style television commercials, Patrick Doyle, the company's CEO, admitted the chain had lost its way in the kitchen and promised to deliver better pizzas in the future. Domino's then went back to the drawing board, giving its pies a complete makeover with new dough, sauce and cheese.

Its Pizza Turnaround campaign worked a treat. Year-on-year sales surged 14.3 per cent, the biggest jump in the history of the fast-food industry. Two years after the apology the company's stock price was up 233 per cent. Of course, the new pizza recipes helped, but the starting-point was Domino's doing what RAF air crews and Exxon employees are now expected to do as a matter of course: acknowledging the error of its ways. This allowed the firm to learn exactly where it was going wrong so it could fix it. It also cleared the air. These days, so many companies trumpet 'new and improved' products that the net effect is a whirlwind of white noise that leaves consumers cold. The very act of owning up to its mistakes allowed Domino's to cut through the din and reboot its relationship with customers.

PR experts agree that the best way for a company to handle a mistake is to apologise and explain what it will do to put things right. This accords with my own experience. The other day a payment into my bank account went astray. After 20 minutes of evasion from the call centre, my voice began to rise as my blood reached boiling point. And then a manager came on the line and said: 'Mr Honoré, I'm very sorry. We made a mistake with this payment.' As she explained how the money would be retrieved, my fury drained away and we ended up bantering about the weather and our summer holidays.

Public apologies can have a similarly soothing effect. When a customer filmed a FedEx driver tossing a package containing a computer monitor over a six-foot fence in the run-up to Christmas 2011, the video went viral and threatened to annihilate sales during the busiest time of year. Rather than stonewall, though, the company apologised right away. In a blog post entitled 'Absolutely, Positively Unacceptable', FedEx's senior vice-president for US operations announced he was 'upset, embarrassed, and very sorry' for the episode. The company also gave the customer a new monitor and disciplined the driver. As a result, FedEx weathered the storm.

Even when we squander other people's money, owning up in order to learn from the error is often the best policy. In 2011, Engineers Without Borders (EWB) Canada set up a website called *AdmittingFailure.com*, where aid workers can post their mistakes as cautionary tales. 'Opening up like that is completely the opposite of the norm in the sector, so it was a huge risk,' says Ashley Good, Venture Leader at EWB. But it paid off. No longer afraid of being pilloried for messing up, EWB staff became more willing to take the sort of risks that are often the stepping stone to creative breakthroughs. 'People now feel they have the freedom to experiment, push themselves, take chances because they know they won't be blamed if they don't get it right on the first try,' says Good. 'And when you push boundaries like that, you get more creative solutions to problems.' One example: after much trial and error, EWB has devised a system that improves water and sanitation services in Malawi by mobilising district governments, the private sector and communities all at the same time. Workers from across the development sector now post their own stories on *AdmittingFailure.com*. EWB's donors love the new regime, too. Instead of dashing for the exit, they welcomed the eagerness to learn from mistakes. Says Good: 'We've found that being open and honest actually builds a stronger bond and higher trust with our donors.'

The same holds true in personal relationships. A first step towards rebuilding bridges after falling out with a partner, friend, parent or child is for all parties to take their share of the blame. Admitting mistakes can ease the guilt and shame gnawing at the wrongdoer and help the victim overcome the anger that often stands in the way of forgiveness. Marianne Bertrand sees the magic of the *mea culpa* every week in her job as a family therapist in Paris. 'Many people sit in my office and cannot even begin to address their problems because they are stuck in the rage and resentment for what went wrong,' she says. 'But when they finally accept and apologise sincerely for their mistakes, and hear the other person doing the same, you can really feel the atmosphere in the room change, the tension subside, and then we can start working on reconciliation.'

Even doctors are warming to the *mea culpa*. Study after study shows that what many patients want after being the victim of a medical mistake is not a lump sum payment or the physician's head on a plate. What they really crave is what FedEx delivered in the wake of that package-tossing incident: a sincere apology, a full explanation of how the error occurred and a clear plan to ensure the same thing will not happen again. Among patients who file a suit for medical malpractice in the United States, nearly 40 per cent say they might not have done so had the attending physician explained and apologised for the mishap. The trouble is, many in the medical profession are too proud or too scared to say sorry.

Those that do so reap the benefits. In the late 1980s the Department of Veterans Affairs Medical Center in Lexington, Kentucky became the first hospital in the United States to tap the power of the *mea culpa*. It informs patients and their families when any member of staff makes a mistake that causes harm, even if the victims are unaware of the error. If the attending physician is found to be at fault, he or she must deliver a clear, compassionate apology to the patient. The hospital also explains the steps it will take to ensure that the error does not happen again, and may offer some form of restitution. But the cornerstone of the new regime is the simple act of saying sorry. This scores well with patients and their families. 'We believe we spend much less time and money on malpractice lawsuits these days as a result,' says Joseph Pellecchia, the hospital's Chief of Staff.

Apologising also helps deliver better healthcare. When medical workers can deal openly with the emotional fallout that comes from making a mistake, they are less stressed and more able to learn from their errors. 'Physicians are not gods, they are human beings, and that means they make mistakes,' says Pellecchia. 'There's been an incredible change here where we've gone from a punitive environment to a learning environment where a physician can ask, "What happened here?" "What went wrong?" "Was it a systems problem?" "Was it me?" – and learn from their mistakes to deliver better care.' Other hospitals around the world have followed suit. In the same vein, state and provincial governments across the US and Canada have enacted what are known as 'sorry laws', which bar litigants from using a physician's apology as proof of guilt. Everywhere the net effect is the same: happier doctors, happier patients and less litigation.

The truth is that any Slow Fix worthy of the name usually starts with a *mea culpa*. Whether at work or in relationships, most of us tend to drift along pretending that all is well – remember the status-quo bias and the legacy problem. Admitting there is a problem, and accepting our share of the blame, can jolt us out of that rut. In the Twelve-Step Programme invented by Alcoholic Anonymous and now used in the battle against many other addictions, Step 1 is to admit you have lost control of your own behaviour. 'Hello, my name is Carl, and I am addicted to the quick fix.'

To overcome our natural aversion to admitting mistakes, especially in the workplace, removing the stick of punishment is often just the first step. It also helps to dangle a carrot to encourage or even reward us for owning up. Remember the Employee of the Quarter accolade bestowed on that young engineer at ExxonMobil. As well as Flight Safety Awards, the RAF pays a cash bonus to anyone who highlights an error that later saves the Air Force money. In the aid world, organisations can win Brilliant Failure Awards for sharing mistakes made in development projects. At SurePayroll, an online payroll company, staff nominate themselves for a Best New Mistakes competition. At a lighthearted annual meeting, they listen to tales of colleagues messing up and what everyone can learn from their blunders. Those who own up to the most useful mistakes win a cash prize.

Even in education, where botching a single question on an exam paper can torpedo your chances of attending a top-tier university, moves are afoot to reward students for embracing mistakes. Worried that its high-achieving pupils had lost their appetite for taking intellectual risks, a top London girls' school held a Failure Week in 2012. With the help of teachers and parents, and through assemblies, tutorials and other activities, students at Wimbledon High explored the benefits of being wrong. 'Successful people learn from failure, pick themselves up and move on,' says Heather Hanbury, the headmistress. 'Something going wrong may even have been the best thing that could have happened to them in the long run – in sparking creativity, for instance – even if it felt like a disaster at the time.' Failure Week has altered the atmosphere in the school. Instead of mollycoddling pupils, teachers feel more comfortable telling them point-blank when they have given a wrong answer, thus making it easier to search for a better one. The girls are taking greater risks, too, pursuing more daring lines of inquiry in the classroom and entering creative writing competitions in larger numbers. Members of the school debating club are deploying more adventurous arguments and winning more competitions. 'Maybe the most important thing the Week gave us is a language to talk about failure as something not to avoid but as an essential part of learning, improving and solving problems,' says Hanbury. 'If one girl is upset by a poor mark, another might now make a friendly joke about it or say something like, "OK, you failed, but what can you learn from it?""

Most workplaces are in dire need of a similar cultural shift. Think of all the lessons that go unlearned, all the problems left to fester, all the bad feelings churned up, all the time, energy and money wasted, thanks to the human instinct to cover up mistakes. Now think of how much more efficient – not to mention agreeable – your workplace would be if every error could be a spur to working smarter. Instead of muddling along, you could revolutionise your office or factory from the bottom up.

There are steps we can all take to harness the *mea culpa* and learn from our mistakes. Schedule a daily Clinton moment when you say, 'I was wrong' – and then find out why. When you mess up at work, pinpoint one or two lessons to be gleaned from the mishap and then quickly own up. When others mess up, quell the temptation to scoff or gloat and instead help them to spot the silver lining. Start a conversation in your company, school or family about how admitting mistakes can inspire creative leaps. Reinforce that message by using feel-good terms such as 'gift' or 'bonus' to describe the uncovering of helpful errors and by pinning up quotes such as this from Henry T. Ford: 'Failure is simply the opportunity to begin again, this time more intelligently.'

It also helps to create a shared space, such as a web forum or a suggestions book, for airing mistakes. Borrowing an idea from Toyota, Patounas has put up a Communications Board in his squadron headquarters where any crew member can call attention to a problem – and every case is promptly investigated and addressed. 'It's very popular already and you see the engineers and pilots gathered round it,' says Patounas. 'It's tangible and something you can put your arms round.'

It certainly helps to know that our errors seldom look as bad to others as we imagine. We have a natural tendency to overestimate how much people notice or care about our gaffes. Psychologists call this the 'spotlight effect'. You may feel mortified to discover you attended a big meeting with laddered tights or egg on your tie, but the chances are hardly anyone else noticed. In one study at Cornell University, students were asked to walk into a room wearing a Barry Manilow T-shirt, a social kiss of death for any self-respecting hipster. While the subjects nearly died of embarrassment, only 23 per cent of the people in the room even clocked the cheesy crooner.

If owning up to a mistake is seldom as bad as we fear, however, it is only the first step towards a Slow Fix. The next is taking the time to work out exactly how and why we erred in the first place.

CHAPTER THREE

THINK HARD: Reculer Pour Mieux Sauter

Don't just do something, stand there.
White Rabbit in *Alice in Wonderland*

If asked to design an office that could make staff look forward to Monday morning, you might come up with something like the headquarters of Norsafe. Every window looks onto a snapshot of bucolic bliss. Clapboard houses nestle in the forest, small boats bob alongside wooden piers, gulls float across a clear sky. In the late morning, the sunshine turns this narrow waterway in southern Norway into a strip of shimmering silver.

For many years the company's balance sheet looked similarly idyllic. Norsafe has been building boats since 1903 in a country where boating is a serious business. With more coastline than the United States, this long, slender nation on the northern edge of Europe has always looked to the sea. Even today, one in seven Norwegians owns some sort of watercraft. But looks can be deceiving. Not so long ago Norsafe was a firm on the verge of a nervous breakdown, where nobody looked forward to coming in to work on Monday morning.

The company manufactures highly specialised lifeboats for oil rigs and supertankers. Enclosed like a submarine, and painted a vivid, regulation orange, they can drop into the sea, with a full load of passengers, from a height of nearly 40 metres. In the mid-2000s, as the global economy boomed, orders flooded in from around the world, tripling Norsafe's turnover. Yet behind the top line numbers, the firm, like Toyota, had lost control of its inner workings and was struggling to keep up. Deadlines slipped, design faults passed unnoticed through the production plant, customer complaints went unanswered. With lawsuits piling up and profits plunging, the design, manufacturing and sales teams were at each other's throats. Everyone knew there was a problem, but no one knew how to fix it.

The turning point came in 2009, when an organisational consultant named Geir Berthelsen delivered a pitch at the Norsafe headquarters. With his shaven head and watchful eyes, the 48-year-old Norwegian exudes the calm of a Zen monk. Since the early 1990s his consultancy firm, Magma, has been mending broken companies around the world with his version of the Slow Fix. Whatever the country or industry, the first step in his recovery plan is always the same: take time to work out the real reason things are going wrong. 'Most companies are in a hurry, so they just firefight with quick fixes that only address the symptoms instead of the problem itself,' he says. 'To identify what is really going wrong, you first have to get a full picture of a company in slow motion, you have to do like Toyota and ask why, why and why, you have to slow down long enough to analyse and understand.'

That is a neat summary of the next ingredient of the Slow Fix: taking the time to think hard about the problem to arrive at the right diagnosis. When asked what he would do if given one hour to save the world, Albert Einstein answered: 'I would spend fifty-five minutes defining the problem and only five minutes finding the solution.' Most of us do the exact opposite. Think of your last visit to the GP. Chances are the appointment lasted no more than a few minutes and you struggled to say everything you wanted to. One study found that doctors let patients explain their complaint for 23 seconds before interrupting. Is it any wonder so many illnesses are misdiagnosed?

By the same token, you seldom uncover the real reason an organisation is failing by reading an email, convening a meeting or skimming the annual report. When things go wrong, as we saw earlier, people usually shift blame and shy away from saying anything that might cause them to lose face or hurt their colleagues' feelings. In a world that prizes action over reflection, and when the clock is ticking, it takes nerve to spend 55 minutes thinking. Yet, from business to medicine to everything in between, a little inaction can be just what the doctor ordered. Some problems are no more than a bit of passing turbulence, or a red herring. Others will find their own solution if left alone. But even for problems needing intervention, inaction combined with deep thought and shrewd observation can be the first step to a smart fix. That is why doctors treating unusual conditions will often spend days, weeks, even months running tests, watching how the symptoms evolve, ordering more analysis, before finally arriving at a diagnosis and starting treatment. 'To do nothing at all is the most difficult thing in the world,' said Oscar Wilde, 'the most difficult and the most intellectual.'

That is why the Magma consultancy firm spends a long time in the trenches, working alongside employees, watching, listening, learning, gaining trust, reading between the lines. 'We always start at the bottom, on the factory floor or wherever the work is done, and live there as long as it takes to understand everything about how all the systems operate and how all the people act within those systems,' says Berthelsen. 'We have to discover the right questions before we can figure out the right answers. Only then can we really fix things.'

After a lengthy tour of duty, the Magma team pinpointed why Norsafe was floundering: it had become a big company that still operated like a small one. As orders had grown more complex, staff had stopped paying attention to the details – a fatal mistake when the most sophisticated lifeboats contain 1,500 parts and are subject to a thicket of rules and regulations. The designers would churn out drawings with scant regard for budgets or the laws of physics. The sales team would green-light jobs without fully understanding the small print. Housed in a separate building beside the headquarters, the manufacturing side of the business scrambled to make ends meet. As recriminations flew, the company degenerated into a rabble of rival fiefdoms. 'We used to struggle to get Sales to show us their upcoming orders or to get any information out of them at all, and no one could break the peaceful silence of the Design people over in their own corner,' says Geir Skaala, the owner and CEO. 'I used to feel like I was the only one in the Head Office who took any interest in what was going on in Production.'

After doing its homework, Magma devised a system that would allow Norsafe to operate like a big company. The first step was to set aside more time for vetting contracts. The sales team now goes through every order with a fine-toothed comb, and Skaala reads every contract himself, marking points he disagrees with in red and those that need clarifying in yellow. Each design drawing now comes with a complete list of all the relevant specifications. Everyone's role in the business has been clearly defined, with staff keeping regular action logs.

Magma also started breaking down the barriers between departments. Employees from design, sales and production now meet regularly, with their phones switched off, to talk about contracts, new plans and what is happening in the factory. Like crews at RAF Coningsby and staff at ExxonMobil, everyone is urged to report even the smallest problems and propose solutions. To reinforce the new spirit of openness, Skaala started eating lunch in the canteen rather than alone in his office.

This Slow Fix did not happen overnight, or without pain. It involved months of explaining, hand-holding and retraining. Egos were bruised and friendships tested. Though dismayed by the status quo, many employees found it hard to embrace the new way of working. 'They felt, "This is how I do it, how my father did it, how my grandfather did it, why should I change?"' says Skaala. 'It wasn't ill will; it's just that it's easier to carry on as before.' The status-quo bias, in other words. But eventually most Norsafe employees embraced the new regime, and the two who did not left.

Staff seem pleased with the change. Hans Petter Hermansen has been the production manager at Norsafe for more than 20 years. With his deep tan, white hair and piercing blue eyes, he looks like a cross between Giorgio Armani and the hero of Hemingway's *The Old Man and the Sea*. 'Magma have taught us to complain, even to stop production, if something is wrong in an order instead of just trying to make it work,' he says. 'Now we all talk and work together as a team, which means we actually do things right the first time, which is way more efficient than fixing mistakes farther down the line.'

This Slow Fix still has a long way to go. A revolution that began in the sales and contracts department is now wending its way through the rest of the company. Rolling out the changes to operations in China and Greece will take longer. Even at the headquarters in Norway, the new system is still bedding in. The day I visit, Norsafe is testing a prototype lifeboat. Several nervous designers are standing on a dock watching the vessel being scuttled in a controlled experiment. Once it starts taking on water, it fails to right itself within the three minutes stipulated by international law. The designers look perplexed, but Hermansen smiles wryly. 'They're scratching their heads, but I told them they needed four centimetres more foam in the sides of the canopy,' he mutters. 'It shows that even with the right processes in the company, people don't always listen to you.'

Even so, Norsafe seems to have turned a corner. Contracts are cycling smoothly through the company, lifeboats are arriving on time and in good condition, and profits are up. No more lawsuits are pending and the gloom in the office has lifted. In 2011, the leading financial newspaper in Norway published an article describing Norsafe as a 'money-making machine'. Skaala is over the moon. 'Everything is working now and it's actually fun coming to the office again,' he says. 'It's not rocket science. It's not hocus-pocus. It's not hard to understand. We just needed to slow down and think hard about exactly what was going wrong with our company before we could fix it.'

Others do the same deep, slow thinking without consultants. In the late 1980s, Patagonia, the California-based maker of smart, eco-friendly outdoor gear, grew so fast that it stopped training new managers properly and lost control of its ballooning network of product divisions and distribution channels. In response, Yvon Chouinard, the founder and owner, went into quick-fix mode, restructuring the company five times in five years. 'I was driving everyone crazy by constantly trying new ideas without a clear direction for where we were trying to go,' he wrote later. To find that direction, Chouinard eventually pulled the Andon rope. In 1991 he took a dozen of his top managers to southern Argentina for a walkabout in the real Patagonia. Like biblical prophets seeking truth in the desert, the company brass spent two weeks rambling through the harsh, windy landscape, chewing over the Big Question: what sort of company do we want to build? They returned from Argentina with a bundle of ideas that eventually crystallised into a mission statement: 'Make the best product, cause no unnecessary harm, and use business to inspire and implement solutions to the environmental crisis.' To embed that creed in the chain of command, Chouinard took lower-level managers on week-long retreats in US national parks. Having taken the time to answer the Big Question, Patagonia was finally able to put its house in order, cutting out superfluous layers of management, streamlining inventories and taming its sales channels. Today the company racks up annual sales over $540 million while continuing the policy it started in 1985 of donating 1 per cent of those sales to environmental causes.

Businesses aren't the only ones to benefit from thinking hard about problems. Under its new safety regime, the RAF uses psychologists to drill down through the so-called 'human factors' that play a part in every accident. 'Each piece of the puzzle has a story, and behind that story is another story and another – whether it's a man who left home early in the morning because he was out late last night, had an argument with his wife or partner, or got to work and the books he was meant to reference weren't there,' says Group Captain Brailsford. 'We're talking about pulling the Andon rope to get to the very bottom of each problem. It means we take longer to think before acting, but when we do act we are able to apply the right solutions to the right problems.'

The same goes for matters of the heart. To mend a broken relationship, you must take time to work out what is really going wrong before seeking the right fix. When counselling couples in Toronto, Dave Perry places a small, ceramic tortoise on the table between him and his clients. 'It's just a little visual reminder that you need to take the slow and patient approach to get to the heart of the matter,' he says. 'At first, people struggle with it because they want a quick fix, but once they feel they have permission to slow down, it comes as a huge relief.'

Taking time to identify and frame the problem is very much the *modus operandi* of IDEO, a global design firm famous for the deep, probing research it does before prescribing a fix. When the Memorial Hospital and Health System of South Bend, Indiana, asked for help in making plans for its new Heart and Vascular centre, the IDEO staffers spent weeks on the wards, observing, listening, asking questions. They interviewed and ran workshops with patients, families, doctors, nurses, administrators, technicians and volunteers. They even recreated the experience of arriving at the hospital for everything from a simple consultation to open-heart surgery from the point of view of the patient and family members. Many of their suggestions went into the final design of the new wing. 'Instead of just investigating people's needs by asking directly, "What would you like?" we take a more meditative, experiential approach that involves immersion and percolation,' says Jane Fulton Suri, Managing Partner and Creative Director of IDEO. 'When you spend more time getting deeply familiar with a problem, that creates space for new and surprising insights.'

It can even lead to a complete recasting of the original problem. If a client requests a new, improved toaster, IDEO might flip the question round to ask: is there a better way to make toast? Or how could breakfast be different? IDEO took a similar tack when helping Apple develop its revolutionary computer mouse in 1980. 'Right from the start we ask, "What is the real problem we need to address?" says

Fulton Suri. 'There is always a danger that the solution is already embedded in the way we frame our original problem. If we take the time to reframe it, we can open up alternative, and often better, ways to address the real need.'

That principle is even paying off in the staid world of traffic management. When accidents occur persistently along a stretch of road, the traditional fix is to tweak the street furniture – install new lights or speed bumps, say, or put up signs urging caution. Why? Because the more guidance you give motorists, the better they drive.

Or do they? After years of watching this golden rule fail to deliver safer roads, some engineers began to wonder if they were posing the wrong question. Instead of asking what can we *add* to our roads to make them safer, they began asking, in the counter-intuitive style of IDEO, what would a safer road look like? What they discovered astonished them. It turns out conventional wisdom about traffic is wrong. Often, the *less* you tell motorists how to behave, the *more* safely they drive. Think about it. Most accidents occur near school gates and crosswalks or around bus and cycle lanes, which all tend to be regulated by a dense forest of signs, lights and road markings. That is because the barrage of instructions can distract drivers. It can also lull them into a false sense of security, making them more likely to race through without paying attention.

Minimise the lights, the signage, the visual cues, and motorists must think for themselves. They have to make eye contact with pedestrians and cyclists, negotiate their passage through the cityscape, plan their next move. Result: traffic flows more freely and safely. Ripping out the signage along

Kensington High Street, one of the busiest shopping strips in London, helped slash the accident rate by 47 per cent.

There are also neurological reasons for taking the time to think slowly and deeply about a problem. Deadlines have a role to play in finding solutions, but racing the clock can lead to sloppy, superficial thinking. Teresa Amabile, professor and Director of Research at the Harvard Business School, has spent the last 30 years studying creativity in the workplace. Her research points to a sobering conclusion: rushing makes us less creative. 'Although moderate levels of time pressure don't harm creativity, extreme time pressure can stifle creativity because people can't deeply engage with the problem,' says Amabile. 'Creativity usually requires an incubation period; people need time to soak in a problem and let the ideas bubble up.'

We all know this from experience. Our best ideas, those eureka moments that turn everything upside down, seldom come when we're stuck in fast-forward, juggling emails, straining to make our voices heard in a high-stress meeting, rushing to deliver a piece of work to an impatient boss. They come when we're walking the dog, soaking in the bath or swinging in a hammock. When we are calm, unhurried and free from stress and distractions, the brain slips into a richer, more nuanced mode of thought. Some call this Slow Thinking, and the best minds have always understood its power. Milan Kundera talked about 'the wisdom of slowness'. Arthur Conan Doyle described Sherlock Holmes entering a quasi-meditative state, 'with a dreamy vacant expression in his eyes', when weighing up the evidence from crime scenes. Charles Darwin called himself a 'slow thinker'.

Slowing down to ponder even makes sense when circumstances do not allow for weeks of patient observation or long, meditative walks in Patagonia. Statistically, police officers become involved in fewer shootings, arrests and assaults working alone than they do with a partner. Why? Because the lone cop is more cautious and circumspect, more likely to take a moment to weigh the options before acting. A slight pause can even make us more ethical. Researchers at Johns Hopkins University have shown that, when faced with a clear choice between right and wrong, we are five times more likely to do the right thing if given time to think about it. Other research suggests that just two minutes of reasoned reflection can help us look beyond our biases to accept the merits of a rational argument.

To make space for rich, creative mulling, we need to demolish the taboo against slowness that runs so deep in 21st-century culture. We need to accept that decelerating judiciously, at the right moments, can make us smarter. When tackling a problem in groups, that means paying less attention to the fast thinkers who hog the stage and more to the shrinking violets who sit back and ponder. Tim Perkins, a coach at Odyssey of the Mind, sees this all the time. 'Last year, we had one kid who sat so silently through the brainstorming sessions you could almost forget she was there,' he says. 'But she was actually taking time to process what was being said, and then 10 or 15 minutes later she would speak up. Often the team ended up taking her solution to the problem.'

We can all take steps to think harder. Even when nothing needs fixing, build time into your schedule to unplug from technology and let your mind wander. When tackling a new problem, make it a rule to sleep on it for at least one night before proposing any solutions. Ask why, why and why until you uncover the root cause. Keep an object on your desk – a piece of sculpture, a wooden snail, a photo of your favourite holiday spot – that reminds you to slow down and think before you act. Above all, test your solutions again and again, no matter how foolproof they seem.

Betting the farm on a quick fix that shows early promise is an easy mistake to make, even when we design systems to stop it from happening. The investigators at RAF Coningsby, freshly trained in the art of parsing 'human factors' and homing in on the root causes of problems, have fallen into the trap. Not long ago, during routine maintenance work, an engineer opened the undercarriage door of a Typhoon jet. It slammed down onto a heavy jack standing beneath it, ripping open a gash that looked like it could have been caused by enemy fire. In the past, the young corporal would have been punished and probably ridiculed by his peers. He might even have tampered with the evidence to deflect blame. Either way, his crew would have replaced the door without really probing why the accident occurred in the first place.

Under the new regime, the engineer filed a report on the spot, triggering a full investigation. Group Captain Simpson's team quickly found that the safety pin that would have prevented the undercarriage door from lowering at the fateful moment was missing. So far, so good. Further digging then unearthed a startling oversight: though the safety pins are plainly listed in all the Typhoon manuals, three out of the four RAF squadrons had never even fitted them.

Simpson was stunned. 'Everyone's following the list. Everyone's trained in accordance with the list. Everyone can see the pictures of the pin in place. And still no one had noticed that we'd never even bought any of these pins,' she says. It felt like a home-run endorsement of the new safety regime. The RAF bought a load of safety pins and then closed the file on the Case of the Damaged Undercarriage Door.

'Everyone said, "Crikey, isn't this new system brilliant? We would never have picked this up before,"' says Simpson. 'We thought, "That's all sorted now, problem solved."' Only it wasn't. A few weeks later another Typhoon door was wrecked in an almost identical accident.

The safety pin was a red herring. When investigators took the time to think harder and dig deeper, they found a host of other factors leading to the mishap with the door: engineers distracted by changing shifts; poor lighting in the hangar; an illustration in the instruction manual suggesting the wrong angle for the jack.

'We were so pleased to find the safety pin, which seemed like such an obvious answer to the problem, that we were completely blinded by it and just stopped looking for other causes,' says Simpson, wincing slightly at the memory. 'But the upside is we learned a very valuable lesson from this: just because you find one factor that seems to offer an almost perfect solution, you don't stop. You have to carry on investigating, digging, asking questions until you have the full picture of what happened and how to fix it properly.'

In other words, if your first fix seems too good to be true, it probably is.

When I ask Simpson if all that hard thinking ever leads to a moment of perfect clarity, she falls silent for a few seconds before answering. 'You do reach a point when you know what has to be done, but it's rarely as simple as firing a magic bullet,' she says. 'There are always multiple factors you have to connect up.'

CHAPTER FOUR

THINK HOLISTIC:
Joining the Dots

All is connected … no one thing can change by itself.
Paul Hawken, environmentalist

They call it the ghetto limp. You've seen it in episodes of *The Wire*, in a million hip-hop videos, maybe even on the streets of your own city. It's that lolloping, loping gait favoured by young men in tough neighbourhoods. It hints at an old gunshot wound, or at packing heat somewhere in those baggy trousers. It's a gang thing, an affectation of the street, another pose designed to send the same message to everyone around: 'Don't mess with me because I am one mean motherfucker.'

When I meet Lewis Price, he is working the ghetto limp like a pro. Hair pulled back in cornrows; trousers on the baggy side; black and red Air Jordans ostentatiously untied; MOB (Money over Bitches) tattooed on his wrist. At 17, he is compact and muscled, with the coiled energy of an athlete on the starting line, or a cat waiting to pounce.

When Price starts talking, however, you realise he is not a mean motherfucker at all. His easy smile and gentle manner belie his appearance. He loves to talk and grabs hold of any conversation, eyes darting round the room as if searching for the next reason to laugh. Unlike many youths caught up in the gang violence that blights South Central Los Angeles, he is not feigning the limp for effect. When he was 14, a rival gang member took a pot-shot at him while he was hanging out on the sidewalk. The bullet sliced through his right leg and wedged so deeply in his left that doctors chose to leave it there. He can no longer play football or basketball and the limp now draws the wrong sort of attention on the street. 'People think I'm walking like that on purpose, that I'm walking like a gangbanger to make a statement or something,' he says. 'But that's the only way I can walk after I got shot. You know, the way I see it, I'm lucky I can walk at all.'

Price tends to look on the bright side these days. He has turned his back on the street, earned a place on the honour roll and plans to go to university – no mean feat for a kid born and raised in Watts.

This corner of Los Angeles has long been on the front line of black struggle. In 1965 the Watts Riots turned 50 square miles of the city into a war zone of charred buildings and pitched battles with the National Guard. Later, the gangs took hold, with the storied Bloods and Crips carving out violent fiefdoms. Over the last decade Latinos have moved in *en masse*, yet Watts remains plagued by the same old list of urban despair: poverty, crime, failing schools, ill health, unemployment, broken homes, drugs, teenage pregnancy, malnutrition, deadbeat dads, domestic violence. With gang members

numbering in the thousands, fistfights, stabbings and shootings like the one that crippled Price are a part of life. Not
many kids from Watts make it to college.

Price is not the first gangbanger to turn over a new leaf.
But instead of crediting church, family or a heroic social
worker, he puts his conversion down to his alma mater. To
the delight, and surprise, of many Watts residents, the local
high school now known as Ánimo Locke has gone from
basket case to beacon of hope.

'If it weren't for Locke I wouldn't be the person I am
today,' says Price. 'Before I came here, I felt like, man, the only
way I'm gonna make it is just survive on the street, but I got
here and they just woke me up.' He falls silent for a moment,
as if pondering the road not taken, before adding, 'If it weren't
for Locke, I'd be like all my old friends, I'd be dead or in jail.
But now, you know, I got a future. I'm a good student now
and I'm gonna make it somewhere.'

Many countries continue to grapple with how to break
the cycle of poor children stumbling through lousy schools
en route to a life at the bottom of the barrel. The problem is
especially acute in the US, where 10 per cent of the nation's
high schools, most of them in tough, urban neighbourhoods,
produce nearly half its drop-outs. One solution is to build
new and better academies in the same areas. This is the
approach taken by the non-profit Charter Management
Organisations (CMOs), which have used public money to
open and manage hundreds of free schools across the US
since the 1990s. The Obama administration took a different
tack, sending in star principals with the money and the
mandate to rebuild failing schools from the ground up. The

two strategies have delivered mixed results. Locke stands out because it blends both approaches to good effect.

In 2007 the Los Angeles Unified School District invited a CMO called Green Dot to engineer a turnaround at Locke. It was the first time a US charter group agreed to take on a failing school, and Locke was failing on a grand scale. Opened in 1967 as a symbol of renewal after the Watts Riots, the school was named after Alain Leroy Locke, the first African-American to win a Rhodes Scholarship to study at Oxford University. But over the years, as jobs and middle-class families drained out of the neighbourhood, the school's fortunes drained away with them. By the time Green Dot stepped in, Locke, which sprawls over six city blocks and houses 3,100 students, was the sort of drop-out factory you see in the movies: buildings riddled with graffiti, smashed windows and broken lights; paint peeling off the walls in every classroom; litter blowing like tumbleweed across the scruffy campus; cars parked all over the place, even on the handball courts.

Students routinely missed class to wander the halls or sit outside in large groups shooting dice or smoking weed. They set fires inside the school and held parties on the roof. Gang members sold drugs outside the gymnasium. Campus security guards spent most of their time breaking up fights and keeping rival gangs apart. Several pupils were shot in front of the school's gates.

Some teachers toiled heroically to give proper instruction to the few students willing or able to receive it, but the tide was against them. Many just gave up. Staff screened movies so often that parents dubbed Locke the 'ghetto cineplex'. Many read newspapers or novels in class while the children horsed around and played cards. Even the Life Skills teacher turned up to class drunk. Locke hit rock bottom in 2007, when the city sent in helicopters and riot police to break up a brawl involving hundreds of students. But while the shootings, rapes and beatings grabbed headlines, the most damning statistic of all was this: of the 1,451 children who started ninth grade in 2004, less than 6 per cent graduated four years later with enough credentials to apply to a California state university.

It is not as if officialdom gave up on Locke. On the contrary, the city hurled initiative after initiative at the school: a new attendance policy here, a fresh reading programme there, a revamped code of discipline some time after that, and so on. The trouble was, the authorities never took the time to look at the big picture. Instead, they churned through one-off initiatives as I churned through cures for back pain. Stephen Minix, the director of athletics, had a front-row seat on this kaleidoscope of quick fixes. 'Year after year, we had people in suits and ties showing up and sprinkling some of this or some of that on the school, and saying "This'll fix it," and then just walking away,' he says. 'They were always sweeping policies handed down by District with no thought for what they would really mean for Locke, so they never made a dent. They were just band-aid solutions to much deeper problems.'

Green Dot therefore faced a lot of scepticism from the start. Teachers at Locke, including Minix, suspected the newcomers of being just another band of quick-fix merchants. Many Watts residents distrusted the smooth-talking outsiders. As one parent puts it: 'For a lot of people, it was like "Here

75

come these white folks, these pilgrims, putting up their tents, their fences, and they're promising to fix our school and our kids but we don't have no say in it, and when it don't work out they'll ride off into the sunset and leave us with an even bigger mess than before.'"

But Green Dot is not in the business of band-aid solutions. It wheeled Locke straight into the hospital for major surgery. The man at the top is Marco Petruzzi, whose trenchant views on our culture of hype and hot air we encountered earlier. When I ask him what the turnaround of Locke tells us about the art of solving problems, he answers without hesitation. 'The main lesson is there is no one policy, one piece of software, one single change to the environment that can fix a broken school,' he says. 'It's a whole host of factors, and you have to figure out what they are, how they are interconnected, and then tackle them all together.'

This brings us to the next ingredient of the Slow Fix: joining the dots to take a holistic approach. In Chapter Three we saw the importance of taking the time to work out the true nature of a problem. This usually reveals a web of interconnected factors that can never be solved with a single magic bullet. Complex problems, from climate change to conflict in the Middle East to a marriage on the rocks, need to be examined through a wider lens and tackled holistically. When US companies began investing heavily in technology in the 1980s, experts sat back and waited for a surge in productivity. But it never came. Or it did, but only after bosses realised that installing sexy new hardware and software was not enough on its own. You also have to make a host of systemic changes, from retraining staff to revamping working practices. A rule of thumb is that, for every dollar spent on new technology, a company needs to pump in another five to ten dollars to reorganise itself to be able to make use of it.

That holistic approach also pays off in medicine, where physical symptoms are usually part of a bigger story. Tapping the link between mind and body, many hospitals now use art, music and even clowns to help combat stress, manage pain and improve healing.

The same goes for mending broken relationships. Marianne Bertrand, the Paris-based therapist we met earlier, finds warring couples often fixate on a single grievance, such as an affair. Yet such things seldom happen in isolation, and are usually the symptom of deeper, more complex problems. Like the RAF unravelling the stories within stories after an accident, Bertrand helps couples unpick the narrative below the surface. 'You cannot understand a Shakespearean play by listening to one soliloquy,' she says. 'A relationship is like a large and complex puzzle, so you need to examine all the pieces and then work out how to fit them together.'

The trouble is that holistic thinking does not come easily to us. As we saw earlier, the human brain often slips into tunnel vision. Remember how more than half of us miss the man in the gorilla suit wandering into that basketball game on YouTube. That is why the best problem-solvers make a big effort to join the dots. 'We try to come at every problem by uncovering what's really going on for people in the system,' says IDEO's Jane Fulton Suri. 'To map out how things are connected, how the activities of the different players combine to form the culture of the place and how those need to be involved in making changes.' In that same spirit, Green Dot set out to revamp Locke from the inside out.

To create a more intimate environment, it split the school into smaller academies, cordoning them off with makeshift fencing and partitions. It also slashed class sizes from 40 to around 30. Every teacher at Locke was dismissed and invited to reapply. After rigorous interviewing, Green Dot rehired a third of them, with the remaining staff made up of hungry young recruits from outside. Constant training and assessment now keeps teachers old and new on their toes.

Instead of stampeding for the exit at the 3 p.m. bell, staff now stay into the evening to give extra tutoring, advise on college applications or just lend a sympathetic ear. They also make home visits and hand out their personal phone numbers. 'The teachers teach us, but they go way beyond that,' says Price. 'They really make sure that if we don't understand something, we can come to them any time. We can call them late at night and be like "I'm stuck with your homework, will you help me out" and they gonna explain to us till we finished.'

To give the academic changes real purpose, Green Dot set out to embed a single idea in the culture of the school: with enough hard work and imagination every child that walks through the door can make it to college one day. This creed is repeated like a mantra. Every pupil is helped to build a college plan from the ninth grade. College pennants and brochures hang in the classrooms alongside photos of recent graduates in cap and gown. Alumni return to give talks about life at university. During classes, teachers pepper their patter with phrases like 'When you're in college …' and 'Your professors in college will …'

At the same time as putting the academics back on track, Green Dot transformed the look and feel of Locke. It started by giving the campus a face-lift worthy of an LA cosmetic surgeon: repainting buildings; cleaning up litter; fixing broken windows and faulty lights; replacing cracked concrete in the centre of the campus with a grassy field fringed with flowers, shrubs and olive and pepper trees; installing smart metal picnic tables with parasols outside the library. Hallways once plastered in graffiti and gang tags are now spotless apart from posters announcing upcoming football games or displays of classroom work. In one corridor I see a clutch of A+ essays on the Second Amendment, some decent poetry and an exhibition of witty political postcards.

The pupils also underwent a makeover. They now wear a uniform of khaki chinos and a collared shirt in one of the school colours. Jackets with red, blue and other bold hues are discouraged in favour of neutral colours with no gang affiliation. Those who turn up out of uniform are sent home or loaned one, except on Wednesdays, when anyone can wear jeans and a college top. Pupils say the new regime has eliminated spats over who is wearing the right shirt or the wrong pants. The uniform also serves as a safe pass through the mean streets around the school. 'You notice that when you're in regular clothes people are watching,' says Maurice Jackson, an eleventh grader with the darting eyes and easy charm of the class clown. 'But put on that uniform and they look right past you, they don't pay attention to who you are. They just think, "Oh, he's just some kid going to school, he's not a threat to me," and they leave you alone.'

Making the children feel safe was a central plank of Green Dot's Slow Fix. No matter how good the teachers, how pretty the campus or how smart the uniform, if students are constantly looking over their shoulders, worried someone will throw a punch or pull a gun, they're not going to learn anything. And Locke was, according to Minix, 'a place where everyone was angry and scared all the time'.

In response, Green Dot overhauled the security regime. Now, when the bell rings between classes, staff carrying walkie-talkies take up strategic positions on campus to direct traffic and keep order. An officer from the county sheriff's department and private security guards patrol the grounds along with a posse of unarmed aides. Regular armed patrols keep a two-block radius around the school safe and free of gangs and sometimes establish safety cordons further afield. Locke also runs buses to bring in children from distant neighbourhoods and shuttle home those staying late for tutoring or sports. Security staff still search the pupils for weapons, but more discreetly than before. Where once they barged into lessons to pat them down in front of their class-mates, they now do the frisking in a private room. 'It's about being more understanding with the kids,' says Jacob McKinney, an unarmed security guard who was a student at Locke in the 1990s.

Understanding the kids meant joining the dots well beyond the classroom. More than a fifth of Locke students are in foster care and nearly half come from single-parent homes. Domestic violence and teen pregnancy are widespread, malnutrition is not uncommon and many children go years without seeing a dentist or a doctor. To ease the burden, Green Dot partners with a day care centre across the street for the more than 200 babies born to Locke pupils. It also hired a team of full-time counsellors, brought in a dentist to treat kids plagued by toothaches and arranged for others to receive prescription glasses. When prostitutes or gang members start pestering Locke children in a nearby park, a staff member wheels over a taco stand to make peace with them. Like many students, Andre Walker, an eleventh grader who lives in foster care, thinks of the school as a second home, a guardian angel watching over every corner of his hard-scrabble life. 'I don't have my parents and some days I don't feel like talking to no one but I go to one of the teachers here, his name is Mac, and tell him what I'm feeling about my past life,' he says. 'Maybe before when I needed to get something off my shoulders I bottled it up or got angry, but now I can go to him. Our staff and teachers are basically like a secondary kind of parent: they lead you where you need to go.'

Green Dot has also persuaded parents and guardians to show more interest in the school. They can attend regular breakfasts with the principal, while office administrators work the phones to keep them abreast of detentions, home-work, awards, late arrivals and other twists and turns in their children's lives. 'They call so much, they call every chance they get, and my mom loves it,' says Price, laughing. 'Every time Locke call, she picks it up real quick, but it's cool though. It's good to know everyone is looking out for me.'

What all this adds up to is that a broken school is now very much on the mend, as I see for myself one lunchtime. Boys and girls play a giggly game of football on the grass. Others lounge nearby in the shade, fiddling with mobile phones or listening to MP3 players. A couple of girls take turns braiding each other's hair. Outside the canteen, four boys play a raucous game of handball against a wall while others show off tricks on BMX bikes and skateboards. Shielding his eyes from the low winter sun, McKinney surveys the scene and a smile creeps across his smooth, round face. In the bad old days lunch hour meant breaking up fights and scouting for hidden guns. Today McKinney is bumping knuckles and trading banter with the skateboarders. 'If I had to give what's happened here a title, I'd call it "The Resurrection of Locke",' he says. 'Alumni come back and they can't believe it. It's like night and day: everyone going to class, behaving, hanging out together. It's like a real school now.'

There is much truth in that. Meet-the-teacher evenings that once drew a few dozen parents now pull in over a thousand. Dressed in Locke T-shirts, some help serve food or tidy up around campus. Test scores and attendance have risen, and the drop-out rate has nosedived. When I visit the athletics department, Minix is almost turning cartwheels over the latest academic news. Of the 200 players on the school basketball and football teams, only two have failed to meet the minimum grades needed to keep their places. Before the turnaround, 60 or 70 would have been shown the door. 'This is really phenomenal, unbelievable,' says Minix. 'I've just been singing the praises all day, I'm beaming.'

Yet the real triumph of Locke is harder to measure than test scores or attendance figures. When you tackle a complex problem from every angle, the various elements of the fix can add up to more than the sum of their parts, yielding a much deeper change. At Locke, Green Dot has conjured a shift in the very DNA of the school, an acceptance that discipline, hard work and respect are the way forward. You would struggle to quantify it in a PowerPoint slide, but you see it in a hundred little moments every day.

My first encounter with the new culture comes at the Advanced Path academy, which helps struggling students earn enough credits to graduate. In a room with 80 children sitting at rows of computers, I spot a girl in the far corner tossing a scrunched-up piece of paper towards the bin. When it misses and lands on the floor, our eyes lock, and a moment of tension ensues. I learn afterwards that she is a 17-year-old single mother with a history of assault. In the old days she would probably have rolled her eyes or flicked me the finger. Instead, she laughs, throws up her hands in an 'I'm busted' gesture and rises to collect the piece of paper and drop it in the bin.

All that banging on about college seems to be making a mark, too. Locke will not be sending legions of graduates to Ivy League schools any time soon, but aspiring to a place at Yale or Stanford no longer invites derision or bullying. Julia Marquez, a quiet eleventh grader who wants to be a paediatrician, loves the new atmosphere. 'What's really changed is that now you're cool if you're smart,' she says. 'Before you had to get in trouble to be cool. Now you're cool if you get straight As.'

Of course, a studious girl like Marquez is low-hanging fruit for Green Dot. The real challenge is to turn around kids like Price. By his own account, he was a lost cause by the age of 12, running the streets, ditching school, smoking pot, fighting and running 'missions' for the gangs. Within his own crew he rose to the rank of OG, or Original Gangster. 'I was on top,' he says. 'I was only 14 and I already had all that power and it felt good.' Even a bullet in the leg did not change his mind. On the contrary, it made him lash out to prove his status as a mean motherfucker. 'I was lying in hospital thinking, "If I leave it alone, people gonna think I'm a sucker or a bitch," so I had to stand up, I had to retaliate,' he says. 'Even before I got home from the hospital, my little crew was on it and it was already war – we drive by there, they drive by here, we shoot at them, they shoot on us, innocent bodies get hit in the crossfire but it don't matter, it's a war thing.' Two of his friends died in the skirmishes, and Price started carrying around his Glock 9mm pistol more often. 'I felt like ain't nobody can protect me but me and my gun,' he says. 'Once you're in a gang, that stuff is mandatory. If you don't have it, you're useless. You're just a walking target.'

Price is a mass of contradictions. Sometimes he talks of his gang past with a wistful bravado, like a kid reliving highlights from a video game. Other times he seems horrified by what happened. On one point, though, he is completely consistent: the staff at Locke helped him apply a holistic fix to his own life.

'When I went there, they were real patient with me,' he says. 'They made me just sit down and think about the whole gang thing. They helped me see that I ain't got nothing from it – no car, no money, no jewellery – that it was just me hurting people and people hurting me. They listened to me without judging me like no one ever done before, and they got me thinking about all the things I could change.'

As well as hitting the books for the first time in his life, Price started buying clothes that were less baggy and threw away his Toronto Blue Jays baseball cap because its blue colouring marked him out as a member of the Crips. He also stopped visiting his old 'hood. His new goal in life is to become a surgeon.

Later, I meet Price at the small two-bedroom apartment he shares with his mother, Sandra, and three younger brothers. He lived with his father until the latter died recently from an old gunshot wound. When we arrive, the apartment smells of the chicken gizzards Sandra is boiling up for a snack. The Shopping Channel is playing on a plasma-screen TV hung on the wall. Sandra looks relieved to see Price. 'He got into a lot of problems before, and I was scared when he got shot, but Locke's been good for him – he's got a future now,' she says. 'But with how he looks, and how he walks, people still target him in the street.' After telling his mom not to worry, Price steers me straight to the bedroom where a certificate awarding him a place on the honour roll is pinned to the wall. When his little brother runs over and jumps into his arms, he gives him a squeeze and a tickle. 'You know,' he says, 'I feel like Locke gotta be the best school in the world.'

Let's not get carried away. Despite the face-lift, Locke remains scruffy, and can sometimes feel like a prison yard. A tall metal fence installed in the 1990s still rings the perimeter. Windows are covered in wire mesh, the snack machines are cloaked in heavy-duty metal caging and there are CCTV cameras everywhere. The armed security guards outside the gates wear wraparound shades and carry spray canisters on their belts.

With expectations rising, the children are quick to list their grievances. They object to the partitions that break the campus up into separate schools, the dated 1960s buildings and the cafeteria food. They want more college mentoring, more parental involvement, more after-school programmes.

Many within Green Dot feel too much academic progress was promised too soon. After years in inferior schooling, children often arrive at Locke without knowing the multiplication tables or barely able to read. Nor did it help that the young teachers received too little support and training at the start. Even now, staff concede that Locke needs more writing programmes, better provision for special needs and help for pupils learning English as a second language. Instead of promising to deliver higher test scores, which took time to start rising, Green Dot says it should have made more noise about more reachable goals, such as slashing drop-out rates and fostering a better climate within the school.

But clearly much has gone right. Impressed by the turn-around at Locke, educational authorities in Los Angeles have hired Green Dot to work the same magic on two other failing schools, with promising early results. The Department of Education in Washington also hails Locke as a model worth studying.

Even if fixing a broken school is not on your agenda, we can all learn from Green Dot's holistic approach. When confronted with any complex problem, take time to figure out all the different variables and how they interact. Map them out on a piece of paper to clarify the connections.

Then devise a solution that tackles them all together. No matter how urgent the need for a fix, never promise too much, too soon.

Taking the long view is certainly the most valuable lesson Price has learned from the turnaround of Locke. 'Green Dot taught us that the people with you now, they might not be by your side later and the only person that's always gonna be there is you, yourself and the books and what you know,' he says. 'Your education is really going to count in the long run, and no matter how tough things are now, you always gotta think of the future.'

CHAPTER FIVE

THINK LONG: Tackling Tomorrow Today

*In this age, which believes that there is a short cut to
everything, the greatest lesson to be learned is that the most
difficult way is, in the long run, the easiest.*
Henry Miller

'I think you'll be impressed,' says Are Hoeidal, pushing open
the door and leading me into the cottage. We step across the
welcome mat into a cocoon of Scandinavian comfort –
exposed wooden beams, bunk-beds with plump white
duvets, wool rugs on the floors. It is early summer in southern Norway, and sunlight pours through the large windows.
The air smells of fresh pine.

In the living room, we sit in leather chairs to admire the
amenities. A plasma screen TV and prints of Impressionist
paintings on the walls. Shelves jammed with *Harry Potter*
novels, boxes of Lego and jigsaw puzzles. A retro chrome bin
standing guard in the kitchen.

Hoeidal cracks open the sliding doors at the back and we step out onto a wooden deck. A picnic table and bench stand on the grass along with a few metal seats, including a blue one with a spinning top, hammered into the ground for children. A gentle breeze riffles the trees and the blackcurrant bushes at the edge of the garden. Hoeidal breathes in the bracing Nordic air and smiles like a man holding all the cards. 'It is a very comfortable place for a family to spend time together,' he says. 'Do you not think so?'

Yes, I do. I can easily imagine a family spending a very happy holiday here. It feels like a million other cottages tucked away in forests and nestled beside lakes around the world. It reminds me of a recent vacation my family took in the Rockies. I can picture myself firing up the barbecue on the deck with my own children horsing around nearby.

Except for one thing: a six-metre-high concrete wall snaking through the surrounding forest as far as the eye can see.

We are standing in the grounds of a new high-security prison called Halden, and Hoeidal is the warden. Convicted drug-dealers, murderers and rapists stay in the cottage with their visiting families. 'People from other countries are surprised by how nice our overnight house is, but to Norwegians it makes sense to have something like this in a prison,' says Hoeidal. 'It is part of a solution that works.'

Around the world, nations are grappling with the failure of penal systems to send inmates back into society as reformed citizens. Jail often does exactly the opposite. Many convicts finish their sentences angry, scared and unsure how to apply for a job, rent a flat or even hold a conversation. Not long after Halden opened in 2010, Ken Clarke, then Home Secretary for the new coalition government in Britain, demolished one of the shibboleths of his own Conservative party when he argued that years of tossing more and more people into jail for longer and longer had backfired. 'Too often, prison has proved a costly and ineffectual approach that fails to turn criminals into law-abiding citizens,' he said. 'In our worst prisons, it produces tougher criminals.' The numbers speak volumes. In the United States, Britain and Germany, more than half of inmates are re-arrested within three years of leaving prison. In Norway, the recidivism rate is around 20 per cent.

I have come to Halden to find out why. Hoeidal himself seems to embody a very different penal philosophy. He is as far as you can get from the ass-kicking, cigar-chomping prison warden of Hollywood lore. Affable and avuncular, he always seems on the verge of smiling. When I emailed him to arrange a visit, he answered with a cheerful 'Hello!' At lunch, he eats salad.

Hoeidal is clear about why the Norwegian approach works. Most countries take a short-term view of prison, he says, making punishment and containment its main, or even sole, purpose. That means popular support for longer sentences. It also means conditions on the inside must hover between spartan and downright unpleasant. Even the slightest hint of creature comforts can provoke convulsions of public outrage. When Halden opened its doors, media across the world mocked 'the world's poshest prison' for its flat-screen TVs, *ensuite* bathrooms and 'luxury library'. American college students moaned that the prison was smarter than their dorms. A French blogger described Halden as an open invitation to criminals across Europe to move to Norway.

Most Norwegians ignored the huffing and puffing from abroad. Set on the northern edge of Europe, this oil-rich nation of 4.8 million souls believes the real punishment for committing a crime is the loss of liberty. Everything else about a prison should help pave the way for convicts to fit back into society at the end of their sentence. On the island of Bastøy, for instance, inmates live in a village-like setting, complete with shops, school and church, and their own red and yellow clapboard houses. A White Paper published by the Norwegian government in 2008 concluded that 'the smaller the difference between life inside and outside the prison, the easier the transition from prison to freedom'.

This brings us to the next ingredient of the Slow Fix. We have already seen the importance of thinking hard about a problem and joining the dots to devise a holistic solution. The success of the Norwegian prison system reminds us that any fix worth its salt must also take the long view. Of course, pondering the future does not come naturally in our shoot-now-ask-questions-later culture. Just think of all the things you have said in the heat of the moment to friends, family and colleagues that came back to haunt you later. Short-term thinking haunts the corporate world, too. Companies often slash costs to survive hard times today without thinking about how they will cope when business picks up again tomorrow. In 1993 General Motors shrank its payroll through a generous early retirement plan. A year later the company was so short of staff in its US plants that it had to lure GM retirees back to work with bonuses of up to $21,000.

When a crime is committed, punishment tops the agenda in most countries. We want to see perpetrators pay for their misdeeds, and we want them off the streets so they cannot carry on breaking the law. Norwegians want that, too. But even after the most heinous crimes, one of the first questions they ask is how to rehabilitate the criminal. 'We don't think about revenge in the Norwegian prison system,' says Hoeidal. 'Instead, we look at what kind of neighbour you want to have when they come out. If you treat prisoners harshly and just keep them in a box for a few years, they will not leave as better people. Our work here at Halden is therefore not just about what we do with the inmates today or next week or next month; it is really about helping them rebuild the rest of their lives by helping them become normal citizens again.'

A big part of that is keeping in touch with loved ones on the outside. Study after study shows that criminals who maintain strong family bonds while in jail are far less likely to reoffend after their release. Yet in many countries prisoners have to rely on the occasional supervised visit or phone call to stay in touch. At Halden inmates can spend up to 30 minutes a week on the phone with their nearest and dearest. They can hang out with their families in private rooms stuffed with wooden toys, bean-bags and photographs of zebras and rhinoceroses. Or they can book a stay in the two-bedroom cottage.

Rather than ostracising convicts, Norway allows them to vote and even take part in television debates from their cells. It also encourages its citizens to visit. When Halden opened its doors, 9,000 people turned up for a tour on the first day.

'There has been a big effort to make prisoners visible, to show their ordinariness, to make it clear they are not that strange, that they are human beings also,' says Nils Christie, a professor of criminology at the University of Oslo. 'In Norway, more than in other countries, the hypothesis that there are lots of monsters running around who need to be locked up for life has been weakened to a large extent.'

That does not mean all Norwegians love every aspect of their penal system. With the maximum jail term fixed at 21 years, right-wing politicians have called for tougher sentences for violent criminals. Many Norwegians think foreigners, who make up about a third of all inmates here, should be housed somewhere less comfortable than Halden. To an outsider, however, the country seems remarkably relaxed about prisons. Elsewhere, jails rank up there with paedophiles and nuclear power stations on the list of Stuff You Really Don't Want in Your Neighbourhood. By contrast, local residents welcomed the new Halden prison as a boost to the regional economy. Despite grumbles about freeloading foreigners, all the mainstream political parties backed its construction.

It helps that crime is not a serious problem in Norway. The country reports ten times fewer murders and incarcerates ten times fewer people per capita than does the United States. Most Norwegian criminals are doing time for petty theft, drink-driving or other run-of-the-mill crimes. The Norwegian media play their part, too. Rather than stoke panic with the sort of sensationalist coverage that is a staple of tabloid newspapers and TV crime shows in other countries, journalists in Norway report on even the most ghastly crimes in measured tones, resisting the temptation to pander to the short-term lust for retribution. Instead, they stress the need to rehabilitate the perpetrator.

That reticence was tested in 2011 when a right-wing extremist named Andres Behring Breivik set off a bomb in Oslo before shooting dead 77 people at a youth camp. In the aftermath, some Norwegians called for his execution, while others vowed to kill him if he is ever released from prison. Still others demanded a new law allowing for life imprisonment. But the overwhelming response was what you might expect from the nation that built Halden prison. I visited Oslo a month after the attack, and found the mood astonishingly moderate. Back in Britain, judges were doling out four-year jail terms to people caught using Facebook to egg on the riots that ripped through that country around the same time. By contrast, Norway, reeling from the worst mass murder in its history, had settled into a firm consensus that the crimes of a single madman must not cause the nation to abandon the long-term goal of rehabilitation for the quick fix of vengeance. 'Kill Anders Behring Breivik' pages on Facebook garnered no more than a few hundred fans, many of them from overseas.

The idea of rehabilitation has deep roots in Norway. In the mid-19th century, Scandinavians began re-imagining prison as a place where criminals could learn to work and find God. After the Second World War, with the memory of Nazi prison camps still fresh, many European countries took steps to make their jails less punitive. In the late 1990s Norway made rehabilitation the cornerstone of its prison philosophy. It renamed its penal network the Criminal Care system and embraced electronic tagging and open prisons. Guards became Personal Contact Officers, charged with acting as coach-cum-confidants to inmates. This is a work in progress. Many convicted criminals still start their sentences in old-style, closed jails, which are much less salubrious than the low-security Bastøy or the high-security Halden. At the gloomy Oslo Prison, where Hoeidal spent 11 years as warden, many inmates spend 23 out of every 24 hours in their cells and drug abuse is rife. But in keeping with the 'normalisation principle' of making inside as much like outside as possible, Norway has pledged to make all its jails more hospitable. Halden is the face of this next stage. 'There is still a big gap between the ideals and the reality, but already we have seen huge changes,' says Hoeidal.

To remind inmates that they are still part of society, and should therefore work on returning to the fold in the future, Norwegian architects designed Halden to feel like a small village. Rather than grim, rain-stained concrete, the buildings are made of brick, larch and galvanised steel. The windows are free of bars and the perimeter wall is partially obscured by trees. Dolk, an über-hip graffiti artist, painted three giant murals here. One depicts an inmate, dressed in stripy pyjamas, using a ball and chain as a shot put. There are plenty of security cameras scattered around the grounds, but then much of the outside world seems to be carpeted with CCTV these days. With inmates dressed in their own casual clothes, and guards gliding around on trendy two-wheel scooters, Halden has, from certain angles, the look of a university campus, or even the headquarters of a tech start-up in Silicon Valley.

Inside, the atmosphere is just as congenial. Filled with natural light, adorned with photographs of daffodils and Parisian street scenes, and stocked with ping-pong tables and exercise bikes, the extra-wide corridors feel spacious and welcoming. The individual cells resemble rooms in a mid-range business hotel, with desks, beds and wardrobes in blond wood. Tall, vertical windows with vents circulate fresh air from outside. Each cell features a flat-screen TV, mini-fridge and *ensuite* bathroom complete with white tiles and large, fluffy towels. In the evening, smart linen curtains and LED lighting lend an almost boutique atmosphere to the environs. To create a feeling of family life, cells are grouped by the dozen and arranged around a communal space furnished with comfortable sofas, tables and a massive flat-screen TV. Inmates can send out for groceries to cook their favourite recipes in the kitchen.

Though confined to their cells from 8.30 p.m. till 7 a.m., the prisoners are encouraged, with the help of a daily payment of 53 kroner (£5.60), to come out and use the facilities. They can play football or basketball; lay down tracks in the state-of-the-art recording studio; work out in the gym or on the rock climbing wall; study mechanics, steelwork or carpentry in the vast workshop; or learn to fillet fish or whip up grapefruit sorbet in the gleaming professional kitchen. They can also perform small jobs for outside contractors. I come across a group of prisoners laughing at a crude joke as they pack plastic clips into boxes. 'Sitting alone all day is not good for a person,' says Hoeidal. 'If they are busy, then they are happier – and therefore less likely to become institutionalised.'

Instead of watching from behind shatter-proof glass or leaning against the walls with their arms crossed, guards at Halden eat meals, play sports and generally hang out with the prisoners. None of them carry weapons. 'We do not need guns because we are here to care for the criminals, to talk to them, not terrorise them,' says Hoeidal. 'Even in other Scandinavian countries you see more distance between staff and inmates, but here we are inside the environment, right there with them.'

It helps that Norway invests more heavily in its prison staff than other countries. Many guards earn an undergraduate degree, often in criminology or psychology, before spending two years hitting the books and completing hands-on training at the prison officers' academy. This is a desirable career for someone who wants to do more than just turn keys and break up fights. The academy receives ten applications for every opening.

A young guard – or rather Personal Contact Officer – named Asmund shows me round Halden. He is educated, polite and gentle in the Scandinavian tradition. As we visit the various blocks, he chats and jokes with the inmates. 'We are more than just guards, we are also social workers,' he says. 'The bottom line here is always security, but a big part of our job is creating as normal an environment as possible based on good relations and trust so that inmates can become responsible for their own lives and be able to reintegrate into the normal world afterwards. Everything we do here is supposed to be an investment in their future.' That thinking is woven into the language itself. The Norwegian words for 'prison guard' translate into English as 'prison servant'. Every detail in Halden is arranged to ease the transition back into civilian life. To stop prisoners turning into muscle-bound menaces, the gym has no free weights. And half the guards at Halden are female. 'It reduces the aggression inside the prison,' says Hoeidal. 'Plus it teaches inmates to feel comfortable around women, which is important for the future return to society.'

The inmates seem to like the regime. The first stop on my tour is the music studio, an Aladdin's cave of shiny new instruments and top-of-the-line iMacs. A poster of the TV show *Prison Break* hangs on the door.

Marcus Nordberg is fiddling with an iMac in the mixing suite. He transferred to Halden from another prison a few months earlier. A fifty-something refugee from the music and film industry, he wears a goatee, shades and flip-flops. He refuses to tell me what he is in for, but is quick to sing the praises of Halden. 'It's high security here but it doesn't feel like a prison,' he says. 'They try to keep the warmth, and cultivate people to be positive, and they help you look to the future.'

'Do the guards live up to their billing as Personal Contact Officers?' I ask.

Nordberg gives a qualified nod. 'Some of the staff still have the "prison" mindset, where they're just door-lockers, but most of the guards get more involved with us,' he says. 'They play sports and cards with us. They sit in the fellowship room and chat. They create an atmosphere of normality and respect, which is good training for going back into society after you've done your time. Most of the inmates like it.'

When I ask if the regime is too cushy, Nordberg shoots me a dirty look. Last month he was denied leave to attend his father's funeral outside Norway. The memory of it makes his voice catch and his eyes redden. 'Prison is prison and just because it's a nice place doesn't make it any less of a punishment,' he says. 'Even in a five-star hotel you can still be locked up and that's horrible, really horrible.'

In the past I might have dismissed that as a self-indulgent whine, but not after a day at Halden. It is an agreeable place with fine fixtures and fittings, but, as Nordberg says, it is still a jail. The loss of liberty deals a crushing blow to the human spirit. The six weeks I spent wearing a cast to heal an ankle injury were among the most depressing in my life. It was not the pain that bothered me but losing the freedom to move around at will. Being denied the right to be with the people that matter to us, or to be with any people at all, can be even more dispiriting. Charles Dickens, who knew a thing or two about hard knocks, once denounced solitary confinement as the cruellest punishment: 'I hold this slow and daily tampering with the mysteries of the brain, to be immeasurably worse than any torture of the body.' After a few hours wandering around Halden, I find myself shooting anxious glances at the perimeter wall. It seems to rise up from the forest like the monolith in *2001: A Space Odyssey*, a dense, solid, implacable reminder that I can no longer come and go as I please. On our way to the library, I suddenly realise I am no longer listening to Asmund: I am wondering how I can get the hell out of Halden.

In the library, Arne Lunde is reading a book about Ole Høiland, Norway's answer to Robin Hood. At 37, Lunde still has the chubby frame and eager, soft face of a schoolboy. He is serving time for killing his own mother.

A former schoolteacher, he is the unofficial philosopher king of Halden. Fellow inmates come to him for help polishing their CVs or preparing for exams. He is studying for a master's degree in history with a view to returning to the classroom after his seven-year jail term. Having read extensively about prisons around the world, he is a firm fan of the Norwegian penal system.

'You feel here that prison is to help you, not hurt you,' he says. 'From the first day you arrive somewhere like Halden you can start rebuilding your life so that one day you will be able to return to the world outside.'

Of course, Halden still has many wrinkles to iron out. Inmates smuggle in drugs, often carried inside plastic eggs from Kinder chocolates and concealed in an orifice. Tempers flare, too, and there are fights. Occasionally an inmate is tossed into solitary confinement in the Security Cell, a bare room with a mattress on the floor and a tiny window. Some prisoners feel the staff spend too much time chumming around with them; others say the less experienced staff are not chummy enough. Critics also wonder up to what point it is possible to be both a guard and confidant. 'This man who reads my letters and listens to my phone calls – is he a psychiatric helper or a hidden spy?' says Professor Christie. 'I get him as a special contact, but how free can I be with him?'

And not even the most ardent optimist thinks Norway can slash its recidivism rate to zero. Hoedial is aiming for 10 per cent. Nordberg agrees. 'I think Halden is too kind for the really hardcore guys,' he tells me. 'They think it's a hotel, and they're waiting their time out so they can go back and do the crime again.'

Even so, Norway continues to help convicts once they leave jail, which experts agree is essential for curbing recidivism. Most spend the final part of their sentence in open prisons that are well integrated into the community. Afterwards, they are guaranteed a job and a place to stay, though that does not always work out in practice. If all else fails, Norway has a generous welfare state to fall back on. Compare that to the United States, where offenders are often released with no more than a bus ticket and a few dollars in cash.

When it comes to reducing crime and recidivism, a strong welfare state seems to be part of the fix. Studies around the world suggest that poverty and social inequality are the main engines of crime – and states that plough more money into health, education and social security usually devote less to their penal systems. California, on the other hand, spends more on prisons than on higher education.

In other words, opening up a Halden tomorrow in the United States would be a doomed quick fix. 'For a Norwegian-style prison to work in the US you would also need to have a Norwegian attitude to crime and rehabilitation as well as the welfare state to back it up,' says John Pratt, a professor of criminology at Victoria University of Wellington and an expert on Nordic prisons. 'It would also help to have much less obvious social divisions and much greater homogeneity within the population so prisoners don't become the fearful, dreaded creatures and dangerous specimens who seem so different from the rest of us.'

Yet other nations have embraced a Norwegian-style penal philosophy – and scored similar success. In the late 1990s

Singapore tackled recidivism by putting rehabilitation at the heart of its penal system. The island state rebranded its prison officers as Captains of Lives and Personal Supervisors, retraining them to work closely with inmates to smooth the return to civilian life. It launched a national media campaign to promote the long-term benefits of rehabilitation, and set up a programme to encourage communities to give ex-cons a second chance. Some prisoners are now permitted to serve part or all of their sentences at home while wearing an electronic tag. Life inside Singaporean jails has changed, too. Inmates are afforded more education and more training for work on the outside. Employers can even conduct interviews in prisons, allowing convicts to land jobs before their release. When someone is jailed, volunteers help the family adjust, tap state benefits and prepare for the return of their loved one. After release, a network of prison officers, welfare experts, social workers and ex-cons is on hand to help every convict re-enter society. As a result, recidivism fell nearly 18 per cent in the 11 years to 2009. The Prison Service now ranks among the most popular employers in Singapore, attracting better candidates than ever before. 'Beyond our focus on protecting society through the safe custody of criminals, we also developed our capabilities to become a leading rehabilitation agency,' says Soh Wai Wah, the country's Director of Prisons. Translation: long-term thinking works.

Sometimes the best way to unlock a complex problem is to set a clear long-term goal, and judge everything you do against it. That is how the Norwegian penal system works. It is also the philosophy behind the Harlem Children's Zone, a social outreach programme that has shown promise in breaking the cycle of inner-city poverty across 97 blocks in New York City. To do so, HCZ goes even further than the holistic approach we saw at Locke High School in Watts. The programme targets every variable that might determine a child's prospects, starting from birth: health, diet, housing, education, leisure, parenting, the environment, policing, street crime, community development. When it became clear that many kids in the neighbourhood were suffering from asthma, HCZ staff lobbied landlords to remove mould and cockroaches from the homes of affected children. They also warned parents about keeping pets and smoking indoors and showed them how to monitor a child's lung capacity and use an inhaler. Result: the proportion of students missing school for asthma fell by a fifth.

Everything the Harlem Children's Zone does is pointed at the same long-term goal: to get every child through college. Between healthy meals and afternoon naps, the three- and four-year-olds at its pre-kindergarten centres learn about numbers, colours and the English language as well as basic vocabulary in French and Spanish. At the one site I visit, each of the three rooms bears the name of a prestigious college: Harvard, Columbia, Spelman. It's a small detail that speaks volumes. 'We start with this very simple concept that every child can get through college, and then do whatever it takes to make it happen,' says Marty Lipp, who joined the HCZ in 2004. 'Taking the long view brings clarity and cohesion to everything you do in the present.'

It can also help curb the temptation to push for a quick fix in a moment of panic. Henry T. Ford talked about 'the calmness that the long view of life gives us'. Tom Butler-Bowdon, the author of *Never Too Late to Be Great*, argues that thinking long makes us more effective and measured in the short term. 'When you have that clarity of purpose,' he says, 'and accept that your solution will develop in its own time, you can relax and focus on doing things properly in the present instead of constantly looking over your shoulder or stressing about the person in the next cubicle.'

That is why firms that make short-term profit their North Star seldom go from good to great. Studies show that companies that devote the most time to guiding analysts on their quarterly earnings tend to deliver lower growth in the long term. They also tend to invest less in research and development. Before its fall from grace, Toyota rose to the top of the car industry by thinking in decades, not days. The advice to its executives: 'Base your management decisions on a long-term philosophy, even at the expense of short-term financial goals.' In the high-tech sector, where companies routinely flame out in pursuit of a fast buck, taking the long view is often the ticket to enduring success. 'We weren't trying to just go public and get rich,' Bill Gates once said of the early days at Microsoft. 'There was no near-term thing. It always was this many-decades thing where there were no shortcuts and we'd sort of put one foot in front of the other.'

Amazon has evolved into a global behemoth by embracing a similar creed. Looking beyond the next board meeting is an article of faith for its founder, Jeff Bezos. 'It's all about the long term,' he wrote in his first letter to shareholders in 1997. Since then, Bezos has irked investors by sacrificing short-term profits in order to back new technologies that might only pay off down the line. Critics scoffed when Amazon started selling cloud-computing services to high-tech firms in 2006, but today the company is a leading player in the field. Bezos argues that thinking long delivers a competitive advantage, allowing us to lay claim to the future while the madding crowd slugs it out over the here and now. 'If everything you do needs to work on a three-year time horizon, then you're competing against a lot of people,' he says. 'But if you're willing to invest on a seven-year time horizon, you're now competing against a fraction of those people, because very few companies are willing to do that. Just by lengthening the time horizon, you can engage in endeavours that you could never otherwise pursue.' Investing in companies for the long haul has helped turn Warren Buffett into one of the most celebrated money managers in the world.

How can we think longer in our own lives? Start by setting an over-arching goal – to have the most loyal customers in your sector; to spend more time together as a couple; to make exercise a pleasure rather than a chore – that is clear enough to be a guiding light but vague enough not to blind you. Write the goal down and put it in places where it will catch your eye – a card in your wallet, a sticker on the fridge door, a Post-It note beside your computer. Judge every move you make by how much it helps you reach that goal.

Measuring progress and offering rewards for hitting milestones can be useful, too, but beware of targetitis. Targets tend to be short term and focused on a single metric, which can obscure the big picture and the long view. When Sears set quotas for its auto repair teams, staff began overcharging customers and inventing faults. In the public sector, a fixation on targets has led to police forces redeploying detectives to easier cases to meet arrest quotas and to doctors moving patients who are less ill to the front of the queue to keep down waiting times. In 2011 investigators uncovered the largest cheating scandal in the history of the public school system in the US. Nearly 180 teachers and principals across 44 schools in Atlanta, Georgia, were accused of routinely correcting their pupils' answers on standardised tests. Whistleblowers were bullied, hit with professional sanctions or fired. Meeting the short-term targets, and harvesting the concomitant kudos and cash, had become more important than the long-term goal of giving children a solid education.

The best Slow Fixes use targets judiciously. ExxonMobil tracks the number of near misses without turning them into a benchmark for performance across the company. Why? To avoid targets becoming an end in themselves. 'If you turn it into a corporate metric, you risk getting the wrong result,' says ExxonMobil's Glenn Murray. 'You can unintentionally encourage people not to report, or increase the temptation to drive numbers down. The real value is in recording these things closer to the workforce.'

It also pays to wield money with a light touch. The starkness of the bottom line, of reducing complex ideas to dollars and cents, has a way of shutting down debate, blowing away nuance, narrowing horizons. Neuroscientists have shown that the prospect of making money has a similar effect on the brain to cocaine, which hampers that deeper System 2 thinking. Even cash rewards designed to bolster problem-solving can end up warping judgement and priorities. Just look at the irrational exuberance that turned the financial markets into an orgy of bonus-hunting. After analysing 51 studies in 2009, researchers at the London School of Economics concluded that short-term financial incentives damage the long-term performance of companies. Another study by Harvard Business School found that professional artists produce less creative pieces when working on commission. 'When I work for myself there is the pure joy of creating and I can work through the night and not even know it,' said one artist in the study. 'On a commissioned piece you have to check yourself – be careful to do what the client wants.'

No wonder many of the Slow Fixes we have encountered keep money on the periphery. On its annual safety review day, ExxonMobil does not talk about profits and productivity. Murray fears that linking remuneration to safety targets might encourage what he calls the 'wrong types' of behaviour. When I ask Group Captain Simpson how much that broken Typhoon wing set the RAF back, she squirms a little in her seat. Like the oil industry, the air force deals in such expensive equipment that even the smallest mistake can cost a fortune in damage. Like ExxonMobil, Simpson prefers to keep money separate from the business of solving safety problems. 'I deliberately try not to work out the financial cost of any damage caused by a mistake,' she says. 'If you do that, then people would go back to the blame culture. You know, pointing the finger and saying, "You've cost us half a million pounds," and that's very much not where we want to go with this.'

Yet the tyranny of short-termism is hard to resist. Jeff Bezos warns that taking the long view often means being 'willing to be misunderstood for long periods of time'. And this is a vital point. When you dare to apply a Slow Fix, the brickbats are never far behind – too indulgent, too expensive, too slow, the sceptics will cry. To weather the storm, make the case that fixing problems thoroughly is never an indulgence or a luxury; it is a wise and essential investment in the future. A problem left to fester now will almost always be harder and more costly to fix later on. Put in the time, effort and resources today, and reap the benefits in your business, relationship or health in the future. One example: after a hefty investment at the start, Green Dot is now running Locke High School for less money per pupil than authorities were spending before the turnaround.

Of course, ignoring short-term metrics altogether would be silly. In the right dosage and spirit, targets can focus minds and channel energy. Counting your pennies today is always a wise investment for tomorrow. After waxing lyrical about thinking big and long, every Slow Fixer will remind you, in the same breath, to focus on the small stuff. Or as Hoeidal puts it: 'You have to cultivate a macro way of thinking about problems, but you always need to take care of the micro, too.'

CHAPTER SIX

THINK SMALL: Devil in the Details

It's the little details that are vital.
Little things make big things happen.
John Wooden,
Hall of Fame college basketball coach

On a clear, cool morning in January 1969, a team of divers set off to inspect a drilling rig 10 kilometres off the coast of Southern California. What they saw alarmed them. 'Everywhere you looked, there were shortcuts,' remembers Hoss McNutt, one of the crew. 'You could see the company had cut corners to save time and money, and that's what we reported when we came back up.' The owner of the rig, Union Oil, chose to ignore the warnings, and three weeks later Platform A blew, eventually spewing 200,000 gallons of crude oil into the waters off Santa Barbara. Black tar washed up on the local beaches and more than 10,000 birds perished along with seals, dolphins, fish and other marine life.

I catch up with McNutt 41 years later at Michigan State University in East Lansing, the setting for the 2010 World Finals of Odyssey of the Mind, an international problem-solving competition for schoolchildren. Every news channel is screening footage of crude oil belching from BP's damaged Macondo well deep below the surface of the Gulf of Mexico. McNutt looks at the grainy images, shakes his head and echoes the verdict handed down by insiders across the oil industry. 'It's history repeating itself,' he says. 'BP ignored the risks and the warnings, went for the quick fixes and now look at the mess they're in.'

When it comes to the art of solving problems, McNutt, a blue-eyed sixty-something, has seen it all. After his days as an underwater trouble-shooter, he became a robotics teacher at Burton Middle School in Porterville, California. He has also spent the last 30 years as a coach with Odyssey of the Mind. Many of his former charges are now solving problems in boardrooms, factories and labs across the US.

Though his teams compete within the confines of a tournament, much of what they do right and wrong holds useful lessons for the real world. Now into its fourth decade, Odyssey of the Mind resembles a giant testing ground for the Slow Fix.

At the 2010 World Finals, McNutt is coaching a team of six ninth-graders. They have chosen to tackle Problem Number 1: invent a human-powered vehicle that surmounts an obstacle, cleans up the environment, encounters wildlife and undergoes a repair while navigating a path through Nature. The boys decided to build a minesweeper, a Mad Max-meets-Blue Peter contraption cobbled together from old circuit boards, planks of wood, metal bars and a complex pulley system of ropes, chains and levers. A gear turns a hacksaw against a tin can to emit a guttural growl that would fend off wild animals. The scoop that collects the styrofoam mines is the casing of an old iMac computer. It takes three boys to operate the vehicle, with the driver sending power to the wheels by pumping a wooden board up and down. My first thought: why didn't I make one of those in ninth grade?

Like every other troupe at Odyssey, the boys from Burton talk with smooth conviction about many of the ingredients of the Slow Fix we have encountered so far: owning up to and learning from mistakes; thinking hard to divine the true nature of a problem; joining the dots to forge holistic solutions; taking the long view. With the certainty of a management guru thrice his age, one tells me: 'There is no such thing as a mistake, just an inaccurate idea.' Another chips in: 'If something doesn't work, you go back all the way through the steps to the beginning, till you find out why it doesn't work – and then you fix it.'

So far, so good. But an hour before the Burton team is due on stage, McNutt is uneasy. He thinks the boys should be fine-tuning their solution to Problem 1 right up to the last minute, but the Odyssey rules forbid him from making that point too forcefully. 'Even now there are parts of this vehicle that could break,' he says, 'and if I were them I'd be panicking before going to war with it.'

Over McNutt's shoulder I can see the minesweeper standing alone in a corner of the gymnasium. The only member of the Burton team in sight is sloping towards the exit. McNutt calls out to him.

'Do you know what time you guys have to be in the staging area?'

'Three o'clock,' the boy answers.

'And how long is that from now?' asks McNutt.

The boy shrugs, miming that he doesn't have a watch.

'It's 50 minutes,' says McNutt. 'Don't you think you should be doing a training run or something or be getting ready?'

The boy says he'll mention it to his team-mates, but, in the end, they ignore the advice.

Just over an hour later, the boys, dressed in robot costumes, are ready to stage their performance in another large gymnasium. Around 200 children and a smattering of coaches and parents sit watching from the stands. Nine months of problem-solving has come down to this moment. The first team to perform sets the bar high, uncoiling long shoots of bamboo to propel their vehicle. The spectacle is breathtaking, elegant and oddly moving. The crowd roars its approval.

When their turn comes round, the Burton boys start shakily. It takes them longer than planned to set up. The minesweeper then advances ten feet before juddering to a halt. The boys make frantic adjustments to restart it, only for it to stall again, this time with a chain hanging limply below the chassis. Two boys remove their robot costumes and climb underneath like mechanics at a Formula One pit-stop. An awkward silence settles over the gymnasium. Odyssey of the Mind is a competition, but there is a gentle spirit of camaraderie and the teams cheer each other on with gusto. Watching children die on stage is no one's idea of a good time. Eventually, though, the crowd stirs into life, clapping and shouting encouragement to the marooned minesweepers.

The team gets the vehicle moving again, but just as they are about to scoop up the first mine, a buzzer sounds to signal that their time is up. The boys are distraught despite a standing ovation from the crowd. A judge moves in to console the youngest, who is in tears.

After an emotional post-mortem, McNutt takes the debacle in his stride. Having seen other teams self-destruct in the same way, he believes the Burton boys will come out of this as better problem-solvers. 'The lesson they learned here is more important than winning,' he says. 'Today, they learned that when it comes to problem-solving you have to be incredibly thorough because the devil is always in the details.'

This brings us to the next ingredient of the Slow Fix. We have seen how widening the lens to think holistically and take in the long view is essential for solving complex problems. At the same time, zooming in on the tiniest details can be just as vital. What caused Concorde to crash in a ball of fire at Charles de Gaulle airport in 2000? The trigger was a tiny strip of titanium alloy that had fallen off another plane and lain on the runway until Concorde drove over it at 500 km/h. That is why RAF Coningsby employs a full-time squadron officer whose only job is to make sure the runways are free of detritus and why all drivers stop and check their wheels for debris before crossing any runway on the base. 'For anything to be true it has to be true at the level of the big picture and the small detail,' says IDEO's Fulton Suri. 'To solve problems well, we have to integrate the two.'

Like other ingredients of the Slow Fix, sweating the small stuff takes time. You usually have to slow down to spot, understand and manage the details. Sometimes we do this as a matter of course. Think how long you spend in front of the mirror before a hot date, making sure every last hair is in place. Or how many times you re-read a job application before sending it in. But in our hurry-up world, such attention to detail often goes out the window. Our minds are prone to brush aside the small stuff that contradicts our pet theories – remember the confirmation bias and the legacy problem. Sweating the details can also be boring, fiddly and unglamorous. It seldom hits the headlines or makes an audience swoon. What catches the eye is the bold, sweeping gesture. Yet no matter how much money, energy and time you invest, and no matter how noble your intentions, even the best fix will flounder if you get the details wrong.

Just look at the history of aid in Africa. Over the years, Western donors have sent container-loads of medical equipment that cannot function in the continent's blistering heat and hearing aids designed for a type of hearing loss seldom found in the developing world. Pesky details also undermined the headline-grabbing reconstruction of Afghanistan. US authorities, for instance, built schools in the war-torn nation but failed to build a single college to train teachers to staff them.

Attention to detail has always been a hallmark of the best fixers. Some believe the finest ceramics in history were made during the Southern Sung Dynasty which reigned in China from the 12th to the 13th century. The Sung ceramicists spent their lives refining, tweaking and massaging simple, sober designs in pursuit of the perfect pot. Their creed was that even the most modest bowl or cup could be imbued with the highest artistry and meaning. By sweating the small stuff they crafted ceramics that continue to lift the spirits and shape design 800 years later. That same attention to detail marks out the winners in every field of endeavour. Think of the obsessive craftsmanship poured into a Savile Row suit, a Rolls Royce Phantom or the mahogany neck of a Paul Reed Smith guitar. If only the Burton boys had emulated Henry Steinway, who built 482 pianos by hand before finally launching his own all-conquering company. What was the secret of Gustave Flaubert's luminously beautiful prose? A manic determination to refine and rework each sentence until everything down to the last consonant was just so. Remember the celebrated scene in *Madame Bovary* where Emma tiptoes out of her house at dawn and runs to meet her lover? Flaubert wrote 52 versions of it before finally hitting on the perfect arrangement of words. Like McNutt, his motto was: 'The good God is in the detail.'

Steve Jobs, founder and former CEO of Apple, took that creed to the level of obsessive compulsion. Towards the end of his life, as he lay dying in hospital, he burned through 67 nurses before settling on three that met his exacting standards. Even when heavily sedated, he tore an oxygen mask off his face to object to the way it looked. The pulmonologist was startled when Jobs demanded to see five other mask designs so he could pick the one he liked best. Yet what sounds like a rampant case of OCD helped turn Apple into one of the most successful companies in history. Deadlines came and went as Jobs drove his designers, engineers and marketers to get every detail just right. The Macintosh computer took more than three years to develop because Jobs kept on fiddling with it, jettisoning the internal fan for being too clunky, redesigning the motherboard for not being elegant enough. To perfect the title bars that run along the top of windows and documents, he forced his software developers to tweak, tweak, then tweak some more. When they complained, after nearly 20 iterations, he yelled at them: 'Can you imagine looking at that every day? It's not just a little thing. It's something we have to get right.' Even when Apple was riding high, Jobs, like a latter-day Sung ceramicist, took an interest in how many screws went into the company's laptop cases. In other words, by the time he took to the stage in his trademark black turtleneck to unveil the latest game-changing gadget, Apple had already dotted all the i's and crossed all the t's in a way that put the Burton boys, and most rivals, to shame.

Sometimes the tiniest detail can mean the difference between a triumph and a turkey. The lack of cheap artificial light is a chronic problem in developing countries. Poor households in rural Africa, Asia and Latin America spend a large slice of their income on lighting in the form of candles, dry-cell batteries and kerosene – cash that could be better spent on food, education, medicine or investing in farms. And despite the heavy expenditure, there is still nowhere near enough light to go around after sunset. That means children cannot study in the evenings; girls skip school to perform chores during the day; and women who venture out after dark are more vulnerable to attack. Cheap kerosene lamps also pollute the air, attract malaria-carrying mosquitoes and cause fires and serious burns. In 2006, Mark Bent hit on a nifty solution to the darkness problem: his BoGo torches are solar-powered, water- and shock-proof and deliver up to five hours of illumination after charging for 10 hours in the sun. Every time you buy one of the devices, Bent donates another to the relief group of your choice. BoGo stands for 'Buy One, Give One.'

Like Geir Berthelsen at Norsafe, but unlike so many aid organisations, Bent did his homework first. Having spent years working across the developing world as a US marine and diplomat and then as an oilman, he knew the value of local knowledge. 'So often I see well-meaning folks with fantastic intentions trying to help other people without knowing what their real morals are, what their real needs are, what causes them to tick, or what economic, social and tribal pressures they face,' he says. 'What it takes is an awful lot of time and an awful lot of listening, because the first thing people throw out is never going to be what the reality is. They'll say everything is wonderful, wonderful, but then after an hour they start saying, well, if the light could be longer, brighter, or I could carry it this way or hang it that way.' Armed with those granular insights, Bent was able to refine the BoGo torch to fit the brief.

In a later chapter we will explore why it makes sense for people to have a hand in forging solutions to their own problems, but for now let's focus on the tiny detail that allowed the BoGo torch to become a game-changer. When the first devices arrived at a UN refugee camp in western Ethiopia, they were finished in a lurid orange colour. 'I wanted something bright that people would be able to find under low light conditions,' says Bent. But right away it became clear that men were seizing the torches, leaving the womenfolk in the dark.

While UN workers proposed tracking each torch by its serial number, Bent hit on a much more simple and elegant fix: he began manufacturing some of the devices in pink. He knew many African men were proud, touchy and superstitious about their masculinity, but he also knew most did not associate pink with femininity. So he distributed the pinkified torches along with the message that no red-blooded male should be seen dead with a pink accessory. It worked. In parts of Africa, men left in charge of a pink torch will use a stick to reposition it on the ground rather than risk being seen holding it. Carrying around a pink torch can even get a man branded a thief. Bent has distributed over 400,000 BoGo torches across the developing world, and African women use the pink ones freely.

Sometimes it pays to revisit a detail that has already been dismissed as irrelevant. Classical music has traditionally been the preserve of white males. In the masculine world of black-suited soloists and silver-haired maestros, it was an article of faith that women simply could not play as well. They had the wrong kind of lips, lungs and hands. They were too weak. They just couldn't *feel* the music in the same way. Time and again, the gatekeepers of the great orchestras saw that view reinforced during auditions where the men always sounded better than the women. Or did they?

Traditional auditions were often informal affairs, with candidates playing for a few minutes in front of the musical director or conductor of the orchestra. That up-close-and-personal encounter was meant to help the experts reach an informed verdict, but in fact it often did just the opposite. Contrary to conventional wisdom, seeing a candidate audition in full view made it harder for the judges to concentrate on the most important skill on every musician's CV: the sound of their playing. Instead, they could be distracted, even swayed, by a host of visual clues: posture, age, hairstyle, jawline, how much the candidates sweated; how little they smiled; how they held their instruments. And gender.

Just how much those visual variables could alter what the orchestral grandees heard became clear when the classical music world began adopting blind auditions in the 1970s. Instead of performing in full view of a committee, candidates were assigned a number and played hidden behind a screen. If they made even the slightest noise that might betray their identity – a brief cough, for instance, or the click of a heel – they were sent away and brought back later in the day with a fresh number. Through that one change, experts were forced to do what they claimed to have been doing all along: judge applicants purely on the sound of their music. And what do you think happened? Suddenly, the women didn't sound so bad after all. They began landing prestigious jobs as violinists, cellists and trombone players. In the three decades since screen auditions became the norm the number of women playing in leading US orchestras has risen fivefold. The general cultural drift towards gender equality played a part, but without the introduction of blind auditions women would probably still sound worse than men.

In sociology, the power of the telling detail is neatly distilled in the 'broken window theory'. This holds that even the tiniest whiff of disorder, a broken window in a building, for instance, or a daub of graffiti on a wall, can set a tone that fuels more anti-social behaviour. In 2011 a group of researchers at the University of Groningen in the Netherlands showed how this works in practice. In one experiment they placed advertising flyers on bicycles parked in an alley with a sign prohibiting graffiti. When the alley was tagged with graffiti, 69 per cent of the cyclists threw the flyer to the ground or stuck it on someone else's bike. After the alley was freshly painted, only 33 per cent did so. In a similar experiment, researchers left an envelope with a five euro note visible through the address window sticking out of a postbox. When the postbox was clean and well-tended, only 13 per cent of passers-by pilfered the cash. When it was covered in graffiti, or the surrounding area was strewn with empty cans, cigarette butts and other litter, that figure doubled.

This is not to say that sanitising every street would put an end to crime: to pull that off you would need to join up a lot of other dots. But it does show that changing a tiny detail, from fixing a broken window to erecting a screen at a music audition, can make a big difference.

This is a point rammed home by the savviest problem-solvers. John Wooden coached the UCLA basketball team to a record-breaking 10 NCAA championships between 1964 and 1975. Though lucky to have stellar players, including Kareem Abdul Jabbar and Bill Walton, come through the ranks on his watch, he is generally considered one of the greatest coaches in the history of college sport. And what did he do when a new crop of basketball prodigies turned up for the first day of training camp? He showed them how to put on their socks. Like a medieval monk unfurling a parchment manuscript, he would slowly roll each sock down over his toes, over the ball of the foot, the arch and eventually around the heel, before finally tugging it up snug. Then he would return to the toes to iron out any wrinkles or creases along the full length of the sock. He would then watch the super-jocks until they did it just right. Wooden had two reasons for this ritual. First, wrinkled socks cause blisters, which hamper performance. But he was also making a meta-point about the need to sweat the small stuff. 'I believe in the basics: attention to, and perfection of, tiny details that might commonly be overlooked,' he wrote. 'They may seem trivial, perhaps even laughable to those who don't understand, but they aren't. They are fundamental to your progress in basketball, business and life. They are the difference between champions and near champions.'

That is what you hear time and again from people who have risen to the top of the business world. When asked on retirement what advice he would give to budding entrepreneurs, Conrad Hilton, founder of the eponymous hotel chain, told them to sweat the small stuff with a memorable one-liner: 'Don't forget to tuck the shower curtain in the bath.' When Sir Richard Branson visits any of the 300 businesses in his Virgin empire, he makes a note of every small failing that catches his eye, from a dirty carpet in an aeroplane cabin to an employee using the wrong tone of voice in a call centre. '[The] only difference between merely satisfactory delivery and great delivery is attention to detail,' he wrote recently. 'Delivery is not just limited to the company's first day: employees across the business should be focusing on getting it right all day, every day.'

Even the hell-raising hard rockers of Van Halen understood that. Back in their heyday in the 1980s the band inserted in the contract sent to every concert venue a rider that became the butt of a million jokes. They asked for a large bowl of M&Ms with all the brown ones taken out. Article 126 read: 'There will be no brown M&Ms in the backstage area, upon pain of forfeiture of the show, with full compensation.' When news of this demand leaked, the media pilloried the mega-haired musicians for being drunk on their own superstardom. Yet Van Halen had a very sound reason for banning brown sweets. As one of the first bands to take a gargantuan stage-show on the road, they had started to notice that staff at arenas in smaller cities were struggling with the engineering complexities of assembling their set. Bungling a detail could mean the sound or spectacle was below par, or worse. At Colorado State University the Van Halen stage sank through the floor, causing $85,000 of damage, after staff failed to clock the weight-bearing requirements in the contract. Another oversight could easily have led to someone being injured or killed. Van Halen therefore came up with the M&Ms as a canary in the coal mine. A bowl free of brown candies suggested a crew that could be trusted to have gone through the band's technical requirements with a fine-toothed comb, to have sweated the small stuff. 'So, when I would walk backstage, if I saw a brown M&M in that bowl,' said David Lee Roth, the lead singer, 'well, guaranteed you're going to arrive at a technical error. They didn't read the contract. Guaranteed you'd run into a problem. Sometimes it would threaten to just destroy the whole show. Something like, literally, life-threatening.'

One way to formalise the M&M test is to draw up a checklist. For years, pilots have used these to guard against forgetting to flick a vital switch or confirm a crucial reading. Lawyers use them to avoid missing the tiny, telling details in complex litigation. Checklists are increasingly common in industries ranging from construction to software engineering, where botching the small stuff can have catastrophic consequences.

The trouble is, many experts balk at being asked to run through a checklist. We have already seen how hard it can be to own up to our own mistakes and limits. Turning to a checklist implies that, despite our many years of experience, we might still make an elementary booboo. Why do I need a checklist to remind me to do stuff I do without even thinking? Yet that is precisely the problem. When we switch into autopilot, when we stop thinking, we can miss the small things that make a big difference. Even Santa checks his list twice.

That is why the medical world also embraces the checklist. Consider the use of antibiotics. To have any effect, they must be given no *more* than an hour and no *less* than 30 seconds before the surgeon makes the first incision. Fall outside that time frame and the chances of infection shoot up by 50 per cent. Every medical student can recite these figures, yet experienced surgical teams often get it wrong. In 2005 the Nationwide Children's Hospital in Columbus, Ohio, discovered that its staff failed to administer the right antibiotic at the right time to more than a third of all patients undergoing an appendectomy. They were giving the drug too early, too late or sometimes not at all. On the face of it, this seems inexplicable. How can seasoned medical pros screw up so often? The answer is that surgery is one of the most exacting forms of problem-solving. Compounding the challenge of cutting open and repairing a human being, the average operating theatre is a minefield of distractions: a last-minute page from the emergency room; a malfunctioning piece of equipment; a missing clipboard; an upset patient; an exhausted anaesthetist. No wonder the antibiotics sometimes get lost in the shuffle.

The director of surgical administration at the Nationwide Children's Hospital was also a pilot in his spare time, so he knew how checklists cut errors and boost safety in aviation. To tackle the antibiotics problem, he fitted every operating theatre in the hospital with a whiteboard bearing a pre-surgery checklist called 'Cleared for Takeoff'. There were two boxes to tick before the surgeon could reach for the scalpel. First, the nurse had to confirm verbally that the person lying on the operating table was the right patient and the correct side of his body was prepped for surgery. Second, the team had to confirm with one another that the proper antibiotics had been given. To encourage staff to sweat this small stuff, the surgical director spent a lot of time speaking to doctors, nurses and anaesthetists about the benefits of checklists. With an eye for the telling detail, he also designed a six-inch metal tent stamped with the words *Cleared for Takeoff*, which nurses were instructed to place over the scalpel when laying out the instruments before surgery. In the early days the tent served as a physical reminder to slow down and read the small print.

These little changes made a huge difference. Three months after the launch of the *Cleared for Takeoff* initiative, the anti-biotics were administered properly in 89 per cent of appen-dicitis cases. After ten months the figure was 100 per cent. Other hospitals have had similar success with checklists, some of which run to 20 or 30 items.

To deliver a breakthrough fix, however, you must often go beyond just remembering the small stuff; you have to see it in a fresh light. This is how many game-changing inventions come about. In 1941 a Swiss engineer named Georges de Mestral returned from a hunting trip in the Alps to find burrs from a Burdock plant all over his socks and his dog's coat. But instead of just yanking off the sticky, furry balls without a second thought, as hikers have done for generations, he put them under a microscope, where he noticed hundreds of tiny hooks designed to attach to any surface with loops, such as clothing. De Mestral suddenly saw burrs in a way no one had before – and used that fresh insight to invent Velcro.

Many medical problems are only solved because someone eventually pays attention to an unexpected side effect during drug trials. In the late 1980s a pharmaceutical research group in England was exploring ways to tackle angina. Their best hope was a compound named UK-92480, which seemed to affect the blood vessels of healthy volunteers. But after disappointing trials the drug was heading for the scrapheap – until test subjects started reporting penile erections after taking it. At first the researchers brushed this aside as an irrelevant, if amusing, detail. But eventually some began to wonder if it might hold the key to a cure for erectile dysfunction. Turns out they were right. After six more years of research and development, UK-92480, renamed Viagra, took the market, and millions of bedrooms, by storm.

That is why sweating the small stuff is a feature of every Slow Fix. Remember how Halden prison banned free weights to stop the inmates becoming over-muscled. Or how kitchen staff at ExxonMobil monitor the temperature of their salad dressings. Mindful that jostling on the stairs can lead to fights, Green Dot installed iron banisters down the middle of every stairwell at Locke High School to separate those going up from those coming down. Staff at the school talk of taking a 'broken window approach' to even the most trivial problems. 'If a window is broken, it's fixed immediately. And the next one and the next,' says CEO Marco Petruzzi. 'The idea is that change is in sweating the details.'

We can all get better at mastering the small stuff. Lists are a good starting point. When tackling a problem, write down every idea, however small, that floats across your radar. Put those that will clearly advance your long-term goal on a To Do list and the rest on a Maybe list in case they turn out to be important later on. Place the latter in a drawer and glance at it from time to time to make sure nothing slips through the cracks. At every stage of your fix, remember the Burton boys: check, check and check again.

Because even Flaubertian attention to detail cannot always guarantee a smooth ride. When Steve Jobs launched the iPhone 4 in 2010 he suffered one of those technical glitches that are the bane of keynote addresses the world over. A faltering connection to the internet made it hard for the device to load photos or start a video chat. To carry on, Jobs had to ask the audience to stop clogging up the wi-fi network in the hall. It was a Burton boys moment from the sultan of the small stuff. 'Even the gods screw up sometimes,' observed one blogger.

Of course, Jobs never suffered the same indignity again. Why? Because he did what all Slow Fixers do when they miss a detail. He learned from the mistake, and came back better prepared next time.

CHAPTER SEVEN

PREPARE: Ready for Anything

The action that follows deliberation should be quick,
but deliberation should be slow.
Aristotle

It looked like his race was over. In the 69th lap of the 2011 Grand Prix in Monaco, Lewis Hamilton took a knock from another driver that smashed the rear wing endplate of his car. In the world of Formula One, where a few seconds can mean the difference between swallowing defeat and spraying champagne from the podium, that sort of damage usually puts you out of the running. While a good pit crew can change four tyres in three and a half seconds, they seldom have enough time to carry out more complicated repairs during a race. On that sunny afternoon in Monaco, however, Hamilton, the *enfant terrible* of Formula One, got lucky. After a rival car was demolished, track officials temporarily stopped the race to clear the debris, giving his McLaren team more time to fix the rear wing.

But the clock was ticking. Dressed in their trademark overalls, the mechanics sprinted out to the grid, and the moment Hamilton's car was stationary they went to work, sizing up the damage, working out the best fix, then carrying out the repairs. As they tightened the final bolts, officials shouted at them to get out of the way so the race could continue. With a new rear wing endplate in place, Hamilton roared back onto the track. He ended up finishing eighth, but getting him back in the race was the kind of coup that enters pit-crew folklore and is talked about over beers for years to come.

'Fixing a rear wing is not the sort of thing you want to be doing in the middle of a race, but they pulled it off,' says Peter Hodgman, liaison engineer of McLaren's Vehicle Technology Department. 'It was amazing, really, when you think how little time they had.'

Such stories are the stuff of legend in the Formula One world, and Hodgman, a genial, bearded 57-year-old, has his fair share of them. At the European Grand Prix at Donington Park in 1993, a McLaren mechanic spotted pools of water beneath a car that Michael Andretti was waiting to drive off the starting grid. The team swung into action, replacing the faulty radiator in under ten minutes. 'Time is always your biggest enemy in Formula One,' says Hodgman.

Though it sounds like a paradox, fast troubleshooting can also be part of the Slow Fix. That's because in the real world there is often no time for *mea culpas*, unhurried reflection or forensic analysis of every last detail. Sometimes problem-solving is survival of the fastest. When our ancestors stumbled across a hungry predator, they either came up with an instant exit strategy or ended up as lunch. In the impatient, on-demand 21st century we are constantly under pressure to supply off-the-cuff solutions. This can lead to the sort of quick-fix bungling we have already encountered in this book. But not always. Under the right conditions, tackling problems at high speed can actually work to our advantage.

The pit crews in Formula One are just one example. What marks out the stars in any field, from medicine and management to firefighting and football, is the ability to handle problems on the fly. In *Blink*, Malcolm Gladwell showed how clever we can be when we learn to 'take charge of the first two seconds'. Among his case studies of people making fast judgements that turn out to be uncannily accurate were art experts who instantly spotted that a sculpture sold for $10 million was a fake and a psychologist who could predict which couples would later divorce simply by watching them converse. This is System 1 thinking in action – and it is not only experts who do it. We all can. When I play hockey my mind is problem-solving on steroids, calculating within fractions of a second how to dodge an incoming defenceman or slip the puck through to a teammate. Most of what we do in ordinary life, from driving a car to chopping carrots, involves the same kind of thinking without thinking.

Finding a fix in the blink of an eye is so common that many disciplines have their own term to describe it. When a basketball player makes the perfect blind pass during a lightning quick counter-attack, we say he has 'court sense'. A general who can size up the terrain of a battlefield with a single glance is said to be blessed with '*coup d'œil*'. We often call this intuition, and hail it as a gift from the gods. Napoleon, himself no slouch on the battlefield, believed *coup d'œil* was 'inborn in great generals'. Yet the truth is more prosaic than that. As we have already seen, our minds switch back and forth between System 1 and System 2 thinking. When we make a snap judgement we still make all the System 2 moves – sizing up the scenario, plucking out the relevant data, joining the dots, pinpointing the best course of action – we just do it a whole lot faster. Psychologists call this 'thin-slicing' because we extract all the necessary information from a tiny sliver of experience.

How does it work? When the clock is ticking, the best thin-slicers tap into a personal database of experience that allows them to spot familiar patterns, pitfalls and possibilities in a problem. While novices get bogged down gathering and parsing irrelevant information, running up blind alleys and analysing doomed courses of action, experts cut straight to the chase, zeroing in on the key data and then leaping to the best solution. How long this takes depends on the problem at hand. Some thin-slicing can happen in seconds, even milli-seconds. At other times we need a little longer, a few minutes even, to make the most of our personal databases. Either way, the ability to thin-slice can transfer across disciplines. Accustomed to making split-second calls in the bear-pit of the financial markets, Wall Street traders turn out to be rather good at war games that demand similar rapid-fire decision-making. Yet the best thin-slicing tends to occur within a single area of expertise because it is built on previous experience. Research across many fields suggests it takes 10,000 hours of practice to master a discipline enough to make the intuitive leaps that separate the winners from the wannabes. As Esther Dyson, the technology analyst turned investor, observed: 'When we call something intuitive, we often mean familiar.'

And that is where the slow part comes in. Most examples in this book, from the turnaround of Locke High School to the new safety regime at RAF Coningsby, involve investing time in solving a problem. That is still true for thin-slicing, but with a twist: you have taken time *before* the problem arises to build up a database of experience that allows you to troubleshoot from the hip when things go wrong. In other words, practice, planning and preparation allow you to fix things quickly when the clock is ticking, which is very different from grabbing the nearest quick fix in a blind panic.

This does not just apply to single problem-solvers. Groups can also hone their thin-slicing prowess. We already know from a mountain of research that experienced teams are more likely to solve problems than are inexperienced ones. According to one study in the United States, nearly three-quarters of the accidents involving commercial aircraft occur on the first day the pilot and first officer fly together. Rookie mistakes seldom happen in Formula One, where the golden rule of the seven Ps (Prior Planning and Preparation Prevents Piss-Poor Performance) is a religion. Teams hire smart people, from engineering wizards to maths nerds, who then build up a database of experience that makes them thin-slicers of the highest order. It helps that most share a monkish obsession with making cars faster. Even after three decades in the racing world, Hodgman retains a boyish enthusiasm for the magic of mechanics. When we meet, he whips out his iPhone to show me photos of the 1957 Austin A35 he is rebuilding in his spare time. 'Most people in Formula One are mad about cars,' he says. 'We're always thinking about better ways to build them or fix them.' Up to 300 people like Hodgman spend days and nights sweating every last detail in the McLaren cars. Using data from the onboard computers, as well as feedback from the drivers, they track every tiny shift in wheel speeds and engine revolutions, gear changes and throttle openings, fuel consumption and exhaust output. Between races, they tweak the design, test parts, experiment with new fixes, investigate faults, practise repairs – honing their personal and collective databases at every turn. During a standard tyre-change, 28 people swarm around a car in the pit, some operating wheel guns or holding the vehicle steady, others pulling off the old tyres or putting on new ones. Unlike the Burton boys, the McLaren team practises the drill over and over and over, even squeezing in a final dress rehearsal on the morning of every race. 'Everyone knows exactly what they're doing,' says Hodgman. 'It becomes so automatic that it's almost like synchronised swimming. You do your thing almost without thinking.' The best pit crews develop a sixth sense about each other. 'You spend a huge amount of time together, probably more than you do with your wife or girlfriend, and you get very close, so you know everything about each other's strengths and weaknesses,' says Hodgman. 'It gets to the point where you don't even have to talk, you just hand over that spanner because you know your mate is going to use it next.'

Formula One pit crews and engineers know their cars so intimately, and are so well drilled, they can often spot signs of malaise – a slight tilt in the chassis, a whine from the engine, a small change in the smell of the exhaust – before the computer spells out the problem in graphs and equations. Even those of us who never set foot in a pit-lane can learn from this. The more you use the ingredients of the Slow Fix – admitting mistakes, pausing to think, joining the dots, sweating the small stuff, taking the long view – the better you come to understand whatever it is you do and the more likely you are to develop the intuition needed to deal with problems swiftly in the future. 'When you have years and years of practice and knowledge behind you, nothing escapes your notice,' says Hodgman. 'Whatever the time constraints, you will spot the problem and find a way to fix it.'

That is true beyond the clock-watching world of motor racing. Gary Klein has spent nearly 30 years studying how people tackle problems under duress. Along the way he has become a leading proponent of the power of intuition. In his book *Sources of Power* he shows how expertise built on practice, training and experience is the most reliable recipe for a good fix when time is tight. Klein found that while novice chess players fall apart when forced to play the game at high speed, the grand masters carry on making all the right moves. By the same token, seasoned fire captains arrive at 80 per cent of their decisions in under a minute.

Many of our Slow Fixers have the same knack. Years of observing clients in offices and factories have given Geir Berthelsen a kind of corporate *coup d'œil*. 'When I go into a company it's like listening to an orchestra,' he says. 'If one player is out of tune, I can hear them right away.' Long experience has taught Group Captain Simon Brailsford to sniff out what lies behind the mistakes and near misses at RAF Coningsby. 'I can spot stuff just by getting on an aeroplane,' he says. 'Even without launching an investigation, I just know that if he'd done x or y it would have been a more successful mission.' Are Hoeidal can gauge what is wrong with a prison in a single visit.

The best thin-slicers never stop building their expertise. No matter how good you are at something, you can always get better. 'Once you start thinking you know it all, you've seen it all before, you're in trouble,' says Hodgman. 'There's always something you don't know, and you have to work hard to stay on top of things.' Japanese businesses call this the art of 'continuous improvement', and it explains why even the finest singers use coaches throughout their careers and why elite athletes undergo endless hours of repetitive drills, practice and visualisation exercises. In improvisational comedy, the best performers can turn on a dime, converting even the most unpromising scenario into comedy gold. Many have a comic gift, but the real stars never stop rehearsing, attending and teaching courses, critiquing one another's performances and pushing themselves into uncharted territory. Odyssey of the Mind also cultivates the ability to troubleshoot on the fly. As well as developing one solution over nine months, every team is given five minutes to solve a problem they have never seen before in an event called Spontaneous. 'When you're tackling any kind of problem in life, you have to know when to be fast and when to be slow,' says Sam Micklus. 'It's like the marathon and the sprint, and the best problem-solvers can do both.'

But here comes a big, fat caveat. No matter how assiduously they build up their database of experience, experts are never as clever or infallible as they (or we) like to believe. Study after study confirms that specialists in almost every field, from law to medicine to finance, overestimate their expertise and underestimate their mistakes. In one study of autopsy reports, doctors who were completely certain of their diagnosis while a patient was still alive turned out to be wrong 40 per cent of the time. Or look at the corporate world, where three of every four large mergers end up destroying, rather than creating, shareholder value, despite the blustering endorsements from legions of CEOs, consultants and pundits. A long-term study of predictions made by 284 leading political and economic commentators delivered equally damning findings. When asked to estimate the chances of wars in the Middle East, the future of emerging markets and the political prospects of world leaders, the pundits performed worse than basic computer algorithms. And the more prestigious the commentator, the more over-confident and off-target their forecasts.

Even Formula One crews mess up sometimes. Two months after fixing Hamilton's rear wing endplate on the grid, the McLaren mechanics sent his team-mate, Jenson Button, back into a race with a nut loose on his right front wheel.

Like the rest of us, even experts can be swayed by stuff that really should not matter. Remember how orchestra bosses automatically dismissed female musicians before auditions were held behind screens. Other studies have found that medical school interviewers green-light fewer applicants on rainy days, and that judges are far more likely to grant parole to prisoners after eating a meal.

Even when the evidence later calls their sixth sense into question, experts find it hard to back down. In 2009 Amanda Knox, an American student, was convicted of taking part in the murder of her British flatmate in Perugia, Italy. Though no physical evidence tied her to the crime scene in the days and weeks after the body was found, police very quickly settled on a theory that never budged: Knox was a sex-mad sociopath with the face of an angel and a Machiavellian flair for deceit. This portrait began to take hold just hours after the murder when Edgardo Giobbi, the lead investigator, saw Knox slip on a pair of shoe covers in what struck him as a provocative manner. 'We were able to establish guilt by closely observing the suspect's psychological and behavioural reaction during the interrogation,' he said later. 'We don't need to rely on other kinds of investigation.' Translation: painstakingly gathering and parsing the physical evidence, or sweating the small stuff, may work for those sissies on *CSI*, but real cops go with their gut. Four years later Knox was set free when an appeals court overturned her conviction for lack of evidence.

The bottom line is that intuition is a double-edged sword. Though it can work wonders when accurate, it can also be blown off course by emotions and biases without our being aware of it. Thinking too hard can also short-circuit intuition. Study after study shows that witnesses are much more likely to pick the right criminal out of a police line-up when they have to make up their minds quickly. By the same token, tennis balls that come lobbing slowly over the net can be devilishly hard to return because we have time to think the shot to death. 'We should be listening to our intuition but not automatically leaping to the end with it,' cautions IDEO's Jane Fulton Suri.

There are steps we can all take to strike that balance and optimise our thin-slicing. The first is to keep on testing and enriching your personal database. Even when there are no problems on the horizon, practise, train and read around your area of expertise. Imagine scenarios where thin-slicing lets you down, and analyse why. To keep intuition as pure and accurate as possible, block out information known to be irrelevant and pull the plug when you start second-guessing yourself. Above all, stay calm and relaxed: studies show that when the heart beats too fast we start falling back on biases and making poor decisions.

The best guard against intuition malfunction is humility. Because thin-slicing will always be an unreliable art, we need to accept that, no matter how impressive our CVs, our intuitive judgements should be checked and sometimes refined by others. That means seeking second, third and fourth opinions when tackling hard problems. Even after 31 years in Formula One, Hodgman would not have it any other way. 'No matter how good you are, you're always better with someone else,' he says. 'No one can do it all on their own.'

CHAPTER EIGHT

COLLABORATE: Two Heads Are Better Than One

In the long history of humankind ... those who learned to
collaborate and improvise most effectively have prevailed.
Charles Darwin

If you had to design a Renaissance man for the early 21st century, you might well come up with someone a bit like David Edwards. A professor at Harvard University who lives most of the year in Paris. A chemical engineer who has written textbooks on applied mathematics and founded a pharmaceutical company. An American whose novels and essays have earned him a place in France's prestigious Ordre des Arts et des Lettres. And still only 50 years old. Does your CV suddenly look a little threadbare? Mine certainly does.

With his pedigree, Edwards could easily be an intellectual snob cloistered away in an ivory tower. But he is exactly the opposite. His dark, tangled locks and leather boots give him a raffish, man-about-town air. Chatty, curious and self-effacing, his instinct is to ask questions, probe the frontiers of his own understanding, soak up the wisdom and expertise of everyone around him. And that omnivore spirit underpins his mission to reinvent the art of problem-solving in the 21st century. Like any good Renaissance man, Edwards understands that reaching across disciplines, veering from the arts to the sciences and back again, can yield remarkable solutions.

Coming after the intellectual stagnation of the Middle Ages, the Renaissance was certainly a fruitful time for solving problems. Between the 14th and 17th centuries mankind came up with a catalogue of inventions that shaped the modern world, including double-entry accounting, the printing press, ball-bearings, logarithms, portable watches and calculus. Like Edwards, many of the best Renaissance thinkers were blessed with a jack-of-all-trades erudition. When he wasn't revolutionising astronomy, Copernicus practised medicine and law. Kepler based his theory of planetary motion on the ebb and flow of musical harmony. Better known in his day as a lawyer, statesman, writer and courtier, Francis Bacon helped to pioneer the scientific method. A theologian named Robert Boyle laid the foundations of modern chemistry. Leonardo da Vinci, the poster boy for polymaths, was a gifted painter, sculptor, musician, anatomist and writer, as well as a startlingly prolific inventor.

Ranging across the disciplines did not end with the Renaissance. Samuel Morse, who invented the telegraph, was a celebrated painter before turning his hand to science. A trained pianist, Alexander Graham Bell used a simple musical game as the starting point for inventing the telephone. A recent survey found that almost all Nobel laureates in the sciences practise some artistic activity. Compared with the average scientist, they are 25 times more likely to sing, dance or act and 17 times more likely to be a visual artist. Max Planck, who won the Nobel Prize in Physics in 1918, prefigured Edwards's devotion to blurring the lines between disciplines when he said: 'The creative scientist needs an *artistic* imagination.'

Nowadays, however, we are often too busy specialising to dabble in other disciplines. Even within fields, the best brains are walled off in ever-narrowing silos of expertise. Economics, biology, chemistry and others have splintered into so many disciplines and sub-disciplines that experts can struggle to understand the work of colleagues sitting next door.

Nor is it humanly possible to be a polymath in the same way as it was during the Renaissance. Five or six centuries ago, someone with a good brain and a lot of free time could become an expert in everything from medicine and astronomy to literature and philosophy, because the sum of human knowledge was modest. And even then there was a danger of spreading yourself too thin. In one of his notebooks, da Vinci wrote: 'Like a kingdom divided, which rushes to its doom, the mind that engages in subjects of too great variety becomes confused and weakened.' Today there is simply too much for one person to know. According to a Google survey, the number of book titles published since the invention of the printing press now stands at 130 million.

Yet the Renaissance ideal is far from a busted flush. It just has to move with the times. In a hyper-specialised, highly complex world, the best way to recreate the mishmash of expertise once found in a single person is to bring various people together. And that is why collaboration is often a key ingredient of the Slow Fix.

This is not a new idea. In *The Rational Optimist* Matt Ridley shows how human beings have always been at their most innovative when connected to large, diverse networks. The Neanderthals were edged out by *Homo sapiens* partly because the latter traded over long distances, allowing their ideas to improve through cross-pollination. Mediterranean societies flourished during those periods of history when trading ships – Phoenician, Greek, Arab, Venetian – were free to sail from port to port, spreading ideas and stitching the region together into one giant social network. When pirates interrupted that flow, as they did at the end of the second millennium BC, during the Dark Ages and in the 16th century, innovation faltered. Throughout history and across cultures, societies that have sealed themselves off from the outside world have tended to stagnate: think Ming China or Shogun Japan, Albania or North Korea. When rising sea levels cut off their small island home from the mainland some 10,000 years ago, Tasmanians went into innovation reverse. 'Human technological advancement depends not on individual intelligence but on collective idea sharing, and it has done so for tens of thousands of years,' wrote Ridley. 'Human progress waxes and wanes according to how much people connect and exchange.'

This partly comes down to good, old-fashioned competition. Mingling with outsiders, especially if they have good ideas, can spur us to raise our own game. But the real problem-solving payoff seems to come from working *with* rather than *against* each other. The latest brain research points to one reason that may be so. Consider the work of two experts in organisational behaviour, Kyle Emich of Cornell University and Evan Polman of New York University. In one experiment they asked 137 research subjects to solve the following puzzle: a prisoner eager to escape from a tower finds a rope in his cell. The rope is only half the length needed for him to lower himself safely to the ground. Undeterred, the prisoner divides the rope in half, ties together the two pieces, and escapes the tower. How did he do it?

Before tackling the problem, half the participants were asked to imagine themselves as the prisoner, while the other half were asked to imagine that the prisoner was someone else. The answer to the puzzle was not exactly rocket science – the prisoner split the rope lengthwise and then tied the two halves together to give him enough length to reach the ground in one piece. But it took some creative, lateral thinking.

And this is where things get interesting. Of those who imagined themselves as the prisoner, only 48 per cent solved the problem. Of those who imagined the prisoner was someone else, 66 per cent cracked it. Conclusion: we are more creative when solving other people's problems.

Nor was this a fluke result. In similar experiments, Emich and Polman found that people come up with more creative presents for total strangers than they do for themselves. They also sketch more imaginative illustrations for a story written by an unknown author than they do for their own scribblings. How to explain this phenomenon? There is already a body of psychological research showing that we think about people and scenarios in one of two ways. When they are close to us – physically, emotionally or temporally – we think about them in concrete terms. When they are distant from us we slip into a more abstract mode of thinking, which tends to be more creative. Jean-Paul Sartre once observed that 'hell is other people,' but it turns out other people may be just the ticket when it comes to solving hard problems.

Working together, or at least drawing on the work of others, has been an article of faith in the world of science since The Royal Society published the first *Philosophical Transactions* in London in 1665. Scientific breakthroughs usually rest on a multitude of advances made by researchers building on earlier findings, learning from each other's mistakes, testing rival theories, adding their own piece to the puzzle. The aim of *Philosophical Transactions* was to spread scientific knowledge so that hunches, theories and flashes of inspiration could cross-pollinate. One early contributor to the journal, Sir Isaac Newton, summed up the importance of leaning on peers and predecessors in a letter to a rival in 1676. 'If I have seen farther,' he wrote, 'it is by standing on the shoulders of giants.' That remains true today. Study after study suggests that scientists solve problems better when they work together. Nobel laureates collaborate more than less garlanded colleagues. Paula Stephan is a professor of economics at Georgia State University and an expert in how science is done. Her research confirms that the founders of *Philosophical Transactions* were right: 'Scientists who collaborate with each other tend to produce better science than do individual investigators.'

A case in point: every six months a company called MathWorks sets a problem in MATLAB, a language it invented to help engineers and mathematicians execute frighteningly complex calculations. Hundreds of contestants submit solutions online in the form of computer code. Each submission is analysed, scored and posted for everybody to see. Anyone can then cannibalise the best bits of code in order to craft a better solution, building on what has come before. If your tweak delivers a more efficient algorithm, even if you have only altered a few lines of code, you go straight to the top of the leader-board. That means participants are competing and collaborating at the same time, which sounds like a recipe for anarchy, yet turns out to be the exact opposite.

Some contestants are smarter than others, but working together makes everyone greater than the sum of their parts. More than a decade of MATLAB contests suggests that collaborative problem-solving usually follows the same path: long periods of minor tweaking punctuated by the occasional great leap forward. 'People will sniff out the slack in an algorithm, like hyenas worrying over a carcass. Then they get exhausted until someone comes along and whips the carcass into a new position, then it all starts over again,' says Ned Gulley, the Design Lead for eProducts and Services at MathWorks. 'We're taught a version of history in which great men, Napoleon for instance, are the sole actors. But the reality is much messier and involves a complex interplay between those that make the leaps and those that make the tweaks.'

This sounds familiar to me. Every so often our family tackles a 1,000-piece jigsaw puzzle. Sometimes the four of us work on it together, at other times we chip away in pairs or alone. Like a MATLAB algorithm, the puzzle evolves in fits and starts. Together, my son and I might assemble one corner, then get stuck, until my wife or daughter comes along and rotates a piece in a new way, which suddenly connects two chunks and leads to a fresh surge of building. Sometimes a visiting friend will break a logjam by joining two pieces in a way that had not occurred to anyone in the family. Each of us could do the puzzle alone, but not nearly as well as when we do it together.

At the end of every seven-day MATLAB contest, Gulley estimates, the winning algorithm is usually 1,000 times better than the best algorithms submitted at the start. 'We have truly brilliant people playing. One of them will make a break-through, and on its own it would have been the best solution in an old-school contest. Just because they're brilliant,' he says. 'But with the MATLAB contest, immediately people are able to come along and tweak it. No single person could do that. It's the swarm, this great big collective brain we have access to.'

Collaborating within a single field, however, has its limits. Small groups with similar backgrounds are prone to tunnel-vision. We say 'great minds think alike' as if this were a good thing, but such uniformity can lead to groupthink. This was a problem long before the Kennedy administration persuaded itself, despite piles of evidence to the contrary, that the Bay of Pigs invasion of Cuba was a good idea. More than 2,000 years ago the Jewish scholars who wrote the Talmud decreed that whenever authorities reached a unanimous guilty verdict in a case involving the death penalty the defendant must be set free. Why? Because the absence of a single dissenting voice is a tell-tale sign of groupthink.

Real problem-solving magic occurs when you start mashing the disciplines Renaissance-style. Bumping up against people from other backgrounds forces us to rethink our assumptions and look at problems with fresh eyes. That explains why group brainstorming works best when participants are encouraged to debate and critique each other's ideas. What's more, something like alchemy occurs at the point where the disciplines touch and overlap. In the 18th century a spectrum of thinkers came together in the coffeehouses of Europe to forge, fine-tune and fight over the inventions and ideas that drove the Enlightenment. The men of science and philosophy who locked horns every Wednesday evening at the Vienna salon run by Sigmund Freud helped lay the foundations of psychoanalysis. The legendary Building 20 at the Massachusetts Institute of Technology, home to a chaotic scrum of engineers, biologists, chemists, linguists, physicists, computer scientists, psychologists, mechanics and military recruiters, spawned a remarkable array of inventions, from high-speed photography to Chomskyan linguistics to the famous Bose headphones, earning the nickname 'the magical incubator' along the way. Ground zero for the personal computer revolution was the Homebrew Computer Club in California, where hackers, scientists, thinkers and entrepreneurs came together to trade ideas in the 1970s. 'Participants flock to these spaces partly for the camaraderie of others who share their passions, and no doubt that support network increases the engagement and productivity of the group,' wrote Steven Johnson in *Where Good Ideas Come From*. 'But encouragement does not necessarily lead to creativity. *Collisions* do – the collisions that happen when different fields of expertise converge in some shared physical or intellectual space. That is where the true sparks fly.'

I witness such collisions every day at work. I rent one of 99 desks in a shared office near my home in London. With the white walls, Buddhist statues and funky meeting rooms, it is a snapshot of urban cool. But the jumble of disciplines also makes it a fertile place to work. Within 15 feet of my desk sit a metals trader, the owner of a network of English-language schools in Asia, a team of architects, an African charity, an acting agency and an app designer. Creative collisions are happening all the time. A software engineer swaps ideas in the kitchen with, say, an interior designer, while at the printer a recruitment consultant discusses with a casting agent how to pitch a client.

Like other ingredients of the Slow Fix, collaboration takes time. You have to find and marshal the right people, and then manage the creative collisions that ensue. But it works even in the fastest-moving sectors of the economy. Steve Jobs once observed that Apple's revolutionary Macintosh computer 'turned out so well because the people working on it were musicians, artists, poets and historians who also happened to be excellent computer scientists'. Nearly three decades later the company is still thrashing the competition with the same recipe. 'It's in Apple's DNA that technology alone is not enough,' Jobs declared after the launch of the world-conquering iPad. 'It's technology married with liberal arts, married with the humanities, that yields us the results that make our heart sing.' Bottom line: the more people that come to your problem-solving party, and the more varied their backgrounds, the more likely it is that ideas will collide, combine and cross-pollinate to spawn the Promethean flashes of insight that pave the way for the best Slow Fixes.

And yet we remain wary of working together, especially across disciplines. We place a steep premium on expertise, spending time and money acquiring and defending it. We flaunt the status it bestows, putting titles before our names and initials after them. We use jargon, certifications and professional guilds to keep outsiders at bay, and then dismiss anyone with the temerity to stray from their chosen field as a jack-of-all-trades and master of none. All those framed diplomas and awards hanging on office walls around the world send the same message: you've come to the right place. I know my stuff. You don't need anyone else now. And let's be honest: in moments of crisis we all crave a safe pair of hands. When you're lying in the street fighting for your life after a car accident, you desperately want to believe the attending paramedic can patch you up all on her own.

Even as we pay lip service to the magic of teamwork, our instinct is to heap glory on the individual. Awards, from the Nobel to the Pulitzer, from the Oscars to the MacArthur 'genius grants', usually go to single winners. Even in team sports we shower the superstars with prizes and praise. Study after study shows that when explaining events we tend to put too much emphasis on the role of individual agency and not enough on circumstances, a phenomenon dubbed the Fundamental Attribution Error. That is why we routinely assume CEOs have more power to shape the fortunes of their companies than all the research suggests. We certainly love the idea of the lone genius, the solo expert toiling away in solitude before finally shrieking 'Eureka!' and emerging into the sunlight clutching a fully-formed solution to a problem. It's simple. It's romantic. It's thrilling. But often it's wide of the mark. Even before the modern era the best ideas seldom sprang whole from a single mind; rather, they were the fruit of cross-fertilisation among various minds. Who invented the light bulb? Thomas Edison. Wrong. Edison was merely the savviest member of a cluster of rival inventors who learned and borrowed from each other. Convinced that small teams with a range of expertise were the most inventive, he presided over a staff of more than 20. Even Michelangelo hired assistants to help him paint parts of the Sistine Chapel.

It does not help that many of our problem-solving institutions are set up in ways that thwart collaboration. University departments often operate like rival fiefdoms. Likewise government ministries, endowed with their own budgets, cultures and agendas, are more inclined to compete than to collaborate. Distrust of collaboration runs especially deep in the corporate world, where the patent system often closes down lines of enquiry. Ego is another obstacle. Researchers who sing the praises of collective toil can bristle when it threatens their patch, and many still prefer to keep their data as private as possible. Even if pooling knowledge and insights serves the greater good, it also makes it harder to assign kudos, tenure and grant money. In 1994, 450 different physicists were credited with discovering the quantum particle known as the 'top quark'. How do you go about rewarding that many people? The MATLAB forum is full of debates over who should get credit for what.

Despite those hurdles, the most creative problem-solvers increasingly reach outside their own intellectual bunkers to tap the wisdom in other bunkers. 'In our highly specialised world, we often get stuck in holes of expertise, which stops us communicating with other holes, which in turn limits our vision and our creativity,' says David Edwards. 'The great creators dream of exiting their holes because they know that pooling knowledge and insight is the best way to solve problems.'

To break down those barriers, Edwards opened Le Laboratoire in Paris in 2007. Housed in a handsome 18th-century building just a few streets from the Louvre, that great repository of Renaissance masterpieces, his brainchild is hard to define. Le Labo is not a college, think tank, science lab, marketing agency, industrial kitchen, art gallery, design studio or shop. Yet somehow it is all of the above, and more. Think of Le Labo as an Enlightenment coffeehouse for the 21st century, a playground for ideas, a space where experts from across the arts and the sciences who would never normally meet come together to tackle problems. You might find a chef showing his latest concoction to a biologist in the gleaming kitchen in the basement, an artist talking quantum mechanics with a physicist in one of the meeting rooms, or an architect arguing product development with a chemist. Or they might all work together in the same team. 'Everyone comes to the problem with their own way of thinking, but then the ideas start flowing and the magic happens,' says Edwards. 'I might see something as impossible from a medical point of view, but someone from the design world sees that it can work. Together we have a bigger picture of the problem that allows us to find a better solution.'

To see Le Labo in action, I track a recent project. The problem: how to create a vessel for transporting water based on the biological cell. The germ of the idea came from Edwards's course at Harvard University, which was attended by students majoring in everything from economics and biology to architecture and visual story-telling. An early proposal was to create a geodesic dome held together by 270 dowel rods, but that proved too fragile and fiddly. The next idea was a cell-like bag modelled on a Chinese lantern.

Later, at Le Labo, Edwards convened a team that included chefs, chemists, designers and a rotating carousel of students from all three fields. They decided to create an edible bottle. Five months later, nine members of the team gather in Le Labo's high-tech kitchen, with its mirrored ceiling and spotless stainless steel worktops. Raphaël Haumont, the lead chemist, shows off some early prototypes for the membrane that will house the liquid. A tattered notebook crammed with handwritten notes about times, temperatures and salt and sugar content lies open on the counter. Haumont points to a slimy, yellow pouch about the size of a tennis ball, which has been sitting with water inside it for two weeks. It has leaked, leaving a stain on the napkin underneath. 'This is clearly not the bottle of tomorrow,' says Haumont. 'We need to do a lot more work on modifying the chemicals and a lot more testing to make the membrane strong enough.' But the sight of this soft, cell-like vessel fires the imagination of the rest of the team, and the ideas start flying.

François Azambourg, the lead designer, suggests attaching a thread that could be used for cutting open the membrane. Or adding a cork or stopper in a different colour. Could the thickness of the membrane vary, he asks, so that sometimes it is hard and other times soft? Another designer wonders if the vessel could be turned into a cube, to make it easier to store and transport. One of the chefs then suggests creating a large circular membrane with smaller spheres inside, each one containing the ingredient for a meal. 'Magnifique,' says Edwards.

Haumont responds coolly to the brainstorming barrage. 'All this design stuff will have to wait because my job as a chemist is to find a stable membrane and I'm not there yet,' he says, a hint of impatience in his voice. Later, he tells me that building a membrane with multiple colours, right angles and a separate break-off cap will never work scientifically.

Edwards watches the tug-of-war within the team with a look of amused indulgence. He plays a pivotal role in most Le Labo projects, tossing in ideas, chiding, praising, marshalling and chivvying along the rest of the crew. He reminds Haumont that the deadline for showing the public the first workable prototype is less than a year away. 'You're very artisanal now, which is fine, but we need to be thinking on a large, industrial scale right from the start,' he says.

Azambourg, every inch the French intellectual in his black jacket and black hat, has been pondering the knock-back from Haumont in silence. He re-enters the fray, hoping to nudge the chemist in a new direction. 'Maybe the idea of an opening in the vessel is a bit primitive,' he concedes. 'Maybe we'll end up with something that you consume all in one without having to open it at all.'

Over the next seven months the team meet regularly to bat ideas back and forth and gradually refine their product. By the time of the first public unveiling they have created a cell-like vessel inspired by the structure of an egg, with external and internal membranes that are both edible and biodegradable. There are two examples on display at the exhibition. One has strawberry juice inside a chocolate membrane. I bite into it. The juice is tasty, but the membrane is too chewy and has an artificial flavour that is off-putting. The second vessel has a much more appealing texture. Its membrane is made from oranges and has a fresh, zesty taste. I find myself eating it all, lapping up the citric juice inside. Both membranes can store liquids safely for several months.

The containers still need work but the first response from the public is favourable. Over the next 18 months, Le Labo, which is funded by charitable donations, sponsorship and the revenue from selling the products it invents, brings in more designers, engineers and food chemists to help refine the formula and experiment with recipes. They eventually christen the new containers 'WikiCells', and the first products hit the market in 2012 amid heady talk of no longer throwing away bottles or pots after consuming their contents. 'Perhaps soon there will be bars and sections in food stores where you can order yoghurts in edible packaging, and where the packaging is made of granola or berries,' muses Edwards. 'Or maybe the membranes – and the shells that will be needed to protect them – can incorporate the vitamins and minerals that are sometimes absent in our diets.'

Though slightly bruised by some of their clashes, the team members are all tickled by the outcome of their combined efforts. 'Science, design and cuisine are completely different universes, and we definitely had our, how shall I say, debates,' says Haumont, with a knowing smile. 'But when universes cross it is hugely enriching and when everyone comes together round the table you get this incredible collision of ideas that takes you places you could never get to on your own.' Azambourg agrees. 'The best thinkers always surround themselves with a good team, whether they admit it afterwards or not,' he says. Julien Benayoun, another designer, likes the way the competitive spark within the group was channelled towards a common goal rather than personal glory or reward. Studies show that creativity nosedives when companies foster too much internal competition, because employees stop sharing information and start obsessing about beating the rival in the next cubicle. That never happens at Le Labo. 'By the end, you don't know who had what idea, this one or that one,' says Benayoun. 'You can't say "that was me" because there are so many influences and inputs from others and everyone nourishes everyone else.'

That is often how collaboration works in a Slow Fix. Check your ego at the door, be prepared to share the credit and let the creative juices start flowing. That was how Monty Python minted some of the most famous sketches in the comedy canon. One member of the troupe, John Cleese, summed up the genesis thus: 'The really good idea is always traceable back quite a long way, often to a not very good idea which sparked off another idea that was only slightly better, which somebody else misunderstood in such a way that they then said something which was really rather interesting.'

IDEO almost never assigns just one person to a project. 'Group critique is key because your ideas will be made better by early exposure to others,' says Jane Fulton Suri. 'Bringing people from different disciplines together is powerful so we have developed a natural bias to mix it up and use teams.'

With so many disciplines converging, that approach makes good sense. As they burrow deeper into the nature of the universe, physicists find themselves contesting the same terrain as philosophers and theologians. The breakthroughs of the future, like the sequencing of the human genome, will therefore rest on input from biology, chemistry, engineering, information technology, design and more. A 2011 white paper from MIT predicted that 'true convergence' and cross-pollination could trigger a 'third revolution' in the sciences.

Thanks to modern technology, working together is easier than ever before. Not long ago it was hard to know what was happening in other fields, so you could waste months trying to work out whether your brilliant idea was good or bad, or if it had even been tried before. Now you can often find out with a few minutes of googling. You can also share data and debate across the planet at the push of a button.

A recent comprehensive survey of patents and peer-reviewed academic papers showed that over the past 50 years teamwork has surged in almost every scientific field and the size of the average team has nearly tripled. Medicine is already well on its way to being a team sport. To deliver better care, health systems now encourage doctors to work together across fields of expertise. Around the world, medical colleges have started to select pupils for their ability to collaborate, and have added 'teamwork' classes to the curriculum. Even the lead character in *House*, the maverick genius played by Hugh Laurie, solves those brain-bending medical riddles by bouncing his theories off colleagues. 'When I entered medical school, it was all about being an individual expert,' says Dr Darrell G. Kirch, the President and Chief Executive of the Association of American Medical Colleges. 'Now it's all about applying that expertise to team-based patient care.'

Collaboration comes in many forms. It can take the shape of a throwaway remark on the phone, a back-of-the-napkin sketch over lunch or a formal brainstorming session with flipcharts and Sharpies. It can also occur in online platforms, among people who never meet or even speak with each other in the real world. One example is the Polymath Project, where mathematicians share problems on a central website. Its first challenge was to find a new proof for the Hales-Jewett theorem. Collaborating remotely, testing, challenging and improving each other's work, 40 mathematicians nailed it inside six weeks.

Another example is the 'idea jam', where experts chew over a problem online. In 2010, 3,800 activists, academics, politicians and military brass spent five days debating 26 topics in global security. Online moderators curated the jam, and later used data-mining software and old-fashioned human judgement to come up with a shortlist of the 10 best ideas. One was to put 5 per cent of all disaster-relief dona-tions into an international crisis preparedness fund. Another was that NATO should set up a civilian wing to handle the non-military parts of its missions. The moral of the story: stirring together a wide spectrum of thinkers can yield richer results than traditional conferences and help guard against what the jam's organisers called 'groupthink or bureaucratic stovepipes'.

Yet the richest collaboration often involves working together in the real world. This can be messy and time-consuming, but it builds the trust that helps us open up, confess errors, take risks and challenge each other – all essential ingredients of the Slow Fix.

When researchers at Harvard Medical School analysed more than 35,000 papers published by teams of scientists, they found that the closer collaborators worked in the real world, the better their research. Scientists based within the same building tended to come up with the best work of all. One of the researchers, Isaac Kohane, concluded: 'Even in the era of big science, when researchers spend so much time on the internet, it's still important to create intimate spaces.'

To help that happen, universities are redesigning their campuses to encourage collaboration, collisions and chance encounters among disciplines. At Columbia, Princeton, MIT and New York University, biologists, physicists, chemists, geneticists, engineers and computer scientists now work together in open-format labs and mingle in shared dining halls, libraries and common rooms. In a similar vein, 'artscience' melting pots in the style of Le Labo are springing up in cities around the world. To build teams with a jumble of expertise, universities have started to recruit by broad research themes, such as 'ageing' or 'energy', rather than following the traditional practice of hiring by department. With governments leaning on scientists to share more data and work together more closely, and pressure mounting for academic journals to open up their publications to the general public, the hunt is on for ways to recognise individual contributions to collaborative discoveries.

Students are being nudged in the same direction. The University of California at Berkeley runs an annual Big Ideas competition in which interdisciplinary teams of students vie to invent new ways to help tackle illiteracy, purify water or help scientists build laboratory equipment using local materials in the developing world. Degree courses are also moving away from narrow specialisation, with biology students, for example, taking classes in technology, business, psychology, innovation and culture. Some call this the T-shaped model of learning, which means going deep in one or two fields while remaining broad across many others. The aim is to hit the sweet spot between the know-it-all Renaissance Man or Woman and the tunnel-vision hyperspecialist. 'I don't think it's about thinking one person can do everything,' says Alan Guttmacher, director of the US National Institute of Child Health and Human Development. 'It's about training people to be exposed to new ways of thinking.'

In a world where no man can afford to be an island, or a one-trick pony, even the most specialised problem-solvers are looking for ways to collaborate and learn from others. In 2012 the Williams Formula One team hired Michael Johnson, the former Olympic running champion, to help streamline their tyre-change routine and bolster their training. Even the crack problem-solvers at NASA now reach out to experts beyond their own laboratories and research centres. Budget cuts are one reason for the shift, but the real driver is the realisation that the world has changed. 'We're mirroring what's going on in academic institutions, the high-tech industry and elsewhere,' says Jeff Davis, NASA's Director, Space Life Sciences. 'With the really complex problems we face nowadays in the world, no one organisation has the resources or expertise to handle the entire suite of challenges that might come up, so it makes sense to tap the broader experience outside the group you traditionally have relationships with.'

Collaboration advances more unevenly in the business world. Many companies only do it within their own walled garden. Like a Californian version of the Kremlin, the famously secretive Apple works its cross-disciplinary magic in-house and would never dream of sharing research like NASA. Yet other firms are taking the leap. Proctor & Gamble, a large maker of consumer products, has signed more than 1,000 partnership agreements with innovators around the world, sharing the sort of R&D that would have remained under lock and key in the past. More than half its new products now involve input from people not on the P&G payroll. 'We want to partner with the best innovators everywhere,' says Bob McDonald, the CEO.

Though few of us have the pulling power of P&G, we can all get better at collaboration. Start by burnishing your Renaissance credentials. Take up hobbies that force you into unfamiliar terrain. If you're a computer coder or an accountant, join a painting class, study an instrument or cultivate an urban garden. If your work involves dealing with people all day, visit a science fair, play Sudoku or attend a course in molecular gastronomy. Make a point of perusing websites that challenge rather than reinforce your view of the world, and read books in fields other than your own.

To maximise collisions with potential collaborators, put yourself out there. Tap into social networks – supper clubs, community choirs, running groups – that throw you up against people from a mishmash of backgrounds. Find a coach or mentor to supply an outsider's view on your fix. Persuade your company to host an idea jam. When confronted with a hard problem, make sure the first question you ask yourself is: who can help me with this?

Sometimes you will find the answer by simply looking across the hall, scrolling down your Twitter timeline or posting a plea on Facebook. Or by hiring one of the new management gurus who specialise in matching people to problems. But at other times traditional collaboration is not enough. There is a lot of wisdom and ingenuity out there that is hard to marshal into an organised team.

Sometimes, to find the right fix, you have to turn to the crowd.

CHAPTER NINE

CROWDSOURCE: The Wisdom of the Masses

Many hands make light work.
John Heywood

'Thetta reddast' is an expression you hear in Iceland a lot these days. It roughly translates as 'Don't worry, everything will fix itself.' To some Icelanders it suggests a dangerous fatalism; to others, a tribute to their native can-do spirit. Either way, this tiny, wind-buffeted island nation in the North Atlantic certainly needed fixing after the global financial crisis in 2008.

Before the crash Iceland was on the mother of all winning streaks. Its banks and businesses devoured rivals overseas. Its overnight millionaires splashed out on yachts and private jets, super-cars and flashy penthouse apartments. Reykjavik, the dowdy capital, began building the world's most expensive opera house. Swept up in the carnival of consumption, ordinary Icelanders borrowed and spent like there was no tomorrow. Yet their much-vaunted 'economic miracle' was a mirage, a bubble of eye-watering proportions. At the peak of the boom Iceland's banks racked up debts worth nine times the nation's gross domestic product. When the bubble burst, the country was one bail-out away from a default.

The carnage of 2008 forced the world to take a long, hard look in the mirror. In many countries the introspection spurred moves to balance the books and rein in the financial sector. In Iceland the soul-searching went deeper. With a population of 320,000, this is a country with very few degrees of separation – and the feeling of betrayal was intense. How could the powers that be, who were in many cases former schoolmates, allow our banks to go so spectacularly off the rails, Icelanders asked. Why did we lose our way as a nation? A consensus took hold early on that electing a new government, reforming the banking sector and balancing the budget were just the beginning: what Iceland really needed was to rebuild itself from the ground up.

Top of the agenda was reforming a political system that had lost touch with the electorate. This problem is not new, nor is it confined to Iceland, home to the world's oldest parliament. Voters around the world have always found fault with their rulers, but over the last generation distrust of elected officials has spiked. Pollsters find that nowadays four times more Britons than in the 1980s think politicians put their own welfare before the national interest. Even in countries where the economy is in decent shape, such as Germany, the relationship between voters and their political masters has curdled. In 2010 the German Language Society chose 'Wutbürger', or 'enraged citizen', as its word of the year. It cited voters' fury over 'political decisions made above their heads'.

To tackle this problem at its root, a group of Icelanders came up with a radical solution that will help us understand the next ingredient of the Slow Fix: they invited the electorate to play a direct role in shaping government policy and writing a new constitution.

This sounds like folly. After all, what do most ordinary voters know about crafting legislation, let alone the finer points of constitutional law and political philosophy? But the Icelandic experiment is not as hare-brained as it sounds. In Chapter Eight we saw how experts can collaborate fruitfully within and across the disciplines. The same can be true when you cast the net much more widely and indiscriminately. That is because a crowd, if properly managed, can be remarkably intelligent. This is hard to accept, given our primal fear of the mob. In the 19th century Thomas Carlyle warned against believing 'in the collective wisdom of individual ignorance'. His contemporary, Henry David Thoreau, would also have sniffed at the idea of enlisting *hoi polloi* to help write a constitution: 'The mass never comes up to the standard of the best member, but on the contrary degrades itself to a level with the lowest.'

Yet that elegant blast of conventional wisdom happens to be completely untrue. Sure, crowds can be crass and barbaric. The riots that erupted near my home in London in the summer of 2011 are grim proof of that. But there is another side to the story. In *The Wisdom of Crowds* James Surowiecki makes a compelling case for enlisting the masses to help solve problems. The book is stuffed with examples of crowds outperforming the experts, from guessing the weight of an ox at a country fair to pinpointing the resting place of a vessel lost at sea. When NASA asked the public to find and classify craters on the surface of Mars, the public, with just a little training, delivered collective judgements that experts deemed 'virtually indistinguishable' from those of a 'geologist with years of experience in identifying Mars craters'.

Jumbling up experts and amateurs has even been shown to boost collective intelligence under laboratory conditions. Scott Page, a professor of political science and economics at the University of Michigan, used computer simulation to design a range of virtual problem-solving agents. Each agent was given a unique set of skills, with some programmed to be clever and others less so. Result: the mixed groups almost always performed better than groups made up solely of clever agents. Why? While experts can outdo the rest of us on a few specialised tasks, they tend to be, as we saw earlier, too similar in background and perspective to bring the fresh eyes needed to tackle many problems. Page boiled down his findings into what he calls the Diversity Trumps Ability Theorem. 'This theorem is no mere metaphor or cute empirical anecdote that may or may not be true ten years from now,' he says. 'It's a logical truth: under the right conditions, a randomly selected collection of problem-solvers outperforms a collection of the best individual problem-solvers.' In other words, the crowd is worth listening to.

When the right sort of crowd turns its mind to the right sort of problem, a surprising alchemy occurs. Imagine a painting by a pointilliste artist. George Seurat's *A Sunday Afternoon on the Island of La Grande Jatte* is made up of hundreds of thousands of individual dots of paint. Peer closely at the canvas and all you can see are tiny points of colour. Step back, however, and the dots merge to produce a vivid scene of people lounging on the banks of the Seine. To understand what has come to be known as 'crowdsourcing', you have to make a similar mental leap. When you aggregate the decisions of the many, even if some of those decisions are bone-headed, the outcome is a single collective decision that is often as good, if not better, than what the sharpest person in the crowd would have come up with alone. That insight is the cornerstone of the Google empire. To organise the ocean of information on the Web, the company uses an algorithm to parlay the billions of decisions we make every day online into a single page ranking. 'You could say it's as if we've been programmed to be collectively smart,' concluded Suroweicki.

And that is why tapping the crowd is the next ingredient of the Slow Fix.

In the preceding chapter we saw the power of working together within and across disciplines. But traditional collaboration tends to involve teams with limited and tightly focused membership. Only a select few are invited to work on projects at Le Laboratoire or conduct research in those open-format labs at Columbia and Princeton.

Crowdsourcing means taking a problem normally tackled by the few and putting it to the many. In the wrong hands it might only deliver a quick blast of publicity or some cheap market research. Used properly, however, the crowd can be a powerful ally in the battle to solve hard problems. You can ask the crowd to gather or mine data. You can invite it to test and judge solutions. Sometimes it pays to limit the interaction

165

within the crowd to avoid groupthink. Just look at the cata-strophic bubbles that inflate when everyone starts singing from the same hymn sheet in the financial markets. But sometimes the crowd does its best work when its members communicate and collaborate.

One of the drivers behind Iceland's experiment in crowd-sourcing is Gudjon Mar Gudjonsson, a boyish, fortysome-thing entrepreneur with a string of high-tech companies and patents on his CV. Surveying the wreckage of the crisis in 2008, he concluded that experts alone could never put Iceland back together again – and ordinary citizens had to play a central role in the reconstruction. 'We all have our own vision for the future and ideas on how to fix our coun-try and that is a valuable resource worth tapping,' he says. 'Our aim was to use the wisdom of crowds to capture the heartbeat of a nation's creativity.'

Working with like-minded reformers, Gudjonsson convened a 'National Assembly' in 2009 based on crowd-sourcing and open-innovation techniques from the private sector. It consisted of 1,500 members, nearly 5 per cent of Iceland's population – a cross-section of 1,200 citizens taken from the national voting register and 300 politicians, business leaders and other 'change-makers'. A blend of amateurs and experts, in other words. During a day-long event, the members sat together in small groups and brainstormed about their vision for the nation's future. What kind of coun-try should Iceland aspire to be, and what can we do to make that happen? A facilitator ran each group and all the input was sifted, ranked, ordered and broadcast on a giant screen. The event was so popular that other, smaller Assemblies were convened around the country. In 2010 the Icelandic Parliament set one up to gather input for the new national constitution. It also canvassed opinions on Twitter, YouTube and Facebook.

To see how crowdsourcing politics works in the wild, I join an Assembly held in a school gymnasium on the outskirts of Reykjavik. Its mandate is to identify the 'core competencies' upon which Iceland should be building its future. Some 150 people turn up on a grey, wet Saturday morning. True to the spirit of crowdsourcing, they represent a cross-section of Icelandic society plus a smattering of parliamentarians, a former mayor and the city's chief of police. Most people are dressed casually, with many men sporting moustaches as part of an anti-cancer campaign. Everyone uses first names, and the atmosphere is relaxed though expectant.

The gymnasium is a reminder that this is an Assembly convened for the people by the people. Posters warn pupils not to smoke, litter or rollerblade. A disco ball hangs from the rafters above, ready for the next dance night. Through the wall you can hear squeaking trainers and the yelps of children playing basketball. Jugs of water and stacks of yellow index cards for taking notes sit on tables around the gymnasium. My place is on Table K along with a software engineer, an unemployed labourer, a chartered auditor, a trainee architect, a music student, a marketing manager, an interior designer and Katrin Jakobsdottir, the young minister for Education, Science and Culture.

After introductions, Sigrun, our moderator, asks us to list Iceland's unique selling points (USPs). The software engineer says the country has a clean, green image that sets it apart.

167

When Sigrun urges him to be more specific, the auditor steps in. 'We have so much fresh, clean water, compared to other countries,' she says. 'Can we find a way to use that?' The architect points out that Iceland is blessed with hot springs. The labourer leans forward, nodding his head vigorously. 'Maybe we could drill into the earth to get geo-heat from the water,' he says. This sparks off a debate about whether water really is a USP and if the energy harvested from it could be exported from Iceland's remote location. Then Jakobsdottir, the minister, gives the hot springs idea a twist. 'Perhaps we could develop and export geo-thermic technology,' she says.

All morning the ideas come thick and fast. We could build wind farms to exploit our climate; brand the best of our cuisine and sell it to the world; turn Iceland into a hub for Nordic fashion. We could harness our high levels of education and tech know-how to become the Silicon Valley of the north Atlantic. Or offer up our small, homogenous population as a giant focus group for companies and research projects. The conversation gradually drifts towards tourism and the prospect of luring foreigners to enjoy Iceland's stunning landscape of geysers, volcanic rock and waterfalls. The music student, largely silent until now, pours cold water all over that idea. 'What's so special about our food and farming or looking at a waterfall?' he asks, in a slightly petulant tone. 'Why would tourists bother going to our museums when we're not even interested in going to them ourselves?' His intervention casts a pall over the table. To lighten the mood, I suggest Iceland's position halfway between Europe and North America makes it the perfect venue for hosting conferences. 'Very true,' says the labourer. 'You see, sometimes it takes an outsider to see our strengths.' And then we are all brainstorming ideas for turning Reykjavik into a hub for conventions and corporate retreats.

After a lunch of lentil and lamb lasagne, we return for more. Jakobsdottir kicks off the afternoon session by observing that Icelandic music is popular abroad, and that another small island nation, Ireland, has built a world-beating music industry. This idea does not go very far, however. Someone points out that Ireland's biggest band, U2, are tax exiles. The marketing manager warns that Bjork, the elfin songstress with the piercing, ethereal voice, is an acquired taste even for Icelanders. Other ideas include making vitamin pills or pet food from discarded fish carcasses and establishing a theme park based on the dwarves, elves and other 'hidden people' that are a central part of Icelandic culture. Eventually, the time comes to draw up a shortlist of Iceland's best selling points to present to the Assembly. We settle on five: water; the blending of urban and rural; transatlantic hub; spas and health; and clean, healthy food. Everyone clusters round a laptop to shape the final presentation, pointing out spelling mistakes, laughing at *double entendres*, chipping in with advice. As the spokesperson from each table reads their shortlist from the stage, the audience whoops and cheers. When our spokesman, the marketing manager, returns from the podium we all give him high-fives. Tourism, fishing, geo-thermal power and agriculture seem to have emerged as the leading USPs.

So has the Assembly done its job? Has Iceland's experiment in crowdsourcing unleashed a torrent of creative solutions to the nation's problems? Sitting at Table K, brainstorming with the locals, I did not feel like I was witnessing problem-solving on a Promethean scale. Sure, we came up with an intriguing list of suggestions, but so too could a few people sitting together in a bar. But that might be the wrong way to the think about it. Maybe I am trying to assess a pointilliste painting from too close up.

When you step back and look at the big picture, Iceland's experiment with crowdsourcing does seem to be churning up useful ideas that might one day make their way into government policy. 'A part of every National Assembly is just blah blah blah, but even if just two or three good new ideas come from a meeting, that's a triumph,' says Jakobsdottir. 'And we are already seeing that happening.' The Assemblies have made it clear how worried Icelanders are about welfare and education and how much they dislike public transport in Reykjavik. An earlier Assembly dedicated to education came up with one solid proposal: put more stress on values and philosophical debate. 'This was missing in my own education, but children should be tackling questions like "What are moral values?" and "Why is society the way it is?"' says Jakobsdottir. 'I am already looking at how to integrate this idea into the national curriculum.'

Many people leave my Assembly optimistic that crowd-sourcing can help reboot Iceland. Some talk of laying the groundwork for a new form of politics. 'What you're seeing here is super-democracy,' says a university lecturer. 'The discussions are so powerful and creative and innovative, but it will take time to trickle up and reshape government.' Even participants of a less academic bent seem delighted with the ideas that have bubbled to the surface. 'To be honest, I expected a boring day but it was actually quite invigorating,' the marketing manager tells me. 'When you put a range of people round the table together, you generate new ideas and new approaches to old ideas.'

Yet such collaboration is not essential. Sometimes you just want to find a diamond in the rough, that one person in the crowd armed with a killer app. In the early 18th century Britain's Royal Navy lost many ships at sea because crews had no way to measure longitude while sailing. Some of the finest scientific minds of the day, including Sir Isaac Newton, had tried in vain to solve this problem. Desperate for a solution, Britain set aside its cosy assumptions about social class and turned to the crowd. In 1714 an Act of Parliament offered £20,000, a vast sum at the time, to anyone who invented a 'Practicable and Useful' way of calculating longitude at sea. Five decades later someone finally won the competition by inventing a highly accurate clock that could take precise readings even in the choppiest waters. The most striking thing about the winner was his biography. John Harrison was not a sailor or a shipbuilder. Nor was he a professor at Oxford or Cambridge or a member of the Royal Society. Indeed, he had very little formal education. The son of a carpenter from Yorkshire, he had taught himself how to make clocks. In other words, he was the ultimate diamond in the rough.

As the discovery of longitude shows, tapping the crowd is not new. What has changed in recent years is that technology makes it possible to marshal and manage larger groups than ever before and unearth ideas in the most obscure corners of the globe. In this high-tech age all the world's a crowd and

171

all the men and women in it potential problem-solvers. Communities of experts and amateurs are just a click away in online platforms such as ideaken and Whinot. InnoCentive solves problems that have stumped the best brains in private research and development labs, governments and non-profit organisations by putting them out to a network of more than 250,000 'Solvers' in nearly 200 countries – tapping the crowd on a scale that would have been unimaginable 20 years ago, let alone in the 18th century. Clients looking for solutions are known as 'Seekers', and range from pharmaceutical giants and consumer product conglomerates to NASA and the *Economist* magazine. Recent offers on the website include: $100,000 for creating an insulin that can respond to the individual needs of people suffering from diabetes; $50,000 for developing a technique that boosts the nutritional value of plant tissues; $30,000 for a saw that can cut through bone without damaging soft tissue; $8,000 for a system that can spot corruption in institutions; and $5,000 for a new way to package beer. Solvers can be anyone from specialists with a bit of spare time to amateurs logging in from their basement, bedroom or garage. They earn money for coming up with workable solutions, making InnoCentive the world's largest marketplace for problem-solving.

The first step is to help Seekers pull the Andon rope to work out exactly what their problem is before working towards a solution. Just like Geir Berthelsen did at Norsafe. 'Most organisations have no idea what their real problems are, and even if they have a basic idea they have real trouble articulating them,' says Dwayne Spradlin, the President and CEO of InnoCentive, which runs training workshops to show Seekers why and how to tap the crowd. 'When you're dealing with deep, complex problem-solving, you can't just set up a quick ad on Craigslist and assume the world will kick in. It's not Yahoo! Answers,' says Spradlin. 'We help our Seekers ask better questions and frame the problem so they get better answers.' Just like IDEO.

Though throwing problems out to a crowd of 250,000 people sounds like a shortcut to chaos, or the lowest common denominator, InnoCentive works rather well. Solvers come up with a suitable fix to more than half of the 'challenges' posted, including many that have foxed the top R&D laboratories in the world. They have invented cheaper and easier ways to manufacture the drugs used to treat tuberculosis and made the water from Lake Victoria in Africa safe to drink. Remember the BoGo torch? While developing the prototype, Mark Bent ran into a problem: his device could not illuminate a whole room in the same way as a kerosene lamp. So he turned to InnoCentive, challenging its crowd to find a way to disperse the light. Within three months an engineer in New Zealand came up with a design that allowed the BoGo to double as a lamp while also putting less strain on its rechargeable batteries. Tapping the crowd through InnoCentive often forges partnerships that would once have been unthinkable. When NASA asked for help improving the packaging used to preserve food on space missions, the winning solution – using graphite foil – came from a *Russian* scientist.

To be sure, the most striking lesson from InnoCentive lies in who solves which problems. A Harvard University study found that the best solutions often come from people operating 'at the boundary or outside of their fields of expertise'. On average, Solvers come up with the goods six areas away from the discipline most closely linked to the challenge. One Solver used his knowledge from the concrete industry to invent a technique for separating oil from water after a spill in freezing temperatures. A patent lawyer from North Carolina came up with a new way to mix large batches of chemical compounds. Four chemical and bioengineering graduate students at the University of Washington invented an electronic device that emits a light signal when water being purified with solar disinfection technology is safe to drink – a potential lifesaver for millions of people in the developing world. Bottom line: it pays to tap the largest, most diverse crowd possible.

That is why InnoCentive tries to frame each problem in such a way that no one feels excluded from trying. A challenge from a drilling company, for instance, will appear with no reference to the oil and gas industry. 'Most people will stop reading the problem as soon as they see "oil and gas", because they will think, "I'm not from the oil and gas industry,"' says Spradlin. 'Our model is about throwing a very broad net to avoid limiting it to the same old experts.'

That means you end up with people like John Lucas beavering away on your problems. The 45-year-old lives in the town of Maidenhead, west of London. In his spare time he has solved four problems through InnoCentive, earning $62,000 in the process. By altering the shape of a bottle, he was able to change the way fizzy drinks feel in the mouth. He later identified an additive that stops the cheese and oil sprayed onto snacks from separating and devised a crust-forming compound that prevents silage stored on farms from rotting. Most recently, he designed a glove that stops soldiers burning their hands while fast-roping from helicopters.

Judging from his scorecard, you might expect Lucas to be a chemist with access to an industrial laboratory. In fact, he is a molecular biologist with a law degree who grew up on a farm in Ohio. 'I don't have a lab or a garage where I can create devices or test compounds, so what I'm doing through InnoCentive is really just thought experiments,' he says. Lucas makes a point of steering clear of problems in his own area of expertise. 'Usually when these companies are stuck on something, it's the people that work in that field that can't solve it, so really it's ripe for somebody else to look at it from a different point of view, to come at it from a side angle,' he says. Like so many Slow Fixers, Lucas approaches every problem with a large reservoir of patience. He never expects to crack the code with his first solution. 'At first you think, "I'm not going to be able to cope with this," but then you let it percolate, you keep thinking about it, ruminating on it, you come up with an idea, do some research on it, which usually leads you in another direction,' he says. 'Most of the time I end up pretty far away from where I started.'

We have already seen how that slow, meandering kind of thinking is the lifeblood of creativity, and cannot be rushed. Nor can you locate your ideal solver in the crowd more quickly by homing in on certain disciplines. If you knew where to look, you would have solved your problem already. Back in the 18th century no one could have predicted that a self-taught clockmaker from Yorkshire would crack the longitude conundrum. By the same token, nobody expected a 15-year-old boy from Maryland to win an international science fair in 2012 by discovering a method for detecting pancreatic cancer. 'It's clear that the best place to put out these problems is to adjacent fields, but the thing is you can never predict which adjacent fields,' says Spradlin. 'It's not about trying to figure out the 1,500 people who might be able to solve the problem; it's about letting go and saying, "I have no idea where the solution is coming from, so I need to get to everybody."'

Despite InnoCentive's best efforts, many Seekers still find it very hard to let go. While government bodies and foundations are usually happy to let outsiders peek backstage, many companies remain terrified of giving away secrets to the competition. Most InnoCentive challenges from the corporate sector are anonymous and a bit guarded, much to the chagrin of the Solver community. 'Several times I've thought I'd definitely solved a problem with a very satisfying solution, only for the company to come back and say "We already knew that" or "We tried that already," which means you've put in all this time and effort and get nothing out of it,' says Lucas. 'If you're going to have people come in and help, you need to be more forthcoming and provide more detail on exactly what your problem is, why you're trying to solve it, what would be a suitable solution and what you've already tried.'

There is a big lesson here for anyone – not just firms obsessed with trade secrets – hoping to tap the crowd: you have to play by the rules. The crowd will only serve up its wisdom if you treat it right. The crowd wants respect. It hates feeling exploited. It expects openness in return for its insights and enthusiasm. If the crowd suspects you are taking it for a ride, it will rebel, disperse or move somewhere else. Nobody owns the crowd.

Companies that open up to the crowd reap the benefits. Sometimes that crowd is your own workforce. Since 2001 IBM has used online idea jams to tap its 300,000 global employees. The internal brainstorming has helped the company reshape its working practices and launch 10 new businesses with seed capital of $100 million.

Tapping the crowd beyond the company walls pays off, too. In 2006, Netflix, an online movie rental company, offered $1 million to anyone who invented an algorithm that could predict user ratings of films at least 10 per cent more efficiently than did its current software. Three years later a team of statisticians and computer engineers spread across the US, Canada, Austria and Israel claimed the prize. That same year Fiat started building the world's first fully crowdsourced car at its flagship factory in Betim, Brazil. The company set up a web portal where anyone in the world could post ideas on how the vehicle should be designed and engineered. More than 10,000 suggestions poured in from 160 countries. At every stage, the crowd, which ranged from experienced Fiat staff to teenagers in their bedrooms, critiqued, debated and refined the ideas. Fiat made sure the dialogue flowed freely in all directions, explaining why ultimately some suggestions ended up prevailing over others. 'This is completely different to the usual design process, which is entirely hidden and secretive,' said Peter Fassbender, manager of Centro Estilo, the firm's design centre. Fiat went a step further than other crowdsourcers by moving from the virtual to the real world, inviting the smartest members of the crowd, which included a civil servant, an IT specialist and a teacher, to inspect the prototypes and mingle with the company's designers and engineers at Betim. The fruit of this experiment was the Mio, a sweet little car that drew rave notices at the 2010 São Paulo International Automobile Trade Show. It also changed forever the way Fiat works. Other manufacturers have followed suit. Pooling ideas from an online crowd of 12,000, ranging from professional designers to weekend enthusiasts, a US company called Local Motors built a prototype military vehicle that could one day run reconnaissance, delivery and evacuation missions in combat zones.

Crowds can also generate fixes for social problems. On IDEO's online platform, OpenIDEO, 34,000 people in 160 countries chew over questions such as 'How can we improve sanitation and better manage human waste in low-income urban communities?' and 'How can technology help people working to uphold human rights in the face of unlawful detention?' So-called 'challenge hosts' winnow down hundreds of ideas into a shortlist and then the crowd brainstorms. The winning solutions are worked up into pilots and prototypes. Thanks to ideas from OpenIDEO, including DIY cheek swab kits, Stanford University inspired more people to sign up to its bone marrow donor register. Sony is now developing an interactive online magazine that pairs local volunteers with local projects, another OpenIDEO solution.

Other organisations are tapping the crowd for ideas on everything from making cities more habitable to combating sexually transmitted diseases. In many fields, academics are turning to the masses for help mining their data, channelling the public's enthusiasm and the human brain's uncanny knack for detecting patterns. By sifting through images from the Kepler telescope that have been posted online, ordinary punters have spotted two planets missed by astronomers using the latest computers. They are also helping to identify cancerous cells, to spot and categorise new galaxies, and to transcribe ancient Greek texts written in a messy, almost illegible hand.

Crowds already help fix problems in our daily lives. What do you do when your computer starts acting up? If you're like me, you head straight for the many online forums, where thousands of people of varying expertise share troubleshooting tips. Unlike company helplines, these do not charge, nor do they leave you on hold for hours listening to Enya. And often they deliver better help. The last time my hard drive went haywire, I spent more than an hour talking to an Apple expert who failed to solve the problem. After hanging up, I tried my luck in an online forum. Within ten minutes I found the perfect fix posted by a teenager in Wisconsin, a kind of John Harrison moment for the 21st century. And computer troubleshooting is just the tip of the iceberg: the Web is crammed with forums where crowds offer advice on everything from relationships to health to home repairs.

Now is the time to sound a note of caution: collaboration and crowdsourcing both have their limits. Working together is not the *only* answer to *every* problem. Even teams with a fine track record can, over time, grow stale and narrow-minded. The crowd can make mistakes or be sabotaged by rogue members. With around 100,000 contributors constantly editing its content, Wikipedia is an example of the perils of crowdsourcing. Though a goldmine of information, the online encyclopedia is prone to inaccuracies and biases. The bubbles and crashes of recent years are a reminder that stock markets, another much-touted example of collective intelligence, are not always so clever. Sometimes, as a character in one of the Icelandic sagas puts it, 'the advice gets worse as more stupid people come together'.

Above all, solving complex problems often entails a conceptual leap, a flash of inspiration, a Cassandra-like ability to see where the world is heading – and that is seldom a collective act. Henry T. Ford did not come up with the idea of building cars for the masses from market research or focus groups. 'If I'd asked customers what they wanted,' he once said, 'they would have said "a faster horse".' Steve Jobs also had a knack for seeing what others did not. It's hard to believe now, but the first iPad was launched into a whirlwind of scepticism from pundits and consumers. Would people really shell out for a device that hovers somewhere between a smartphone and a laptop? Is there even a market for tablets? The answer, it turned out, was a walloping Yes. 'For something this complicated, it's really hard to design products by focus groups,' Jobs said later. 'A lot of times, people don't know what they want until you show it to them.'

Working together can also be counter-productive. Just think of all those hours we waste in boring, pointless meetings at work. You can also take collaboration and teamwork too far. At its headquarters in Emeryville, California, Backbone Entertainment built an open-plan office where everyone could see and hear everyone else. The company develops video games and hoped that stirring its workforce together into one big pot would yield a rich stew of collaborative magic. What it produced was a load of disenchanted developers yearning for some privacy. Eventually, Backbone reconfigured its office with cubicles – those derided symbols of Dilbertesque drudgery. 'You'd think in a creative environment that people would hate that,' says Mike Mika, the company's former creative director. 'But it turns out they prefer having nooks and crannies they can hide away in and just be away from everybody.'

It has always been so. Though Rembrandt worked closely with other painters in his studio in Amsterdam, each artist was assigned a private space for working alone. When consultants compared 600 computer programmers across 92 companies to pinpoint what separated the top performers from the pack, they found the secret ingredient was not higher pay or more experience, but having a private work space that minimised interruptions. Human beings are profoundly social, but we also crave privacy and personal freedom. Research shows that open-plan offices can make us anxious, hostile, tired and prone to illness. They also bombard us with the distractions that undermine deep thinking. To carve out a place of quiet solitude in my shared office, I seek refuge in one of the private suites. Some are built for just one person, their pink, padded walls sealing you off from the world in a womb-like embrace. 'People can only take so much of other people,' says Peter Spencer, who designed the office. 'A lot of the best thinking happens when people are left alone with their thoughts.'

That is why, throughout history and across disciplines, the best problem-solvers, the big beasts of creativity who conjure earth-shaking breakthroughs, have cherished solitude. Einstein spent hours staring into space in his office at Princeton University. William Wordsworth described Newton as 'A mind for ever/Voyaging through strange seas of Thought, alone.' Every major religion has prophets – Buddha, Muhammad, Moses – who went out into the wilderness to grapple with the big questions on their own. Picasso once said, 'Without great solitude, no serious work is possible.' This remains true in the modern, high-tech world. In his memoir, Steve Wozniak described how he built the first two Apple computers working by himself late into the night: 'Most inventors and engineers I've met are like me … they live in their heads. They're almost like artists … And artists work best alone.'

That is why we all need to be careful when tapping the crowd. Ask yourself if your problem really will benefit from being thrown open to everybody. If it can, take the time to figure out exactly the right question to ask and how to manage and reward the crowd. And never pin all your hopes on the multitude.

It is no coincidence that every Slow Fixer we have met so far, from IDEO to Le Laboratoire to NASA, warns against fetishising the group. Instead, their aim is to forge a symbiotic relationship between collective and individual toil, giving everyone the freedom to nurture their own ideas in splendid isolation, before pushing them through the filter of the team or the crowd. The introverted Newton bounced his insights off peers in letters and the pages of *Philosophical Transactions*.

After his long, lonely nights of the soul, Wozniak chewed over ideas with fellow nerds at the Homebrew Computer Club. Even Einstein collaborated. 'The secret lies in striking the right balance,' says David Edwards. 'The group is crucial for developing and improving ideas, but often the best ideas start with a single person. The individual is supremely important.'

CHAPTER TEN

CATALYSE: First among Equals

*Every great institution is the lengthened shadow
of a single man. His character determines the
character of the organisation.*
Ralph Waldo Emerson

Rush hour in Bogotá is not what it used to be. At least not for people like Manuel Ortega. These days, the 42-year-old banker commutes from the suburbs on a bus that has helped turn the Colombian capital into a darling of the green movement and a case study in urban renewal.

The TransMilenio is no ordinary transport network. In the middle of its widest boulevards, Bogotá has carved out nine dedicated bus lanes that crisscross the city like an overground rail network. Each lane is set apart from the remaining road space by low walls, allowing fleets of red articulated buses to glide along unimpeded by ordinary traffic. Instead of waiting outdoors at conventional bus stops, passengers use swipe cards to enter enclosed stations made of metal and glass. Like a train or subway, the TransMilenio pulls up alongside the platform and opens all its doors at once, allowing large numbers of people, including the elderly, the disabled and parents with push-chairs, to embark and disembark quickly and easily. The name of this system is bus rapid transit, or BRT.

Ortega takes the H13 route, and when I catch up with him he looks like a poster boy for public transport. Trim and dapper in a charcoal suit and yellow tie, he is poring over a quarterly report spread out on his lap. A call comes in on his Blackberry from a colleague eager to schedule a meeting. 'I'll be in the office in ... 17 minutes,' says Ortega, glancing at his watch. 'Make sure my coffee is ready.'

Such punctuality would be unthinkable for commuters in much of the world. Your bus may be just three or four stops from the office in London, Boston or Taipei, but how do you know a broken-down truck or a full-blown traffic jam isn't lurking round the next corner?

As the H13 coasts serenely through downtown Bogotá, the streets flanking the TransMilenio route are a portrait of pandemonium. Lane after lane is clogged with decrepit taxis, antediluvian minibuses belching clouds of smoke and horse-drawn carriages piled high with scrap metal. Motorcycles wade through the swamp of stalled traffic, dodging beggars panhandling for spare change and street vendors hawking everything from breath mints to bootleg DVDs. Car horns, growling engines and salsa music merge into a very Colombian cacophony.

Sitting at a window seat in the TransMilenio, looking down on this vision of urban hell, Ortega shudders. 'It's like another world out there,' he says. 'Thank God I'm in here.'

In Latin America, as in much of the developing world, the rich inhabit a separate universe, travelling in private cars from gated communities and country clubs to offices and boutiques patrolled by armed guards. The TransMilenio has struck a blow at this social apartheid by winning over well-heeled *bogotanos*. Swanky neighbourhoods now run their own feeder buses to nearby stations and real estate developers build malls and smart apartment blocks as close to the network as possible. At any time of day, you find yuppies yakking into iPhones alongside maids and labourers from the city's poorest *barrios*.

Many of Ortega's colleagues at the bank now commute by TransMilenio. Across the aisle from him sit three young men with dirt-encrusted hands travelling to work on one of the flower plantations that ring Bogotá. Two rows back, a stylish young lawyer is inspecting the varnish on her freshly mani-cured nails. Behind her, Victoria Delgado, a young biology student travelling to the Universidad de los Andes, is texting her boyfriend. 'It's a good social mix,' she says. 'Everyone is equal here.'

But *bogotanos* do not rack up nearly 2 million trips every day on the TransMilenio in order to boost social solidarity. They have embraced bus rapid transit because it offers some-thing that did not exist before: a comfortable and efficient way to travel across this anarchic city of 8 million souls. Delgado's journey to university takes 25 minutes instead of three times longer by car. Using the TransMilenio has slashed Ortega's daily commute from two hours to 40 minutes a day.

And he can schedule meetings on the fly knowing he will arrive on time.

Women like Delgado also feel safe on the TransMilenio, no mean feat in a city that was once a byword for urban violence. There is still a lot of in-your-face security in Bogotá, with many public buildings and company headquarters protected by guards with guns and sniffer dogs, but the TransMilenio system points the way to a more relaxed future. There is no security on the buses, and stations are patrolled by cheerful young staff wearing bright yellow and red jackets emblazoned with the slogan 'The Friendly Face of the City'.

The TransMilenio is still a work in progress. Bogotá is building new routes as well as underpasses to allow the buses to skirt beneath troublesome intersections without having to wait for green lights or for traffic to clear. Nor is the system without flaws. The ride can be bumpy on routes where poor drainage has caused the paving to crack and buckle. Though Bogotá has a moderate climate, commuters still pine for air-conditioning in the dog days of summer. Women sometimes grumble about amorous male passengers, and everyone has to watch out for pickpockets. But the chief complaint is that there are not enough seats at peak times because so many people ride the system. Translation: the TransMilenio is a victim of its own success.

As a result, BRT is hailed as a solution to one of the world's most pressing problems: how to move people around cities comfortably and cleanly. Across Asia, Africa and Latin America, rising prosperity is clogging urban streets with cars, motorbikes, trucks, scooters, jeeps, motorised rickshaws, buses and other vehicles. Pedestrians are left cowering on the fringes of public spaces, coughing and spluttering through the pollution. Even as emissions from industry fall, traffic is forecast to spew out 50 per cent more environmentally unfriendly gases by 2030, with much of that rise coming from the developing world.

The TransMilenio is not carbon-neutral. To keep costs down, its caterpillar buses run on diesel rather than on cleaner fuels that are more expensive and less suited to the high altitude of Bogotá, which sits 8,500 feet above sea level. Nevertheless, a TransMilenio engine is so efficient that it emits less than half the pollution of an old-fashioned mini-bus. By embracing BRT, Bogotá has taken more than 9,000 small private buses off the roads, slashing the overall consumption of bus fuel since the first line opened in 2001. Some private cars vanished, too. Last year, Ortega sold his Audi sedan and now travels round Bogotá either by TransMilenio or taxi – a big step in a society where having your own wheels is the ultimate status symbol. 'I just don't feel like I need a car any more,' he says. 'You can live differently in this city now.'

In 2009 the TransMilenio became the first large transportation project in the world to win the right to generate and sell carbon credits under the Kyoto Protocol. That means nations and companies that exceed their emissions limits, or simply wish to polish their green credentials, can buy credits from TransMilenio, thus pumping an extra million dollars a year into Bogotá's coffers.

BRT stacks up well against rival forms of transport. It is much cheaper to build and maintain than a subway, yet can carry just as many passengers. Not surprisingly, cities across the world, from Cape Town to Jakarta to Los Angeles, have built or are planning their own versions. More than a dozen municipal governments, from Mexico to China, are already, or will soon be, selling carbon credits for their BRT lines. International delegations flock to Bogotá to study the TransMilenio, and urban development is now a trendy university degree for young Colombians.

Of course, the TransMilenio did not spring up in isolation. In the early 1990s Bogotá was a basket case, blighted by kidnappings, terrorist attacks and one of the highest murder rates in the world. Its infrastructure was poor even by Latin American standards thanks to years of underinvestment and unfettered immigration from the countryside. Parachuting a shiny bus rapid transit system into such anarchy would have been the worst sort of quick fix. Other cities in the developing world have learned that lesson the hard way. New Delhi erected its own BRT without re-educating local motorists, who promptly subverted the system by invading the dedicated bus lanes. In Johannesburg, taxi drivers blocked BRT routes and vandalised buses and stations because they saw the network as a threat to their livelihood.

To make the TransMilenio work, Bogotá had to engineer a broader transformation, which included many of the ingredients of the Slow Fix we have seen so far. It started with a long-term goal: to create a city where everyone felt comfortable mingling in public spaces. Tackling poverty was identified as an essential part of making that happen. The city brought potable water and sewers to nearly all its citizens. Snazzy new schools, swimming pools and libraries sprouted in the poorest neighbourhoods. To crack down on crime, Bogotá modernised its police force with bigger budgets, better training and more accountability. Through amnesties and mandatory searches, it collected and melted down thousands of firearms. All of these measures were underpinned by Colombia's success in pushing the guerrilla forces deeper into the jungle and bringing economic stability.

At the heart of Bogotá's transformation was the effort to redress the balance of power between traffic and pedestrians. In the early 1990s the city was in thrall to the car. Motorists ignored traffic lights, rampaged through pedestrian crossings and parked all over the pavements. A small bribe to one of the city's notoriously corrupt transit police officers was the only sanction they faced. To start clawing back territory colonised by traffic, and to put the car firmly in its place, Bogotá created a new corps of traffic cops that actually enforced laws preventing drivers from stopping and parking wherever they pleased. The city barred 40 per cent of vehicles from the roads at rush hour. It installed hundreds of concrete bollards to stop drivers mounting the kerbs to park illegally. It then removed a third of the city's street parking to clear the way for the TransMilenio. It widened and repaved many pavements, too.

Bogotá also set about reclaiming parks from the drug dealers, beggars and prostitutes. It built new green spaces and spruced up the old ones, planting thousands of trees and staging open-air concerts by rock, jazz and salsa bands as well as performances of opera, theatre and poetry.

All these measures went hand in hand with a campaign to foster what was dubbed a 'culture of citizenship'. To draw

190

attention to the carnage on the roads, Bogotá officials painted stars on the pavement where pedestrians had been killed. They sent 420 mimes into the streets to use art, music, dance and humour to encourage *bogotanos* to behave like good citizens: to put litter in pavement bins, help the elderly cross streets and respect the rules of the road. A jaywalking pedestrian might be pursued by a white-faced mime wagging a disapproving finger or poking gentle fun at her gait. A driver who blocked an intersection or crosswalk might be accosted by a mime feigning horror and holding up a red scarf emblazoned with the word 'Incorrecto!' Bogotá also handed out 350,000 cards with a green thumbs up on one side and a red thumbs down on the other to allow pedestrians to pass instant judgement on the behaviour of motorists. To ram home the message, City Hall used TV ads to challenge the supremacy of the car.

Every Sunday the balance of power now swings sharply in favour of the pedestrian as Bogotá closes 120 km of its streets to traffic. People of all social classes pour into thoroughfares normally jammed with cars to run, cycle, stroll and play football and frisbee. With bands playing in the parks, and aerobics and yoga teachers leading classes in the open air, there is a carnival atmosphere, a giddy sense that the natural order has been reversed, or restored.

Like most *bogotanos*, Delgado, the biology student who commutes to campus on the TransMilenio, loves Sundays. She goes jogging down the middle of the normally busy boulevard in front of her apartment. Or she goes cycling with her boyfriend. 'It's a moment when everyone can taste what it would be like to have a city run for people rather than for cars,' she says. 'And once you taste something, it becomes a possibility in your mind. That is very powerful.'

In the same spirit, Bogotá has built more than 300 km of cycle routes through its knotted neighbourhoods. You can now pedal right across the city, snaking between apartment blocks, across parks and alongside roads and rail lines, without ever sharing space with a motor vehicle. Though cycling through most Latin American cities is like playing Russian roulette, parts of the Colombian capital, with its cycle rickshaws for hire, remind me of bike-friendly Holland. On a warm weekday afternoon the cycle route in the Tintal neighbourhood is a melting pot of Bogotá society: a pensioner cycling back from the market with vegetables in her handlebar basket; a builder in a yellow hard hat overtaking a woman in a business suit, shooting her a cheeky smile on the way past; children returning from school, friends perched on the backs of their seats.

The bottom line is that Bogotá is safer, greener and more pleasant today than seemed possible in the mid-1990s. After the launch of the TransMilenio, bicycle use rocketed while injuries and deaths from traffic accidents nosedived. The air quality along the BRT corridors also improved markedly. In 2007 the national tourist board adopted the slogan 'The Only Risk Is Wanting to Stay.'

The transformation of Bogotá reminds us that sweating the small stuff and thinking holistically and long term are essential elements of the Slow Fix. But it can also teach us something just as valuable. You may have noticed I attributed the changes wrought in the Colombian capital to the 'city' itself or to nameless municipal officials. The truth is more nuanced. It turns out Bogotá is a vivid example of the next ingredient of the Slow Fix: having a strong figure to drive the search for a solution.

So many fixes in this book have multiple authors, and the participants are usually quick to hail the collective effort. We solved this problem together, they say. We were greater than the sum of our parts. All hail collaboration, crowds, teams and networks. But remember the caveat from Chapter Nine: even the smartest team and the wisest crowd can only take you so far. The best problem-solving usually blends individual and collective brilliance. At the very least, you need someone to manage the group, as do the moderators who curate the debates and brainstorming on OpenIDEO and in the National Assemblies in Iceland.

Examine any Slow Fix, and you often find one person who embodies or even supplies the underlying vision, who stitches together the team, acts as a hub for the network or a lightning rod for the crowd, who inspires others to strive, make sacrifices and overcome the resistance and inertia that the most ambitious problem-solving always entails.

This comes as no surprise to Tony Silard, founder of the Global Leadership Institute in Washington, DC. Over the past 20 years he has coached thousands of leaders across the private and non-profit sectors, including the CEOs of Fortune 100 companies. He believes every Slow Fix needs a single figure at its core. 'Solving complex problems always involves change and the number one thing people look for during a change process is security,' he says. 'Ideas change, circumstances change and teams change, so people need a single person who has a clear idea of where they are going and is ultimately going to be responsible for what happens and who makes them feel safe. They want a leader.'

Every Slow Fix we have encountered so far has such a figure. With his gentle, genial manner, Are Hoeidal sets the tone inside Halden prison. Group Captain Simon Brailsford is the catalytic force behind the safety revolution within the RAF. At Locke High School, where dynamic figures are a dime a dozen, staff point to Kelly Hurley, the former head-master and now Greed Dot's vice president of human capital, as the linchpin of the turnaround. 'He's a crack-of-dawn, leaving-after-dark kind of guy who meets with all the schools, the teachers, the parents, the management, the secu-rity, and you run everything by him,' says Phil Wolfson, head of Locke's special education department. 'Kelly is the glue that holds it all together.' Even David Edwards, a crusader for collaboration, remains the invisible hand behind many projects at Le Labo. 'The vision and passion of a core creator is essential,' he says.

Though Apple relies on collaboration and teamwork to forge its game-changing gadgets, it also encourages project leaders to act as 'auteurs', who lead from the front and stamp their personality all over the final product. Jonathan Ive was so central to designing the iMac, iPod and iPad that he is sometimes credited with inventing the devices. And then there was the auteur-in-chief, Steve Jobs. Friends and foes likened his knack for winning over people to a 'reality distor-tion field'. His keynote speeches were hailed as masterclasses in the art of persuasion. By the time he died in 2011, Jobs had achieved the kind of rock star status seldom granted to CEOs, with fans leaving flowers, messages and even apples with a bite taken out of them at Apple stores around the world.

When it came to forging a Slow Fix for Bogotá, the city leaned heavily on two visionary mayors who served back-to-back terms starting in 1995. The first was Antanas Mockus, an eccentric mathematician and philosopher with a flair for the theatrical. Among his stunts, he donned a superhero costume and dubbed himself 'Supercitizen' to promote a 'culture of citizenship' as part of the city's transformation. His successor, Enrique Peñalosa, is a sparky, well-travelled economist with a Marxist past. Less colourful than Mockus, who once resigned as rector of the National University after mooning a lecture hall full of rowdy students, Peñalosa nevertheless rammed through most of the reforms that redrew the urban landscape of Bogotá, including the TransMilenio.

To explore the role of a single, catalytic figure in the Slow Fix, I arrange to spend some time with Peñalosa. We meet on a balmy evening in early spring in Zone T, a pedestrianised area he created in 2000. Lined with smart bars and restaurants, the streets are thronged with people of all ages, strolling, sipping beer, dining al fresco. It is a snapshot of fashionable urban living.

Peñalosa arrives on a bicycle, listening to Sarah Brightman on his iPod. Tall, slim and bearded, he looks like a Don Quixote with star quality. Though a decade has passed since he left office, several passers-by give him a friendly nod. We sit down to dinner on the terrace of an Italian restaurant and within seconds the manager comes up to embrace the former mayor. 'When I took over this city, Colombia was in its worst

195

ever recession and the guerrilla war was out of control,' says Peñalosa. 'But in some ways that was an advantage, because people were ready for change, for a fresh vision, even to try something a bit crazy.'

His quixotic dream went much farther than just building the TransMilenio. It was to transform Bogotá into a city that belonged to everyone and was at ease with itself. 'A good city is one where rich and poor meet as equals in parks, on buses, on sidewalks, at cultural events,' he tells me, setting down his cutlery to free up his hands for gesticulation duty. 'Human beings are natural pedestrians, we are animals that need to walk not just to survive but to be happy. A bird in a cage the size of a cathedral is happier than one in a small cage, but the happiest bird is the one that can fly freely with no cage at all.'

He pauses to scan the scene at Zone T. A young family ambles by, eating ice cream and pushing bicycles. A smile spreads across Peñalosa's face as he warms to his theme.

'To be able to sit outside at a café and not be drowned out by cars, to read a newspaper in silence, to hear birdsong, to see children playing without fear in the street and listen to their laughter, to see couples kissing on the sidewalk, to feel safe enough to cycle to work or to meet a friend in a park, to fill the city with butterflies and flowers – all these things change your life in a way that is better than doubling your income,' he says. 'My vision for Bogotá was to create a city where people want to be outside, where they can live life as it is meant to be lived.'

It is a moving speech, and I feel stirred listening to it. And that matters because a Slow Fix needs someone to rally the troops. You could fill a Kindle with the books, articles and essays dedicated to the art of leadership, but much of it boils down to one thing: inspiring others to follow you into battle. 'If people sense you lack passion, or you are all about self-aggrandisement, they won't invest in you,' says Tony Silard of the Global Leadership Institute. 'When you have true passion for an idea, then people will follow you.'

Many of our Slow Fixers have that fire in their bellies. Julien Benayoun, a designer who worked on the WikiCells project, describes David Edwards as the catalyst-in-chief at Le Laboratoire: 'He believes enough for one, two, three, four or five people,' he says. 'When you feel down, when you get discouraged by the complexity of a problem, he can pull you along. Some people just have that knack.'

Peñalosa clearly does. Though his failure to win re-election in three separate attempts points up his shortcomings as a campaigner, you can easily imagine him firing up the troops at City Hall. Many of his old team remain firm fans. 'Enrique has a way of talking to people where they feel like the most important person in the world,' says one former advisor. 'He is a maestro at inspiring you to dig deeper when the going gets tough.'

It helped that Peñalosa arrived at City Hall with a powerful vision. To inspire people, you must do more than just master the details. You have to think big and think long. You don't galvanise the electorate by promising more cycle paths or better buses. You do it by pledging to revolutionise their city. 'Even the most humble street sweeper understood that he wasn't just cleaning the sidewalks but transforming Bogotá,' says Peñalosa. 'He knew what we were doing and why because we had a vision, and it permeated.'

Today, most locals concede that Bogotá has made big strides since the 1990s, but changing ingrained attitudes was an uphill battle. Motorists refused to cede ground in the early days. 'It was an endless war to get the cars off the sidewalks and then to make the sidewalks wider,' says Peñalosa. 'Car-owners were the ones who held the power in town, they were the rich and no one had ever dared touch them before. They felt they had a divine right to drive and park wherever they wanted. They looked down on buses as the transport for the poor. It was a war to the death.'

Peñalosa paid a steep price for that. Just over a year after he took office, opposition to his plans for urban renewal grew so virulent that he and his wife sent their then 12-year-old daughter away to live in Toronto. 'I was public enemy number one; the only person more hated than me was the head of the guerrillas,' he says. 'I remember praying in the morning: "God, please just let me get through this day." I didn't even ask for the week, the month or the year. I just wanted to survive each day.'

Many politicians would have buckled under the onslaught. That Peñalosa held his ground tells us much about his character. It also suggests Slow Fixers need more than just the power to inspire: they also need a deep reservoir of self-belief. Peñalosa certainly brought that to bear on the problems of Bogotá. 'I was able to persevere because I knew I was right,' he says. 'Even if people opposed my vision for the city, I knew it was the right thing to do. When you have a clear long-term vision, you have the confidence to confront the whole world, to take on public opinion, because you have the tranquillity of knowing that in 15 or 20 years you will be proved right.' And there it is again, the calmness that taking the long view can bring.

Such bullet-proof conviction often flows from taking the time to build up a deep understanding of the problem at hand. Just look at the CVs of our other Slow Fixers. Hoeidal worked for nearly two decades in the Norwegian prison system, including a wardenship, before moving to Halden. Hurley spent years running some of the toughest schools in Los Angeles County before taking the helm at Locke. Edwards had been studying creativity and the interplay between the arts and sciences for years before he established Le Labo.

Peñalosa had seen enough quick fixes go horribly wrong in Bogotá to be in no rush to unleash his revolution on the city. He knew he needed to do the intellectual heavy lifting first, to build the knowledge and expertise that would allow him to fix his home town properly. Back in the 1970s, as a student in Paris, he began thinking about how the urban landscape shaped people's behaviour. 'Paris taught me that in a city that gives you security, cultural life, the chance to walk, to do sport, to go to parks – it becomes less important if you are rich or poor,' he says. 'That got me thinking in new ways about Bogotá.' Around the same time, his father's involvement in the United Nations Habitat conference introduced Peñalosa to the latest trends in urban development.

After studying how the Dutch and the Danes tamed traffic to recapture their cities for pedestrians and cyclists, he started a debate about cycle paths in the Colombian press. He investigated how Lima, the capital of neighbouring Peru, had reclaimed its parks from delinquents. He also explored the pros and cons of the BRT system that Curitiba, a city in southern Brazil, had built in the 1970s. 'I was a bit afraid because no one else in the world had followed their example, so I felt there must be a problem I wasn't understanding or seeing, something I needed to work out before moving from theory to practice,' says Peñalosa. 'Visiting other places gave me ideas and helped me to develop my thinking, but maybe the most important thing it gives you is motivation to see that problems can be solved.'

Once the homework was done, he was ready to hit the ground running. 'I spent 25 years studying, reading, thinking about how to sort out this city,' he says. 'By the time I took office I was ready to make radical changes and make them quickly.' Translation: his personal database was locked and loaded.

But like other strong figures we have seen in the middle of Slow Fixes, Peñalosa does not hail from the autocratic school of leadership. On the contrary, he is a big believer in teamwork and tapping the crowd. To keep ideas and feedback flowing freely, he set up a voicemail system that allowed any of the 1,500 members of his administration to leave a personal message for any other member, including the mayor himself. Every three months, like Patagonia's Yvon Chouinard, he took key members of his team on a retreat outside the city to review their progress. Despite having iron faith in his own vision, and a ferocious resolve to see it through, he went out of his way to praise colleagues for good work and constructive criticism. 'If you are going to solve a complex problem, you have to be arrogant but also humble. You cannot convince yourself that you are an oracle with all the answers,' he says. 'If people thought I was wrong, we talked, we debated, we made adjustments. Yes, I was tough sometimes. I had to be. But I did not force my team to accept my vision, I persuaded them. The key was that everyone in the team contributed and felt part of the vision, and the result was that together we achieved things I could never have dreamed of, let alone done, on my own.'

This is in line with the best academic work on leadership. Research shows that group debates are more fruitful when a leader ensures everyone is given a chance to speak, and that powerful people start making bad decisions when they begin dismissing input from others. When Jim Collins conducted the research for his influential book *Good to Great*, he was surprised to discover that those who take solid companies into the stratosphere over the long term are not the macho blowhards who catch the eye on *The Apprentice*. Yes, they have the fierce, get-it-done-at-any-cost resolve. But they are also humble enough to listen. Just like Peñalosa. 'Self-effacing, quiet, reserved, even shy – these leaders are a paradoxical blend of personal humility and professional will,' wrote Collins. 'They are more like Lincoln and Socrates than Patton or Caesar.'

That approachability fits the times. In our flat world, where celebrities and CEOs speak directly with fans and customers on Twitter, and where the misdeeds and foibles of the great and the good are exposed like never before, the very idea of an infallible, go-it-alone, all-knowing leader seems out of date. Yet welcoming input from others is just the start. The best leaders usually have plenty of what psychologist Daniel Goleman dubbed 'emotional intelligence', the ability to understand and get along with other people. When Goleman studied 188 leading global companies, he found that EI was the key plank of success. 'When I analysed all this data, I found dramatic results,' he wrote. 'To be sure, intellect was a driver of outstanding performance. Cognitive skills such as big-picture thinking and long-term vision were particularly important. But when I calculated the ratio of technical skills, IQ and emotional intelligence as ingredients of excellent performance, emotional intelligence proved to be twice as important as the others for jobs at all levels.'

Google arrived at a similar conclusion when it tested its own assumption that the best managers are those endowed with bags of technical expertise. After months of data mining, which included analysing feedback surveys, performance reviews and nominations for managerial awards, the company reached a verdict: managers who made time to talk one-to-one, who tackled problems by asking questions instead of simply imposing solutions by diktat, and who showed an interest in employees' lives and careers were not only the most popular – they also led the best-performing teams.

That is why so many leadership gurus invoke Ernest Shackleton, the former British naval officer who led an ill-fated journey to discover the South Pole in 1914. Along the way, his ship, the *Endurance*, became trapped in the ice, drifting for ten months before finally being crushed like a matchstick model. Shackleton then had to solve one of the toughest problems in the annals of Antarctic exploration: how to rescue 28 men stranded on an ice-field more than 1,000 km from civilisation. To keep them alive, he put on a masterclass in leadership, giving orders while fostering a strong *esprit de corps*. He set up regular meal times, helped to nurse sick men

202

back to health and insisted that even officers perform the lowest chores. He encouraged his crew to express themselves by playing games, writing poetry to recite at parties and performing tasks that suited them. Eventually, Shackleton and six of his men sailed a small boat across 1,300 km of freezing ocean and then hiked over a snowy mountain range in search of help. They found it and returned to rescue their comrades. After two years of polar hell, all 28 crew of the *Endurance* lived to tell the tale.

'Someone called Shackleton a "Viking with a mother's heart", and what better epithet for a leader: you're a Viking, you're strong, you're assertive, you really care about something and are not afraid to speak up about it, and at the same time you have a mother's heart – you're nurturing and supportive of others,' says Silard. 'The most effective leaders strike that balance between empathy and authenticity. People want to see that you have a strong vision for how to tackle a problem, but at the same time they want to be listened to.'

Many of our Slow Fixers combine that silk and steel. Consider how Wolfson describes former headmaster Hurley at Locke High School. 'He's a very good listener and supportive, but if he needs to make a point on the direction he wants to go he can do that, too,' he says. 'He knows how to walk that tightrope of giving us the freedom to contribute our own ideas while also bringing us all along together down a single path.'

Not all successful leaders have a mother's heart. Steve Jobs is the classic counter-example. Apple insiders described him as a tyrannical control freak who could be obnoxiously rude to his staff, shouting them down, passing off their ideas as his own, displaying zero interest in their private lives. Would Apple have thrived even more had his EI matched his IQ? We will never know. But perhaps Jobs was that very rare thing: a genius you walked away from at your peril.

To what extent lesser mortals can work the Mr Nasty leadership style is up for debate, but there is no doubt that fixing a complex problem often depends on a driving, central figure. It is certainly hard to imagine that Bogotá would have transformed itself, or taken the TransMilenio to heart, without men like Peñalosa at the helm.

Whatever the problem, you should put a catalytic figure at the heart of your fix. Think Viking with both a mother's heart *and* a rich background in the subject. If you yourself don't fit the bill, shelve your ego and bring in someone who does. If that person moves on, find a replacement swiftly. Never leave your fix rudderless, or it will drift, and might even go backwards.

Witness how much momentum for reform in Bogotá has ebbed away in recent years, with subsequent mayors putting less energy into public works, poverty reduction and traffic calming. Crime, or at least the fear of it, has risen again. In 2011 the then mayor was forced to step down thanks to a corruption scandal that also paralysed construction of the new TransMilenio line to the airport. At the same time, rising prosperity has put more cars on the roads. Result: the balance of power has tilted back towards private motor vehicles in Bogotá.

After dinner in Zone T, Peñalosa takes me for a walk round the neighbourhood. He is clearly proud of his accomplishments. 'We set out to change the underlying culture and we did that in Bogotá,' he says. 'Obviously 10,000 things are still missing, and there is much more to achieve, but the key is we changed the vision of the city. We established the idea that progress should not be measured by the number of highways we have but by the quality of our public transport and public spaces. Without that, the TransMilenio would never have worked. Nothing we did would have worked. It would all have been nothing more than a meaningless quick fix.'

But he is irritated by the slippage since he left office. When we stroll past three cars parked on the pavement outside a *ceviche* restaurant, he throws up his arms in disgust. 'They shouldn't be there; it's completely illegal,' he says, in a voice that carries in the warm evening air. A security guard in a nearby doorway hears his lament, and looks away sheepishly.

Before he pedals off into the night, I ask Peñalosa what he would change if he could tackle the transformation of Bogotá all over again. He answers in a flash. 'We would do a lot more to win over the man in the street,' he says. 'To solve difficult problems, you really need to involve the people who live with those problems as much as possible.'

CHAPTER ELEVEN

DEVOLVE: Self-Help
(in a Good Way)

Good solutions exist only in proof … Problems must be
solved in work and in place … by people who will suffer the
consequences of their mistakes.
Wendell Berry

Ricardo Pérez can still remember the first time he tasted his own coffee. It was early 2005 in San José, the capital of Costa Rica, and the experience changed his life. Like so many farmers in this small, peaceful Central American nation, Pérez comes from a family that has grown coffee for generations. But neither he nor his ancestors had ever sipped a cup brewed properly from their own beans. What little crop they held back for personal use was processed so ineptly that even the memory makes Pérez wince. 'It wasn't anything you looked forward to drinking,' he says. 'It was bad, very bad.'

What Pérez drank that morning in 2005 was the holy grail for coffee aficionados around the world: an organic, single-estate brew that was refined, roasted and poured to perfection. 'I had been living and working in coffee my whole life without every truly tasting my own product, so it was an incredible moment,' says the 50-year-old. 'The flavours were amazing – I remember the surprise of the lovely citric quality – but it was very emotional, too. I was thinking, "This is *my* coffee, I'm drinking *my* coffee, it's not a coffee from somewhere else, it's *mine*, it belongs to *me* and it tastes beautiful." Everything changed from that moment.'

Coffee is a serious matter in Costa Rica. Arabica beans were first brought over from Ethiopia and planted here in 1779. Spotting the crop's potential, the state offered small plots of land to anyone willing to grow the stuff. Booming exports gave birth to a new class of coffee barons with enough clout to overthrow the country's first president and dominate its politics and economy well into the 20th century. But the cash also helped transform Costa Rica from a colonial backwater into a modern state. Like fish in Iceland or wheat on the Canadian prairies, coffee is woven into the culture. School holidays used to coincide with the harvest, and the tax year still reflects the trade by starting in October. Coffee remains one of Costa Rica's leading exports.

Many of us carry around a Hollywood view of coffee farmers, coloured by more than 50 years of advertisements featuring Juan Valdez, the fictional farmer invented by the National Federation of Coffee Growers of Colombia. With his trademark moustache and trusty mule, Conchita, he is a cut-out from central casting, a salt-of-the-earth *cafetero* living a simple yet deeply fulfilling life in harmony with nature. Television commercials depict him caressing and smelling his beans with a beatific smile and a soundtrack to pluck at the heartstrings. 'Juan Valdez was definitely a very good tool for promotion,' says Pérez. 'But it gave a very idealised picture of the life led by most coffee farmers.'

In the real world the industry is plagued by problems common to all cash crops. Whether it's sugar, cocoa or coffee, farmers live and die by the yo-yoing prices on international commodity exchanges. Nor is it just the little guy that suffers. Howard Schultz, the CEO of Starbucks, accused speculators of artificially inflating the global coffee price in 2011. Of course, volatility matters less to growers when the market is on a long bull run like the one that buoyed Costa Rica in the 1970s. During that 'golden age' Pérez's parents bought three cars and sent all their children to university. He himself earned a degree in political science and international relations. But the following years brought instability and hardship, and when the price of coffee collapsed in 2002 many Costa Rican farmers went to the wall. Pérez, who owns a 15-hectare plot 60 km north-west of San José, was ready to give up on coffee altogether. 'I was thinking about switching to dairy cattle or even selling the land and doing something else completely,' he says. 'It would have meant the death of a family tradition, but coffee just felt like a dead end.'

That might come as a shock to anyone who has ever forked out $5 for a macchiato in New York or London. To be sure, there is always plenty of money sloshing around the coffee market; the problem is that not enough of it ends up in the pockets of those who grow the beans. As a result, small producers like Pérez usually lack the cash or incentive to turn their farms into thriving, sustainable businesses.

Now that is changing. Throughout Costa Rica farmers are doing the unthinkable: processing and marketing their own coffee under their own labels. Instead of trucking their crops directly from the field to the giant mills that have dominated the coffee market here for more than a century, they have installed their own equipment and refined their own beans.

This so-called 'micro-mill revolution' was sparked off in response to changing trends in the coffee industry. In the 1990s Starbucks, Illy and other large players scoured the world for higher-grade beans. Not for them the anonymous stuff churned out by the mega-mills of Costa Rica. As the coffee-drinking revolution gathered pace, small, speciality roasters entered the market in search of the perfect bean to sell to customers willing to pay for a killer cup.

As with so many other Slow Fixes, one person played a key role in making micro-mills work in Costa Rica. Francisco Mena, a coffee exporter, spotted their potential early on. He introduced Pérez and other farmers to their own coffee. He helped them weather the backlash from the mega-mills and navigate the red tape involved in expanding their businesses. He also helped set up the annual taste awards that have done so much to boost standards and raise the profile of Costa Rican coffee. With his fluent English and easy charm, Mena brings overseas roasters together with local producers. Even after the introductions are made, many farmers, including Pérez, continue to export their coffee through his company. When I arrive in San José, he is hosting a dinner for the judges of the Cup of Excellence awards. As coffee cognoscenti from England, Norway, Germany, Singapore and the United States mingle with farmers and their wives, Mena works the room like a pro. 'Francisco is the guy with the vision who brings it all together,' one coffee-grower tells me. 'Without him, I'm not sure we'd even be talking about a micro-mill revolution.'

'Revolution' may be a big word, but the rise of the micro-mill is certainly changing lives in Costa Rica. In the old days coffee farmers like Pérez were little more than purveyors of raw material. 'You worked a bit, sweated a little, and then by 2 p.m. or 3 p.m. in the afternoon you sat down with your legs crossed because there was nothing else to do for the rest of the day,' he says. 'You felt that putting in more effort wasn't really going to yield any more benefits.'

That all changed in 2005, when Pérez joined forces with two neighbours to install a micro-mill on his farm, which stretches across the slope of a lush valley in the Llano Bonito de Naranjo region. These days he works from dawn till dusk. As well as tending the coffee plants, he and his partners manage the workers who operate the Helsar de Zarcero micro-mill where the crop is pulped, fermented and dried. On my visit, farm hands are feeding coffee beans into machines that rip off their shells, making a thunderous clatter and sending plumes of dust into the air. At the other side of the warehouse, beyond a mountain of white sacks stuffed with beans ready for export, seven women sit picking out sub-standard beans from a fast-moving conveyor belt. In a new bungalow looking out across the valley, the soft-spoken Pérez fields enquiries from around the world on a Hewlett-Packard notebook that his teenaged daughter taught him to use. Next door, in the tiny kitchen, he and his partners roast, brew and taste their own coffee. During the harvest season between December and March, two or three international buyers visit every week to join in the tastings and place orders for the coming year. 'The change is unbelievable,' says Pérez. 'We are no longer just delivery boys who dump our coffee at someone else's mill and then forget about it; now we are specialists, entrepreneurs, managers, quality controllers, financiers, marketers, publicists and agronomists all wrapped up in one. We have gone from a sleepy farm with no future to a business with a strong foothold in the global marketplace.'

Life has certainly been good for Pérez and his partners since they won a prestigious Cup of Excellence award in 2007. These days they cannot produce enough coffee to meet demand, and most of their beans are sold even before they finish ripening in the fields. Search for 'Helsar de Zarcero' on Google and some 20,000 pages pop up, many festooned with glowing reviews. One fan hails the 'fresh blackberry aroma and mellow acidity' of their coffee. Others rave about the 'honeycomb sweetness, vanilla overtones and the exotic, dry aroma of dark fruit'.

Eight neighbours now bring part of their crop for milling at Helsar de Zarcero, which provides jobs for about 35 people. More important, far less of their income goes to middlemen. Out of every dollar his coffee beans fetch from a roaster in Seattle or Seoul, Pérez reckons 85 cents ends up in his pocket, four times more than before. Best of all, he is now much less vulnerable to price fluctuations on the global market. From Osaka to Ottawa to Oslo, buyers are willing to pay top dollar for boutique beans from small producers with a nice story to tell about tending the environment and regenerating local communities. Prices for micro-milled coffee rise and fall, but not with the same ruthless volatility as they do on the global commodity markets. Micro-millers often forge strong, long-term relationships with their roaster clients abroad to help insulate them from short-term setbacks. In the same way as a wine merchant stands by a good vineyard in a bad year, or a publisher accepts a below-par book from one of its established authors, roasters will try to buy what beans they can from a farmer after a poor harvest. When production costs spiked at Helsar de Zarcero a little while ago, Pérez's buyers in Tokyo simply rewrote their contract to guarantee him a higher price.

Thanks to the micro-mill revolution, Pérez lives in a comfortable house, drives a shiny SUV and plans to send his two daughters to university. True to his Latin roots, he seems most tickled by the pride of his mother. 'It is very moving for my parents, too, because they would have loved to do this with our coffee,' he says. 'My mum gets very emotional thinking that her kids are carrying on the family tradition and doing really well: it is like their dream come true through their children.'

We have already seen the wisdom of tapping a wide range of views, both expert and amateur, when tackling a problem. We have also explored how a single figure with fire in her belly can drive the search for a solution. The micro-mill revolution blends these bottom-up and top-down approaches to add another ingredient to the Slow Fix. In other words, it often makes sense to put problem-solving in the hands of those who live with the problem every day, to give people on the front line the chance to call the shots.

This is not a new idea. In Ancient Greece the Athenian assembly expected the demes and regional magistrates to solve local problems. Towards the end of the 19th century the Vatican began embracing 'subsidiarity', the principle that decisions should be taken at the most local level possible. In 1931, in an encyclical entitled the *Quadragesimo Anno*, Pope Pius XI asserted that it is 'gravely wrong to take from individuals what they can accomplish by their own enterprise and industry'. By tasking distant bureaucrats and desk-bound apparatchiks with solving even the simplest problems of everyday life, the Soviet Union signed its own death warrant. Today, subsidiarity is a core principle, at least on paper, of the European Union.

The micro-mill revolution works because it puts farmers like Pérez in the driver's seat. Coffee is now a vocation rather than just a way to pay the bills. 'I love my coffee now,' he says. 'Before, nobody around here said they loved their coffee because it was just a thing we sold to make a living, but now we have a deep feeling of responsibility and ownership. Our coffee is like our children that we give birth to after lots of work, and we follow them right up to the day when we say to them: You are ready to go out into the world now!' Like a proud and pushy parent, Pérez is never finished seeking new ways to solve the old problem of how to earn a decent living from coffee. 'Always now, from the moment you wake up to the moment you go to bed, you're thinking about how to improve your coffee – how to process it better, how to roast it better, how to tend your plantation to yield a better cup,' he says.

That feeling of ownership can boost problem-solving beyond the coffee farms of Costa Rica. Companies that award stock options across the workforce usually see their profits, productivity and share price rise faster than do those who restrict them to top management. A 2010 study by Cass Business School found that firms owned by their employees are more productive and more resilient in a recession. Research has shown that people work better, and seek out problems and find solutions with greater alacrity, when they feel some ownership in the company they work for.

Britain's John Lewis group, which includes department stores and the Waitrose supermarket chain, is a good example. Business experts hail its 'partnership model' as the cornerstone of its success. Every one of its 76,500 staff owns a share of the company through an independent trust, and five are elected to sit on the board. All John Lewis employees, from the CEO down to the cleaning staff, take home the same percentage bonus on their salaries. Many have been with the company for over 20 years. 'Everywhere else I've worked people sat back and let others take the lead or the blame when things went wrong,' says Maggie Shannon, who started on the sales floor a decade ago and now works in management. 'But when you are all owners of the company, the culture changes: you see a problem, and you want to do everything you can to solve it.'

People down in the trenches are often better equipped to tackle problems than those sitting in corner offices with framed certificates on the wall. 'An expert in a laboratory in the United States is not the best person to fix my farm in Costa Rica,' says Pérez. 'The expert can help, of course, but the person who must take the lead is the farmer himself. We dig the soil with our own hands. We roll these beans between our fingers. We know this land inside and out. Give us the power to control our own destiny and there is no limit to the solutions we can come up with.'

Pérez now has the means and motivation to respond instantly to even the smallest shifts in the market. Not long ago, a Japanese buyer in search of new flavours asked him to leave more of the honey on his coffee beans by washing them less vigorously. After tinkering a bit in the mill, Pérez produced a brew with a slightly sweeter taste that scored well with coffee fans in Tokyo. 'Buyers are always looking for something new, and now we can react to their demands,' he says. 'Instead of just watching our prices fall when tastes change, we can adapt in order to stand out from the pack.'

The environment also benefits. To boost yields, and egged on by experts and cash from the developed world, coffee farmers in Costa Rica ditched traditional farming methods in the 1970s and 80s in favour of a high-tech approach. That meant cutting down trees to expose their plants to direct sunlight and embracing chemical fertilisers and pesticides. Today, micro-mill farmers are turning their land back into small ecosystems. Pérez has planted banana, erythrina and avocado trees, which cast shade over his coffee plants and create a natural habitat for animals and insects. Instead of spraying chemicals to fertilise the fields, he now scatters composted coffee pulp enriched with micro-organisms cultured from soil taken from the surrounding mountains. Bean for bean, his micro-mill also uses a fraction of the water that bigger rivals need. Not only is his land kinder to the environment; it also yields more coffee.

The micro-mill model has its pitfalls. When the commodity price of coffee soars, farmers can start wondering if it is worth the extra toil to process their own beans. If they decide instead to dump their harvest at the nearest mega-mill, the carefully nurtured relationship with the roaster can suffer. Another downside of direct trade between small farmers and small roasters is that the latter now bear much more financial risk. And despite all the noble talk of forging relationships with growers, some roasters remain more interested in hawking the latest coffee *du jour*. Poul Mark sells micro-mill beans from Pérez and other Costa Rican farmers at his three stores in my home town of Edmonton, Alberta. He worries that the love 'em and leave 'em approach of some roasters could undermine the micro-mill movement. 'You still get a lot of people who are just looking for the next hot thing, so they visit a farm, photograph themselves smiling with the producer, put the pictures up on their website, sell the coffee and then next year they move on somewhere else,' he says. 'For the micro-mill model to work, it has to be more of a marriage than a one-night stand. You have to take the time to build up stable, long-term relationships. That way you can work together through the good times and the bad times. It's all about trust.'

Running a micro-mill carries risks for the producers, too. The specialist coffee market is growing, and will probably continue to do so as consumers in newly wealthy nations like China discover a taste for lattes and espressos. But there are clouds on the horizon. Costa Rica has higher costs than cheaper rivals, such as Vietnam, that are eyeing up the specialist end of the coffee market. And even on their home turf competition is tightening as more farmers try to grab a piece of the micro-mill action. The difference is that growers like Pérez now feel equipped to tackle such problems head-on. 'We know the coffee won't look after itself and there is risk in everything,' he says. 'But at least the micro-mill movement gives us the power to find our own solutions and shape our own future.'

Setting people to work on their own problems fits into a broader cultural shift. Everywhere, technology is spreading power from the centre to the periphery, from the few to the many, by making it easier to communicate and share information. Informed and connected as never before, ordinary people are tackling problems that once seemed beyond their reach. Just look at how mobile phone-wielding citizens rose up and toppled entrenched dictatorships during the Arab Spring.

Devolving power also pays off in the workplace. Inviting nurses to carry out their own research projects helped improve the care given to patients at Georgetown University Hospital in Washington, DC. One nurse described how her colleagues' old apathy gave way to a can-do spirit where everyone began asking: 'How can I make this place better?' A Cornell University survey of 320 small firms found those that gave their staff real autonomy grew four times faster and had one-third the turnover of those that took a command-and-control approach. The same applies to big companies.

When Jan Carlzon became the CEO of SAS in 1981, the airline was in a bad way, bleeding money and drawing scorn for its late flights. Carlzon decided to focus on the business-class market. He streamlined the management and poured time, energy and $45 million into upgrading every detail of the service aimed at corporate travellers. SAS was the first airline in the world, for instance, to introduce a separate Business Class cabin. But Carlzon's real coup was giving staff on the front line the power to fix things on their own. 'Problems are solved on the spot, as soon as they arise,' he said at the time. 'No front-line employee has to wait for a supervisor's permission.' It was the corporate equivalent of the micro-mill revolution – and it worked. Within a year, SAS was the most punctual airline in Europe and back in profit. A year after that it won *Air Transport World*'s Airline of the Year award. SAS became a fixture on business school curricula, and its training model was later exported to other companies ranging from Japan Airlines to Hewlett-Packard to Marks & Spencer.

Devolution makes sense on the factory floor, too. On the traditional assembly line each worker operates in a bubble, master of his own task and oblivious to those on either side. Toyota turned that model on its head, giving its factory workers enough skills, know-how and freedom to understand and improve the production process from start to finish – very much like Pérez. Toyota also fostered teamwork and gave even the lowliest worker the power to tackle problems through the Andon rope. The upshot: before the brass stopped listening to the rank and file, Toyota grew to become the leading carmaker in the world.

The more control we have over our working environment, many studies show, the better we perform. In one well-known experiment, researchers asked two groups of people to solve puzzles and carry out proofreading tasks with random, intrusive sounds playing in the background. The first group was put in a room with a button that could be pressed to silence the soundtrack. The second group was left to tackle the assignment without that option. As you might expect, the first group proofread much more accurately and solved five times as many puzzles. But the twist is they never once pushed the button. Simply knowing they could, that they were in charge, was enough to help channel their problem-solving mojo.

Empowering the little people can also help in the war on poverty. Many traditional aid projects fail because they are conceived, developed and implemented by experts based in air-conditioned offices hundreds or even thousands of miles away, leaving the poor as little more than bystanders, or pawns on a chessboard. When drought ravaged the Horn of Africa in the 1980s, killing livestock and threatening famine, Norway's development agency came to the rescue with what looked to outsiders like a clever fix. The semi-nomadic cattle herders of Turkana, a remote corner of north-western Kenya, lived beside a lake packed with fish. Why not help them turn that piscine wealth into a steady source of food and income? Teach a Kenyan pastoralist to fish and you feed him for a lifetime. So the Norwegians built a state-of-the-art fish-freezing plant on the shores of Lake Turkana, taught the cattle herders how to make the most of the fish reserves and waited for living standards to rise. But they didn't, and the factory flopped. If the Norwegians had taken the time to listen, they would have realised that nomadic culture is incompatible with fishing and working in a factory, that Nilotic nomads like the Turkana look down on fishing as the last resort of the failed cattle herder, and that in any case the lake was too far away from the nearest fish markets. 'It was the old top–bottom approach,' said Cheanati Wasike, a government fisheries officer for Lake Turkana. 'The lake was identified by outsiders as a resource but they never consulted the Turkana, never asked them what they thought of fishing it.'

Today the most successful aid projects make the poor partners in solving their own problems. One example is Bolsa Familia in Brazil. Launched in the 1990s when Latin American governments began rolling out what have come to be known as conditional cash-transfer (CCT) programmes, Bolsa Familia gives the poor money in return for doing things that are in their best interest. Every month poor Brazilian families can tap the programme for 22 reais per child up to a maximum of 200 reais. In return for these cash transfers, parents undertake to keep their children in school and take them for regular health checks. Bolsa Familia now reaches 12 million families, making it the largest CCT programme in the world. It is also one of the most successful, having helped to cut poverty and rural child malnutrition, reduce income inequality and boost school attendance – all at a fraction of the cost of traditional welfare. Brazil's mainstream political parties all favour expanding the programme, which has been lauded by the World Bank and copied by more than 20 countries.

Why does it work? By combining several ingredients of the Slow Fix that we have already encountered. It takes a holistic approach by tackling three of the main pillars of poverty – low income, truancy and patchy healthcare – in a single package. If a child starts cutting school, or fails to turn up for a doctor's appointment, the family gets less money for food. Bolsa Familia also addresses both the short and long term: cash to pay for necessities today linked to investing in health and education for tomorrow. Another key is the way conditional cash transfers give autonomy to the poor. Instead of just collecting food handouts, and listening to lectures on the benefits of schooling and regular hospital visits, they are given the freedom to make their own choices. Fears that poor Brazilians would fritter the money away have proved unfounded. Most families spend the Bolsa cash on food, clothes and school supplies for their children. 'When you give people money with conditions attached, you are saying to them: "You have rights but you also have responsibilities, and we trust you to live up to those responsibilities,"' says Paulo Moreira, a charity worker in São Paulo. 'That is a powerful shift in the whole dynamic of aid or welfare. Suddenly, the recipient goes from being a passive agent waiting for other people to come up with ideas to playing an active role in solving their own problems.'

Some aid groups have gone one step further by handing over funds with no conditions attached at all. In 2006 the British charity Oxfam issued one-off grants to 550 poor households in eight villages in An Loc, a commune in a rice-growing region in central Vietnam. The payments were large, with one villager pocketing three times his annual wages in a single shot. Apart from having to promise not to splash the cash on alcohol, drugs or gambling, the households were free to use the money as they saw fit.

And how did they spend it? Very wisely, as it turns out. Most villagers invested in better water and sanitation for their homes as well as seeds, fertilisers and cows to guarantee their food supply in the future. Four years after the one-off cash injection, school attendance was up, poverty was down by two thirds and many more villagers were participating in community activities. 'We felt that poor people clearly have the right to decide how the money is spent,' says Steve Price-Thomas, who was Oxfam's director for Vietnam at the time. 'What better than to put money in their hands and let them decide what to do with it?'

That same thinking underlies the microcredit movement, where specialist banks, funds and brokers funnel small loans to those too poor to pass muster in the mainstream financial system. My favourite example is Kiva, whose website brings together borrowers in the developing world and lenders willing to back them with loans as low as $25. Recipients display the same can-do entrepreneurial spirit as Pérez. Lend $575 to Sixta and she will buy a freezer for drinks and ice creams to diversify the tortilla stall she runs in Nicaragua. Naftary will use the same sum to buy a cow for his farm in Muranga, central Kenya. Since 2005 more than 600,000 people have lent over $240 million through Kiva. Most impressive of all is that the community boasts a repayment rate that would make any Wall Street bank envious: nearly 99 per cent of its borrowers pay back their loans in full.

Empowering people to find their own fixes works especially well in the arena of human conflict. As part of a push to make its schools more democratic, Finland set up a programme to put children in charge of solving playground disputes. While teachers still handle cases of bullying, injury or damage to property, pupils now mediate most other tiffs. Schools set aside a fixed time each week when the so-called VERSO sessions are held in a special room. A hearing, which usually lasts 10 or 15 minutes, can be triggered by a formal request from any child or parent. Each session is overseen by mediators who are slightly older than the plaintiffs. Adults are never present during sessions, and mediators never propose solutions. Once the mediators explain the rules of engagement the plaintiffs tells their side of the story and how the conflict made them feel. Both parties propose steps to resolve their differences once and for all. If the pair can agree on a solution, they write it down and sign a pledge to put it into action.

Like any Slow Fix worthy of the name, VERSO involves taking time to get to the root of a problem. Even if a case involves several children, the hearings are always one-to-one to allow enough time to talk. Plaintiffs agree to reconvene one or two weeks after their hearing to confirm that the problem is fixed. In trickier cases, follow-up sessions might carry on for months after the initial clash. In fact, the insistence on giving children time to hammer out a lasting fix rubs some teachers up the wrong way. 'There is still a strong culture that the teacher has the power and does not want to cede it to the pupils,' says Maija Gellin, the education and youth work specialist who devised the VERSO programme. 'They think to themselves, "I can sort out this problem faster and easier myself so we can get back to teaching." But that quick fix approach creates a superficial peace that leaves the deeper problem unresolved.'

To see VERSO in action, I drop by Lotilan Middle School in Lahti, a small city 100 km north-east of Helsinki. It is winter and the children arrive at their desks with rosy cheeks and hair full of static electricity from their woollen hats. About 30 conflicts are mediated through the VERSO system every year. Sessions are available daily at noon in a small staff room. Posters of Charlie Chaplin and a Picasso nude look down on a long, IKEA-style table with an orange and yellow sash draped down the middle. There is a sink, a microwave and a black vase with fresh flowers.

Today brings the case of Mikko and Oskar, two 12-year-olds who traded punches in gym class 11 days earlier. They are friends and also play on the same ice hockey team. Unable to bury the hatchet, they filed for VERSO the day after the fight.

The boys enter the room wearing hoodies and looking chastened and a little tense. It is the first time either has been through VERSO. Ritva, the 14-year-old mediator, invites each boy to give his version of events and explain how the incident made him feel. These being adolescent males, what follows is not a deluge of emoting. Instead, there are plenty of shoulder shrugs, monosyllabic grunts and Pinteresque pauses. But there are also moments of real tenderness, as the boys grope for common ground. At one point, Mikko reminds Oskar that he set him up to score a goal in a hockey game the other night. Oskar looks directly at his friend for the first time and smiles. Eventually they come to a consensus about their fight: both are stubborn and competitive, and both had had a bad day. Their solution is simple – to apologise sincerely to one another and not fight again – and the pair leave the room smiling and relaxed.

Later, I ask the boys what they think of VERSO. Both seem delighted. 'If we hadn't come to VERSO, things would go on and on in your head and we would have more fights,' says Mikko. 'Talking about it like this makes it easier to forget revenge and try to get along again.'

Oskar is also pleased. 'It is definitely easier without adults because children understand children better. We speak the same language and think the same way,' he says. 'It was cool that we were able to work out what our problem was and then fix it ourselves.'

Finland now has over 7,000 trained VERSO mediators. Every year 20,000 children attend a hearing and 90 per cent go on to keep their promises. New schools continue to join the scheme every year, and Gellin has helped set up programmes from Russia to Italy.

Other countries run similar schemes. Through weekly classes embedded in the school curriculum, Peace First has taught over 40,000 pre-teens in Boston, New York and Los Angeles how to resolve their own conflicts and tackle social problems in their communities. Though school staff oversee the programme, and young adult volunteers teach the material, the kids, like their Finnish counterparts in VERSO, take the lead. In participating schools violence is down 60 per cent, while cases of children breaking up fights and helping their peers are up more than 70 per cent.

Putting people in charge of solving their own problems might also help reinvent public services. Traditionally, the state delivers these like a department store sells clothes. It sets out racks of programmes, entitlements and benefits, and if one happens to fit you off the peg, you walk out happy. If not, you can wander through the system for years, endlessly trying on garments that pinch round the waist or come up short in the arms. 'People are conditioned for a quick fix, so you go see an expert, they do a quick assessment, come up with an answer, make a referral, provide you with a service and it's happily ever after,' says Eddie Bartnik, the Mental Health Commissioner for Western Australia. 'But of course life's not like that. If you don't give people the power to design their own solutions, they can end up with lots of services that don't really solve their problem, which leaves them feeling profoundly lonely and disconnected.'

In 1988, Bartnik, who was then a director with the Disabilities Services Commission in Western Australia, persuaded the state government to try a new approach with its disabled citizens. Local Area Coordination, as the system came to be known, turned the status quo on its head. Instead of telling people what services they needed, the state would, in the counter-intuitive style of IDEO, ask them, 'What does leading a good life mean to you?' It would then help to make the answers come true. Acting as the cornerstone of the system are the Local Area Coordinators (LACs), who take the time to get to know their clients as people rather than as case files. A blend of advocate, confidant, adviser, networker and friend, the coordinators play the role of the catalytic figure who, as we saw in Chapter Ten, is central to so many Slow Fixes. They help clients to pinpoint suitable off-the-shelf services and to plug into the local community, arranging for them to join a knitting group, a choir or a football club, say, or lend a hand in a neighbourhood church. More radically, they also help them obtain public money to design bespoke solutions to their problems. 'People have had years of being told by experts what to do, what to expect, what they need,' says Bartnik. 'The Local Area Coordinator turns that around by listening to the person in front of them, asking the right questions and then empowering them to build the support they need.'

Peta Barker agrees. She runs a painting and decorating business with her husband in a suburb of Perth. Their 20-year-old son, Kirk, is autistic. By the time he was three, the family felt completely bamboozled by the state. 'We tried to get help but we always found that if you didn't fit into the box, then it was "No, I'm sorry, we can't help you," and you got passed around like a parcel from doctor to doctor, department to department,' says Barker. 'It was very frustrating because you felt like you wanted to do something but didn't know where to begin.'

Local Area Coordination changed all that. At last the Barkers had an ally who knew them *and* the system inside out. Their first coordinator worked with them for 11 years, and her replacement has been on the job for five. 'Sally-Anne knows my husband, my children, my cats, my dogs,' says Barker. 'She even goes round the back and asks, "How's your budgie doing?"'

When we meet at the LAC office near her home, Barker, an energetic woman with an infectious laugh, tells me the programme has been a godsend. At the very first meeting her original LAC encouraged her to think hard, holistic and long. 'All those years ago I had in my head a list of things that Kirk required, and she said actually we should also focus on what the family needs, because without supporting you, without making sure all the family are helped and looked after, you can't look after your son,' says Barker. 'This struck me as amazing because I had never thought of it like that, but it was quite true.' With an LAC in their corner, the Barkers tracked down the perfect school for Kirk and tapped public funds to pay for his swimming and cricket. They also found money to finance the occasional night away from home when things got too stressful. 'Without that, life would have been a lot harder and I'm not sure how our family would have survived,' says Barker.

Today the Barkers feel they have designed the best life they could. Kirk is thriving. Every Tuesday he attends a life skills course where he learns to cook for himself. On Thursdays a care worker teaches him how to use his bike on the roads. Two days a week he cycles alone to a supported workplace in a neighbouring suburb, where he performs tasks such as putting labels on olive bottles or packaging shoes for a local retailer.

A slew of studies show that the LAC approach slashes the cost to the state of supporting a disabled person. Authorities in other Australian states, as well as in New Zealand, Scotland and England, have implemented similar programmes. Above all, LAC is hugely popular with disabled people and their families, who welcome the chance to play a part in solving their own problems.

Even if our own lives are untouched by disability, we can all benefit from similar empowerment. Sharpen your problem-solving edge by taking more control of your working conditions, from your schedule to your use of technology. When seeking a Slow Fix, always ask, 'Who am I trying to help? How can I involve them in finding the right solution?' Invest time in learning what really makes those people tick – not just what they think and say but what they actually *feel*.

As Barker gathers her things to go and meet Kirk, she tells me that helping families like hers devise their own fixes is not the only reason for the success of Local Area Coordination. Just as crucial is the way it humanises the system by building strong emotional connections. 'Sometimes all you need is someone in your corner, somebody you can ring when you're having a bad day,' she says. 'The LACs put everything aside to listen to you, maybe offer some quick suggestions, and suddenly you're feeling better and ready to handle whatever life throws at you. The emotional part is so important.'

CHAPTER TWELVE

FEEL: Twiddling the Emotional Thermostat

There can be no transforming of darkness into light and of
apathy into movement without emotion.
Carl Jung

Marta Gomez wanders through the corridors of Reina Sofía
hospital like a shell-shocked soldier stumbling across a battlefield. Her mother has been in a coma since suffering a stroke
at the dinner table a week ago. Doctors are trying to revive
the 81-year-old, but her fate remains unclear, leaving Gomez
in an agonising limbo. Her eyes are bloodshot, her hands
tremble and she speaks in a slow, whispery voice. 'I'm sleeping badly and have a headache all the time,' she says. 'There
are so many feelings that it is very hard to know what to
think or do or say.'

But even in the middle of this emotional tempest, one
thing is crystal clear: when her mother dies, the family will
give the hospital permission to use her organs for transplant.

And the story behind their decision points up the next ingredient of the Slow Fix.

With demand for transplant surgery climbing rapidly, hospitals around the world face a serious problem: not enough people are donating organs. Many refuse to surrender any part of their bodies after death, often for religious or cultural reasons. Others fail to make clear their wishes before dying. But often it is the family that refuses to sign on the dotted line. The result, in many countries, is waiting lists that are lethally long. In Britain the average patient in need of an organ waits three years for a transplant. Three die every day waiting. In the US the annual death toll tops 6,000.

That is why hospitals like Reina Sofía, which is in Córdoba, a city of 350,000 in southern Spain, are now in the spotlight. When it comes to persuading people to donate their organs after death, the Spanish seem to have cracked the code. Back in 1989 their donation rate was low by international standards. Today it is the highest in the world. Eighty-five per cent of Spanish families consent to organ donation at the moment of death. That is double the European average and 30 per cent higher than in the United States, the nation that pioneered transplant surgery.

When it comes to boosting donation rates, a popular solution is to create a so-called opt-out system. That means everyone is registered by default as an organ donor – unless they specifically apply to be removed from the list. In practice, though, this delivers mixed results. Sweden, for example, has an opt-out system and one of the lowest donation rates in Europe. The same was true for Spain until 1989. Why? Because at the moment of death most doctors still seek the approval of the family – and that is where consent, whatever the law dictates, is often denied.

Spain understood that the only way to tackle the organ crisis was to overhaul its approach before, during and after death. In 1989 it set up a National Transplant Organisation (ONT) with the power and budget to fine-tune every step of the donation process: from detecting potential donors to winning consent from families to finding recipients and carrying out transplants. One result is that Spain is now a trailblazer in experimental surgery. In 1997 surgeons at Reina Sofía carried out the first triple transplant on a single patient in Europe. Spanish doctors were also the first to implant a windpipe made from a patient's own stem cells. In 2011 surgeons in Barcelona carried out the first full face transplant, complete with new jaw, palate and teeth, on a young man wounded in a hunting accident.

But what really raises eyebrows abroad is Spain's success in persuading families to donate the organs of their deceased loved ones. This turnaround is partly the fruit of a vigorous public awareness campaign to rebrand donation as a supreme act of generosity, kindness and solidarity. And nowhere has the effort to win hearts and minds been more vigorous than here in Córdoba. In early June, while the rest of Spain celebrates the Day of the Donor, Reina Sofía runs an entire Week of the Donor. At concerts, parades and street parties, glamorous bullfighters, sports stars, flamenco dancers and pop singers exhort the public to donate organs. The hospital has published two books of donation-themed verse by 40 poets and staged an exhibition of works by well-known artists exploring what it means to give and receive organs.

Córdoba's professional football team has worn the red sash of the organ donation campaign and the city's taxis are festooned with stickers trumpeting the cause. Every Tuesday a busload of schoolchildren tours the transplant wards at Reina Sofía where they listen to patients and doctors sing the praises of donation.

A sprawling complex with 1,300 beds and 33 operating theatres, Reina Sofía hospital beats the donor drum at every turn. Posters asking for organs hang in corridors and waiting rooms. An entire wall is given over to a photomontage telling the history of transplants in the hospital, complete with portraits of smiling surgeons and thankful patients. Near the main entrance stands a school of red papier-mâché dolphins – the striking artwork created by mentally ill patients expressing their feelings about donation. Sixteen tableaux bearing the images and stories of recipients stand like regimental banners on the lawn outside the hospital. An imposing monument to donors squats beside the main entrance of the hospital, with poems and letters from grateful organ recipients taped to its side. One says simply: 'Thank you for the miracle.'

After nearly 25 years of raising awareness, and more than 70,000 organ transplants, Spain has entered a virtuous cycle: the more people that know someone who has donated or received organs, the more comfortable they feel doing the same. 'Every transplant speaks, every family speaks, every neighbour speaks,' says Juan Carlos Roble, the lead transplant coordinator at Reina Sofía since 1997. 'They are all like disciples spreading the message so that every day more people understand that donation saves lives.' Signing over your organs is now almost as much a part of the culture in Spain as the *siesta* and the *fiesta*. Even Pedro Almodóvar, the mad genius of Spanish cinema, has made an Oscar-winning movie, *All About My Mother*, which revolves around a transplant ward. Spaniards take pride in their role as a world leader in the field of organ donation. *Cordobeses* tell you their city has two jewels in its crown: the exquisite eighth-century mosque in the old quarter and Reina Sofía hospital.

It certainly helps that Spain boasts an enviable public health system, which the World Health Organisation ranks seventh best in the world. Everyone in the country can tap state-of-the-art medical care for free. Spanish hospitals have plenty of critical care beds and patients often convalesce in well-appointed private rooms. What's more, medical teams carry on trying to resuscitate patients longer than their peers in other countries. That means most people die in Spanish hospitals hooked up to a ventilator, the ideal scenario for organ donation. It also means families arrive at the moment of death feeling grateful to the powers that be.

That is certainly the case with Gomez. Plagued by problems with her heart, bladder and stomach, she herself has undergone four free operations at Reina Sofía over the years. And now she sees doctors sparing no expense trying to revive her elderly mother. 'The hospital is amazing, and I know they are doing everything possible for my mum,' she says. 'I feel very, very grateful.'

Yet the anchor of Spain's donor miracle is its network of highly trained transplant coordinators. In other countries, staff charged with seeking out organs and obtaining consent to harvest them are often removed from the day-to-day business of patient care. In Spain they are embedded in every major hospital in the country. The majority are also practising specialists in intensive care, meaning they handle the patients most likely to die and can give accurate medical updates to family members. At any given moment the four transplant coordinators at Reina Sofía can tell you all the potential donors in the hospital, how their treatment is progressing and about the emotional state of their respective families. While a traditional doctor focuses on saving her patient, a Spanish coordinator can look at the bigger picture and the long term. 'We have a different chip inside our heads,' says Dr Robles. 'For a coordinator, it is not just about trying to save the patient, but also thinking that if the patient dies he could help to save others by donating.'

Most important of all, the coordinators are rigorously trained to negotiate the emotional roller-coaster of bereavement. From the moment a potential donor is admitted to hospital, they start building a relationship with his family. Each coordinator has her own style, but all are experts in how and when to bring up the delicate subject of donation, blending medical knowledge with the right bedside manner. After placing Spanish-style coordinators in their own hospitals, both Italy and Portugal saw donation rates rise. 'You can spend millions on publicity campaigns to inform the public, you can be in the streets 24 hours a day telling people to donate, you can have the best equipment, the best surgeons and the best medical system in the world, but if you do not know how to speak to the family at the crucial moment, then everything falls apart,' says Dr Robles. 'The cornerstone of our system is that relationship between the doctor, the patient and the family. If you get that right, everything else will flow from there.'

What is the secret of a good transplant coordinator? Approaching every family with humility, compassion and boatloads of patience. 'My philosophy is a coordinator never looks at his watch,' says Dr Robles. 'Every family is unique, so you have to explore all the avenues, listen, pay attention to the silences, because that is how you learn about the people in front of you, how you help them deal with their emotions so they can make a decision about donation that is right for them.'

During my visit, Dr Robles is steering the Gomez family through this process. He has spoken with them every day since their mother arrived last week at Reina Sofia. The meetings take place in a room painted a soothing shade of peach, with a vase of wooden flowers on the table and a poster and calendar about organ donation on the wall. Dr Robles is wearing spectacles and green scrubs. At 52, he has short, dark hair, kind eyes and the quiet, reassuring solidity of someone who has seen it all before. When he talks to a family, he speaks slowly and clearly, with a disarming softness, part doctor, part therapist. Seeing him in action reminds me of how clumsily the doctors spoke to my wife and me when our baby was in intensive care years ago. 'Dr Robles is a very, very good person,' says Gomez. 'The other day I was crying and he held me to comfort me. You can see that he feels our pain very much.'

After a couple of days Dr Robles gently brought up the subject of donation. The Gomez family had never properly talked about it before. 'We had heard a lot about donating

236

organs on TV and radio,' says Marta. 'My mother never said very clearly what to do with her organs when she died, but I remember she was very happy when she heard how transplants saved other people.'

Even so, one of her mother's sisters was against donation. Dr Robles laid out the case, then backed off to give the family time and space to reach a consensus. Eventually the recalcitrant sister came around. 'The doctor explains things well, he listens to you. He gives you peace,' says Gomez. 'We never felt pressured by him, but by the end we all very much wanted to say yes.'

Other families can be harder to persuade. When the child of a divorced couple dies, finding common ground between the warring parents can take hours of talking, listening and handholding. The other day, a 67-year-old man died at Reina Sofia. His family was split down the middle on whether to donate his organs, with five of his children in favour and the other five against. Like a diplomat marshalling support at a UN summit, Dr Robles spent a whole afternoon shuttling from brother to sister and back again, allaying fears, massaging egos, building bridges, explaining how their father's death could save the lives of other people. Eventually the whole family said yes.

Coordinators like Dr Robles never seek to bully or trick people into donating organs against their will. That might boost donation rates in the short term, but it would also undermine the system as more and more families complained of being duped. To its credit, Spain has so far dodged that quick fix. A recent study at Reina Sofia could not find a single family that later regretted giving its consent for donation. Certainly, no relative has ever complained of being hoodwinked to Dr Robles. 'We always think of the long term and that means our aim is for donation to unite the family, not divide it,' he says. 'You have to find out why a person says no and then try to convert them in such a way that they feel proud to say yes. You want to transform the tears of sadness that fall for the death of their loved one into tears of happiness for the lives that person's organs can save. Ultimately it's all about managing emotions.'

And with that, Dr Robles puts his finger on the next ingredient of the Slow Fix: taking the time to understand and channel emotions. Too often we reduce problem-solving to a science of spreadsheets and flow charts and Venn diagrams. If you want to fix something, the experts tell us, do not get emotional. Run the numbers instead. Be logical. Be rational. Be scientific.

Of course, there is little to be gained by losing your temper or flying into a blind panic, but that does not mean we must approach every problem like Mr Spock. We are hardwired to feel. 'Human behaviour flows from three main sources,' said Plato. 'Desire, emotion and knowledge.' Even when we think we are being rational and logical, we are often guided by feelings. Over the years, economists, sociologists and psychologists have amassed a library of research showing that emotion, and the biases it can trigger, often trumps rationality. You may believe in racial equality, yet you still clutch your handbag more tightly when you see someone like Lewis Price ghetto-limping towards you on an empty street. Or consider an experiment known as the ultimatum game, in which two subjects – let's call them Max and Mary – are given £10 and invited to share it. Max proposes how to divvy up the cash and Mary can either accept or reject his one-time proposal. If she turns down his offer, neither receives any money. In a purely rational world Mary would accept every proposal from Max apart from a split that gave him all the cash. Even if Max proposes to keep £9.99 for himself, Mary still goes home one penny better off. But in the real world most people turn down much more generous offers than that, leaving both parties empty-handed. Why? Because our decision is influenced by our feelings about what is fair. We dislike unfairness so much that we are willing to sacrifice free money to punish anyone who visits it upon us. Around the world, people tend to walk away from any split less favourable than 80–20.

Feelings set the tone in workplaces around the world. Study after study shows that when we disengage emotionally from our job we become less creative and productive. On days when employees feel happy, they come up with more new ideas. Someone content with her job is more likely to let work problems simmer at the back of her mind outside the office, and then come back in the next morning with a clever solution that has incubated overnight.

We have already seen emotion at work in many Slow Fixes. Remember how Enrique Peñalosa made the members of his team feel cherished, how treating prisoners with dignity helps combat recidivism in Norway and Singapore, and how much it means to the students of Locke High School that staff treat them like family. 'It's like there's a positive attitude every day,' says Price. 'Even on a bad day you walk in that gate and it's like, "Man, there are people everywhere encouraging me, how can you get mad in an environment that's so loving?"'

When I ask Ricardo Pérez about the role of emotion in the micro-mill revolution in Costa Rica, he tells me that, for an entrepreneur, a simple pat on the back can be just as valuable as seed capital, modern machinery or a business plan. In 2007 he visited Stumptown Café, a funky emporium that roasts and sells his coffee in Portland, Oregon. Standing by the counter during the morning rush, Pérez was blown away by the sight of American hipsters ordering Helsar de Zarcero coffee by name. 'It was one of the most beautiful things that have ever happened to me, seeing our name up there on the board, and hearing people asking for it. I had tears in my eyes thinking of all the work put into this by my family, my parents, my grandparents, over so many years,' he says. 'For centuries no one told us our own particular coffee was any good, and if you make something and year after year no one tells you it is any good you lose heart, you lose interest in making it better. Seeing someone in another country enjoying your coffee, having people tell you that you are doing good work and making a contribution to the world – that is the kind of motivation a producer needs to get better and better. Emotion is essential to human beings.'

Many complex problems can only be solved by persuading people to make sacrifices, or do something they would not naturally wish to do. Appealing to reason can only take us so far down that road. To engineer a deeper change in the culture of a classroom, company or community, to earn the buy-in that is crucial for most Slow Fixes, you need to tap what Vincent Van Gogh called 'the little emotions (that) are the great captains of our lives'.

How can we do that? One way is to train problem-solvers to engage emotionally. To build empathy in the medical profession, hospitals around the world are encouraging staff to take art, music and photography classes. All oncologists in Britain are now required to attend a three-day course where experts and actors teach them how to speak to cancer patients. Medical colleges have broadened the curriculum to include courses in the humanities to develop students who combine stellar exam scores with emotional intelligence. In the same vein, Harvard Medical School has tweaked its entry requirements so that, starting in 2016, all applicants must 'be fluent and have a nuanced facility in English'.

In Chapter Eleven we saw how recruiting people to tackle their own problems can tap deeper reservoirs of creativity. It can also generate an emotional buy-in for the solution. Even if the fix that people come up with is not perfect, it is *their* fix. Let's be honest: we all love to see our own ideas come to fruition, or at least feel we have been listened to. This is Psychology 101. When Bruno Frey, a professor of economics and behavioural sciences, analysed data from happiness surveys and the levels of autonomy and direct democracy across the 26 cantons of Switzerland, he unearthed a very clear correlation: the more input people have in the democratic process, the happier they are. Frey identified two reasons for this. The first is that democracy is more likely to produce better governments. But the main reason is that we derive a sense of well-being from feeling we can influence events in our lives, which is why the loss of liberty in prison

241

can be so crushing. Frey also found the Swiss enjoy a happiness boost even when they do not vote. In other words, the mere fact that our voice *can* count is enough to make us *feel* better about life and the political system we live under.

That may well be the main legacy of the post-crash experiment in Iceland. Even if not one single suggestion from the National Assemblies makes its way into the new constitution, or into government policy, the investment in crowdsourcing may yet pay off. Voters will feel they have been consulted, that their ideas count for something, and that they have a real stake in the process. 'In recent years, politics felt like something that other people did to me,' says Dagur Jónsson, a schoolteacher in Reykjavik. 'Now I feel like the government doesn't just have to be some external thing that operates separately from the people. We can be the government.' That is sweet vindication to Gudjon Gudjonsson, the main man behind the Assemblies. He thinks crowdsourcing is the perfect tonic to reinvigorate electoral politics around the world. 'In this new model of democracy, you crowdsource vision and values to give you a guiding light from the population,' he says. 'And that gives the population a feeling of ownership in the political system.'

To gain support for the VERSO programme, organisers seek student input from the start. 'When we arrive in a school, we ask the children how mediation should work and then we add some ideas, mention what other schools are doing, put on some dramatisations, building it all up slowly, so we're gently steering them to the right place, but they feel like it's their idea, they feel real ownership,' says Maija Gellin. 'If the people involved in a conflict feel the solution has not been imposed, that it has come from them, they are more likely to make it work.'

If only the authors of the Treaty of Versailles had understood that in 1919. The Slow Fixers at IDEO certainly do. 'We've started to think differently about what it means to bring stakeholders along,' says Jane Fulton Suri. 'We can't just hand down tablets of stone. To get the best out of the people involved in solving a problem, it's better if we can make the experience feel participatory.'

Harnessing our emotional need for acceptance is another way to win buy-in. As social animals, we want to belong. We want to feel part of a larger whole. We want to know that others are both relying on and looking out for us. Why else does simply placing an image of a pair of human eyes beside an honesty box make us cough up more money? And how else do you explain passing fads for kipper ties, polyester jumpsuits and mullets? To change ingrained behaviour, organisations such as Alcoholics Anonymous and Weight Watchers motivate members through group meetings. The micro-credit movement also uses peer pressure by tying borrowers into small groups where a single default can cut off everyone else's access to capital. In war, soldiers do not risk their lives to achieve government policy or follow orders; they put themselves in the line of fire because that is what is expected by their band of brothers. In *Cohesion: The Human Element in Combat*, Colonel William Darryl Henderson, who has taught military psychology at West Point, wrote: 'The only force on the battlefield strong enough to make a soldier advance under fire is his loyalty to a small group and the group's expectation that he will advance.'

If the need to fit in can persuade us to risk enemy fire, then maybe it can also help us overcome behaviour and biases that stand in the way of so many Slow Fixes. Peter Whybrow, the psychiatrist-cum-neuroscientist we met earlier, thinks so. 'We are self-interested and self-driving, but we are also social,' he says. 'If we can figure out how to engage our wish to be well regarded by others, we can start to offset the self-interest to give us a lever to pull for long-term thinking and solutions.'

One way to win that approval is through humility. When the people at the top admit to their own frailties, those further down feel more inclined to sign up to the fix on offer. By owning up to his error over the North Sea, Dicky Patounas inspired members of his squadron to admit their own. 'If they feel the top of the shop hasn't bought in, they're not interested because they're exposing themselves,' he says. 'That's why I make it known that I'm for it.'

Humility often means keeping open the channels of communication. There is nothing people like less than being kept in the dark, especially in times of crisis and change. That is why companies seem to survive restructuring better when management is open with the rank and file. In 2001 the telecom crash hammered Dallas-based Marlow Industries Inc., a producer of thermoelectric equipment for the high-tech industry. When orders fell off a cliff, the firm retrenched in a hurry, automating parts of its assembly line, shifting low-end production to China and slashing the payroll from 779 to 222. Those who remained agreed to a pay cut. Barry Nickerson, the company president, kept up morale by adopting the motto: 'Communicate. Communicate. Communicate.'

In monthly face-to-face meetings he explained to all his employees the thinking behind every piece of restructuring, how the overhaul was going, what was coming next and when full pay would be restored.

Like other Slow Fixers we have encountered, Nickerson anchored every reform in a long-term vision for the company, promising to establish the Dallas plant as a world-beating centre of high-end production, with China shouldering the low-end work. 'Every time we had a change we had a meeting to explain exactly what we were doing,' says Nickerson. 'We were very open with our employees about where we were financially. We would explain exactly the current status and where we were.'

Marlow Industries weathered the storm and bounced back stronger than ever. More than a decade later it is a global powerhouse in thermoelectric technology. The Dallas workforce has reached 1,100 and Nickerson remains at the helm.

Communicating with the troops is part of Sir Richard Branson's *modus operandi*. Like Peñalosa, the goateed, globe-trotting entrepreneur makes a point of being available to every employee in the Virgin Group. 'Great delivery also depends on great communication, which should start at the top,' he wrote recently. 'Be brave: hand out your e-mail address and phone number. Your employees will know not to misuse it or badger you, and by doing so you will be giving them a terrific psychological boost – they will know that they can contact you any time a problem comes up that requires your attention.'

Sometimes even the smallest emotional connection can have a dramatic effect. Studies in a range of fields show that groups solve problems better when members know one another's names. Hospitals where surgical teams introduce themselves before an operation – 'I am Sameena Tewari, the attending surgeon' … 'I am Rachel Jankowski, the operating room nurse' … 'I am the anaesthetist and my name is Paul Chang' – report that communication during surgery improves markedly, with everyone more inclined to point out problems and proffer solutions.

The lesson from every Slow Fix is to start communicating as soon as you have something to communicate. Green Dot learned that lesson the hard way. By failing to launch its charm offensive early enough, the charter-school chain allowed nay-sayers in Watts to poison local opinion against their plans for Locke. 'We should have got out there faster with our message,' says Ellen Lin, the school's business manager.

Learning to twiddle the emotional thermostat is certainly within everyone's grasp. Start by listening more. When discussing a problem, make it a rule not to interrupt when others are explaining their arguments. Pay attention not just to the words but to the emotions behind them. Be as open and honest as you can. Schedule enough time to forge bonds with the key players in your Slow Fix. Pay more attention to relationships in your private life and expose yourself to literature, music, nature, art – anything that helps tune your emotional antennae.

Remember, though, that the touchy-feely approach is not always enough. To break entrenched patterns of behaviour, you often need to jolt people into action. Long years in the private sector taught Marco Petruzzi that companies in free-fall are extremely hard to rescue – and those that do pull back usually start their recovery with a short, sharp shock to the system. 'Without that initial jolt, the inertia sets in and the blob eats you,' he says.

To create the right amount of shock and awe at Locke, Green Dot made sure all the elements of change – the uniforms, new teachers, grassy quad, repainting and repairs, beefed-up security – were in place from the very start. 'The idea was when the kids came back from that first summer everything would be different, so shockingly different that it captures their attention that it is a different world, that they need to act differently, behave, respond differently, and that more is asked of them,' says Petruzzi. 'Introducing that whole-sale new environment on Day 1 was what I really tried to bring from my knowledge of the business world.'

Walking through the gates on that first day, Lewis Price remembers feeling Locke was opening a new chapter for him and Watts. 'We figured the new Locke would be just like our community, a place where we gotta watch our back, that people go there to cause trouble or drop out, but on the first day we knew it was gonna be different,' he says. 'We came through the gates and they greeted us so friendly like we was family. The campus was all clean and nice and stuff and everybody was wearing the uniform.'

Did that really jolt Price and his buddies into a new mindset?

'Definitely. Everything *felt* different, so we knew we had to *be* different,' he says. 'It was kinda like a game – they made their move so we had to make ours.'

CHAPTER THIRTEEN

PLAY: Solving Problems
One Game at a Time

People rarely succeed unless they have
fun in what they are doing.
Dale Carnegie, author of
How to Win Friends and Influence People

What is the hardest problem in the world? Some would put climate change, poverty or terrorism at the top of the list. Others might opt for crime, racism or consumerism. In many homes, though, it sometimes feels like the thorniest problem facing mankind is housework.

It is not chores themselves that cause trouble. Dusting, vacuuming and polishing are all pretty straightforward: when was the last time you met someone taking a course in domestic cleaning? The real problem is finding a fair way to split the workload. Several waves into the feminist revolution, women are still doing the lion's share of household chores. A 2010 study in Spain found more than half of women in dual-income couples did all or most of the housework, with a third of men doing absolutely none. In Italy 70 per cent of men have never used a stove and 95 per cent have never operated a washing machine. Even in parts of the world where gender roles are less rigid, such as Scandinavia, men still do less than half the chores.

This causes friction. One study found that performing household chores can raise blood pressure more than work meetings in those who feel saddled with more than their share. In homes across the world, women chafe against the unequal distribution of labour. Chat forums thrum with the fury of the put-upon. On one parenting website, a Montreal mother using the moniker DomesticSlave tore into her family: 'They don't do ANY chores and it's driving me FUCKING crazy!' Is it any wonder studies show that the more housework a man does, the less likely his marriage is to end in divorce? The chore wars are even raging in families that can afford plenty of hired help. When Barack Obama ran for President of the United States in 2008, his wife chided him in public for dumping his dirty socks on the floor.

Does all this have a familiar ring? It certainly does to me. In our family, my wife is the one chiding. It's not that I don't help. I cook and make a big effort to keep the kitchen clean. I perform the home repairs and occasionally do the laundry. Even though I struggle with all those cushions, I often make the bed. But the truth is I could do more, starting with picking up my own dirty socks from the floor. Our children are not exactly pulling their weight, either. For everyone in our family, apart from my wife, the housework report card reads: Could Do Better.

Why don't I do more? The state of my office suggests that tidiness is less important to me. My desk is clogged with papers and notebooks and dotted with biscuit crumbs and stray bits of dried fruit. A sticky fork rests on a jar of home-made salad dressing. At my feet, a pile of sports equipment and unfolded clothes, in various states of cleanliness, nestles against the wall.

Though I know such bachelor pad anarchy is unacceptable at home, I still struggle to muster any enthusiasm for house-hold chores. Apart from cooking, I just don't enjoy them. Nor do I get a kick out of walking into a tidy room. My children feel the same way. My daughter once said to me: 'If housework is so important, why don't they invent a way to make it more fun?'

Well, in 2007 someone did. Chore Wars is an online game that turns housework into something you might actually want to do. To play, you form a virtual group made up of people who share the same real-world space – a household, say, or an office or social club. Each player chooses an avatar and then together you draw up a list of chores to be performed in return for prizes ranging from virtual gold to points that enhance your avatars. You can also assign real-world rewards in return for that digital treasure: a trip to the movies for the children, perhaps, or a foot massage for a partner.

Like all role-playing games, Chore Wars gives reality an epic and heroic twist. Chores are 'adventures'. Putting out the rubbish, for instance, might be described as 'removing toxic waste from the kingdom', while mopping up the melted snow on the porch might be called 'rolling back the flood waters from the gates'.

I know what you're thinking, because I thought the same thing. Lame, silly, childish. You can't make people love housework by turning it into a version of *Dungeons and Dragons*. Well, what do I know? Chore Wars has inspired housework-phobes around the world to reach for the mop and duster. Players report children springing out of bed to tidy their rooms and hang up the washing; colleagues sneaking into work early to do the dishes in the office kitchen; even students jostling for the right to scrub toilets in a hall of residence. Chore Warriors are stunned by their own damascene conversion to the joys of dusting, scouring and vacuuming. 'I've never seen my eight-year-old son make his bed,' exclaims one mother in Texas. 'I almost fainted when my husband cleaned out the toaster oven.'

I'm not crazy about spending more time sitting in front of a computer screen, but the endorsements for Chore Wars are too glowing to ignore. When I first mention the game to my children, I expect them to bristle and accuse me of trying to trick them into doing chores. But their reaction is the opposite. Even before I finish explaining the rules of the game, they start suggesting possible prizes – Moams, Skittles, Jelly Beans. Before I can say, 'I love it when a plan comes together,' they have whipped out a piece of paper and started designing their own avatars.

One lesson of this book is that inspiring us to do things we would not normally do often lies at the core of a Slow Fix. Recruiting people to solve their own problems is one way to achieve that. Remember how the VERSO scheme inspires children to broker their own peace deals in the playground conflicts of Finland. Another is to manage the

251

emotions like the organ donation system in Spain. The success of Chore Wars suggests gaming can have a similar effect, which brings us to the next ingredient of the Slow Fix: harnessing the human penchant for play.

The gaming instinct is hardwired into us. Long after play has helped build our brains in childhood, we carry on loving games, from *Scrabble* and *Sudoku* to charades and chess. Seventy years ago Johan Huizinga, a Dutch sociologist, identified play as a basic human need in his book *Homo Ludens*: 'Play cannot be denied,' he wrote. 'You can deny, if you like, nearly all abstractions: justice, beauty, truth, goodness, mind, God. You can deny seriousness, but not play.'

You certainly cannot deny that a gaming revolution is washing through our culture. Today, human beings rack up 3 billion hours playing video games every week. Screen-based games now earn more than movies and DVDs combined. To anyone over the age of 40 this can all seem slightly baffling. Older generations remember video games in their infancy: the monotonous bombardment in *Space Invaders* or the soporific rallies of *Pong*. Gaming has come a long way since then.

Today many games are dazzling, complex and hugely addictive. The stereotype of the gamer as a spotty teenaged boy blowing away zombies in a lonely bedroom no longer holds true. Many games now have a strong social component: think of *The Sims* or all those invitations you receive to water your friends' gardens in *Farmville*. The average age in the gaming community is now 30, and more than a quarter are over 50. Nearly half of gamers are female.

With four decades of fine-tuning behind them, game designers know all the psychological and neurological buttons to push to keep us fully engaged. In Chore Wars rewards for completing adventures are immediate, and you can always monitor how powerful and skilful your avatar becomes. That might sound trivial, but constant, measurable and incremental progress is precisely what the brain craves.

To persuade players to do things they normally don't want to do, Chore Wars favours the carrot over the stick. Each adventure yields different rewards, and players are free to decide which ones to tackle. This removes the sting of coercion and turns housework into a series of voluntary acts and creative strategising.

Chore Wars is also profoundly social. Players receive feedback from rivals, a thumbs-up for finally unblocking the gutters, say, or some good-natured ribbing for shunning the tougher adventures. As social animals, we like nothing better than interacting with other players in a game, especially when it delivers peer approval.

My wife is sceptical when I sign us up for Chore Wars. 'What is the point of turning housework into a game?' she asks. 'Why not just offer prizes or rewards for doing chores?' Our daughter sees the point right away: 'Because it's way more fun if it's a game,' she says.

After my wife opts out, the rest of us create a party called the Bennerley Band. My avatar is a bearded Peasant dressed like a Roman centurion. My son opts for a masked Enchanter with steely eyes. My daughter chooses a glamorous Ranger in a purple hood. We draw up a list of adventures, ranging from setting and clearing the table to pairing socks and making beds. We then assign the rewards. Completing an adventure earns a fixed number of experience points. But it also generates an unpredictable number of gold coins and the chance of winning a piece of treasure like a cloak of invisibility, potions or a sword.

That means you never quite know what your total reward will be, which is neurological catnip. Studies show that the brain releases feel-good dopamine when we achieve a goal, win a prize or score a victory. But it releases even more when the rewards are novel and uncertain, which is why gambling is so addictive. In games like Chore Wars, sweet but unpredictable triumphs flood the brain with dopamine and keep us coming back for more.

The Bennerley Band starts with a surge. The three of us fan out through the house to hunt down adventures. My son takes an armful of dirty clothes up to the laundry basket in the loft, while my daughter brings three empty loo rolls down to the recycling bin. Both firsts. At the same time I find myself neatly arranging all the shoes, boots and skates in the cloak area, another first. My fear that the novelty will wear off turns out to be misplaced. One evening, five days after we start, I overhear the children threatening to make each other's beds in the morning. A week into the game the front door opens and closes during breakfast. I wonder if someone is breaking in until my daughter enters the kitchen carrying the morning milk, earning herself 10 experience points, 24 pieces of gold and a dagger.

We decide that our coins and treasure can be turned into real-world goodies ranging from an iTunes song and an ice cream at the local gelateria to a ticket to see a Chelsea match. But it is clear the prizes are only part of the charm. We have also fallen for the game itself, the thrill and the pleasure of playing together, the rush that comes from nudging ahead of the competition or scoring an unexpected piece of treasure. My son sends me a text gloating that he has surpassed my gold coin total by tidying his room. Later, I catch myself logging on to the Chore Wars website at work to check the standings and plan my adventures for the evening. I have to confess that the first time the game awards me a piece of treasure out of the blue – a magic compass, as it happens – I punch the air. The clincher comes 10 days into the experiment, when my daughter corners me in the kitchen with a request that would have been unthinkable before Chore Wars: 'Please, please, please, can we pair socks together?'

That is why Chore Wars is just the tip of the iceberg. Around the world, schools find teaching through video games can spur children to tackle their homework with relish. Without any prompting, my daughter will fire up the kitchen computer to test her arithmetic against kids around the world in an online game called *Mathletics*. In 2010, when it emerged that British members of parliament had been fiddling their expenses on an epic scale, the media needed to raise an instant army of researchers to find further evidence of chicanery buried in nearly half a million pages of documents. How many outraged citizens would have volunteered to help if simply emailed the papers in a giant PDF? Exactly. Instead, the *Guardian* newspaper turned the hunt for dodgy expense claims into a Web-based game. Result: more than 30,000 people joined the race to unearth every last nugget of scandal in return for nothing more than the thrill of the game.

What motivates highly skilled programmers to devote hundreds of unpaid hours to those MATLAB competitions?

Certainly not the prospect of winning the grand prize, a MathWorks T-shirt. What drives them is the rush of the game, and the pleasure and kudos that come from playing well with their peers.

Gaming can even help us overcome the inertia that locks us into bad habits. Take the humble pedometer. Like true gamers, fans count their steps with a nerdy obsessiveness and compete, cheerlead and swap tips in vast online communities. As a result, the average pedometer user ends up walking 2,000 more steps per day. In 2011 residents living on a single street in Brighton, England, began recording their daily electricity use. With the help of a graffiti artist and a box of coloured chalk, they tracked their average consumption in a funky, gaming-style infographic running down the middle of their road. To get the competitive juices flowing, the display compared the street's energy use with that of other parts of Britain and beyond. The pressure was on for each resident to save more energy than the person next door, and for the street as a whole to out-green rivals around the world. Within weeks the street's average electricity consumption fell 15 per cent.

The medical world is also warming to the joys of gaming. One of the most vexing problems facing physicians, insurers and the pharmaceutical industry today is our refusal to follow the doctor's orders. Send us home with medication, and around half of us fail to take our pills as directed. In the US this 'non-compliance' leads to at least 125,000 preventable deaths and piles an extra $100 billion onto the nation's health-care bill.

Gaming may help change that. Many Type-1 diabetes sufferers, especially teenagers, fail to keep a close eye on their blood sugar levels, which determine how much insulin they need. After all, who wants to prick their finger with a glucose monitor at school four times a day? To get round this aversion, the Centre for Global eHealth Innovation in Toronto devised a smartphone app that gives the process a gaming twist. Each time teens check their blood they get an electronic pat on the back and win credits to spend in the iTunes store. Result: users increased their monitoring by 50 per cent.

When it comes to changing ingrained behaviour, one element of gaming shows special promise: feedback. Have you noticed the spread of those electronic signs that flash your current speed as you drive past? At first blush they seem utterly pointless. After all, the speedometer on your dashboard can tell you how fast you are driving. Nor are the signs backed up with coercion: there are no cameras, no cops hiding nearby with radar guns, no threat of a ticket or a fine. At most, you might be flashed to 'Slow Down'. Around the world, however, such signs are remarkably good at inspiring us to obey the speed limit. When flashed, drivers cut their speed by an average of 10 per cent – and carry on driving more slowly for several miles afterwards. One of these signs appeared recently near my home in London. It is fixed to a lamppost on a long, wide, straight road where I find it easy to drift above the speed limit without noticing. Actually, that's not quite true. Before the sign went up I knew when I was breaking the limit, and kept an eye out for police and cameras. But now, whenever the sign flashes, I ease my foot off the accelerator. Each time my speed falls closer to the legal limit I get a small thrill. When the sign tells me I have reached the magic 30 mph I feel a modest version of the same rush of accomplishment that keeps gamers welded to their seats for hours on end.

You could take that as evidence that I need to get out more. But the game I play with that electronic sign is a perfectly natural response to what psychologists call a feedback loop. Since the first cavemen started messing around with sticks and stones, we have been solving problems through trial and error. Fast, clear, regular feedback is at the core of that process: you need to know how you are doing *now* in order to work out how you can do better *later*. In other words, the human brain is wired to respond to the challenge implicit in those blinking Your Speed signs.

When you recycle bottles or newspapers, or take some old clothes to the charity shop, there is no feedback loop. Nobody tells you how much you slashed off your weekly carbon emissions, leaving you only a vague sense of having done the right thing. Contrast that with wearing a pedometer, which gives a running step-count in real time. Or with driving a Toyota Prius, whose dashboard tracks and displays your current mileage per gallon in increments of five minutes. Ease off the pedal, and the figure rises. Speed up or turn on the air-conditioning, and it falls. This is just the sort of feedback loop to transform a prosaic task into a personal challenge, a game even. Like users of pedometers, Prius owners go online to boast about their mileage per gallon and trade tips on how to improve it. Danny Hernandez, a restaurateur in San Francisco, hums the tune to the Queen song 'We Are the Champions' whenever his dashboard hits 60 miles per gallon. 'There's something about seeing that mileage number go up and knowing you made it happen that's kind of cool,' he says. 'It's actually turned me into a total mileage nerd.' It has also made him a better driver, solving a speeding problem he has had since his teens.

Not all feedback loops are created equal. Too subtle, and they dissolve into the white noise of daily life; too aggressive, and we filter them out. The secret lies in the middle ground with a signal that, like the Your Speed signs or the Prius dashboard, is noticeable but not overbearingly so. Whether persuading people to drive more slowly, take their pills, use less energy, stop smoking or eat more healthily, feedback loops tend to deliver around 10 per cent improvement in behaviour. Not earth-shaking, to be sure, but enough to earn a place in the toolbox of every Slow Fixer, which is why feedback plays a role in so many of the solutions we have already encountered. Remember pedestrians in Bogotá passing instant judgement on motorists by brandishing thumbs-up or thumbs-down cards and how the RAF telephones crew members who report a mistake or a near miss within 24 hours and then keeps them apprised of progress in the case.

A leading proponent of the push to harness gaming is Jane McGonigal, a thirty-something game designer based in San Francisco. Her book, *Reality Is Broken: Why Games Make Us Better and How They Can Change the World*, is a call to arms, a manifesto for how online games can help solve problems in the real world. Organisations ranging from the World Bank to the US Department of Defense to McDonald's beat a path to her door.

We meet in London. With her startlingly blue eyes and thick, curly blonde hair, and her black jeans, black T-shirt and cashmere arm warmers, she looks like a Silicon Valley take on the Pre-Raphaelite muse. She is a small bundle of crusading energy, the words pouring out of her like text on a stock-market ticker. As soon as we sit down she starts telling me how gaming can shift us into a problem-solving frame of mind.

'When we play games we feel like the best versions of ourselves. We feel so smart and capable and self-confident. We have all these allies who can help us solve our problems, and that makes us more likely to set really ambitious goals and stick with them, to be really resilient in the face of failure,' she says. 'It's a very special kind of energy. Spending the same amount of time watching TV doesn't make people jump off the sofa and want to save the world. Gaming actually puts us in a state of mind and a state of heart that makes us more likely to do something extraordinary in the real world.'

McGonigal goes further to explain why games can be a key ingredient of the Slow Fix. Not only can they inspire us to get up off the sofa and tackle challenges (and chores) we would normally duck, she says, they can also unleash the creative energy needed to come up with the best solutions. 'Games are all about solving problems,' McGonigal says. 'The best games teach us to start solving a problem before we know all the parameters; to explore a world, testing what different resources can do, interacting with systems just to figure out how they work; to be open to whatever challenge presents itself; to approach it with curiosity and equanimity; to be totally mindful of the environment and the big picture; to carry on making our best effort even when our first solutions don't work out; to have optimism and positive energy.'

This is not as fanciful as it sounds. Play can be a profound way to engage with the world and the self. Artists have always known that a playful mind can unlock the richest secrets. Picasso talked of remaining child-like in order to paint. Henri Matisse noted that 'a tremendous spirit of adventure and a love of play' is the hallmark of creative heavyweights. In science, too, a playful testing of the boundaries is often the first step towards the lightning bolts of genius that win Nobel prizes. Sir Isaac Newton once wrote that 'to myself I seem to have been only like a boy playing on the seashore, and diverting myself now and then finding a smoother pebble or a prettier shell than ordinary, while the great ocean of truth lay all undiscovered before me'. Albert Einstein put it more pithily: 'To stimulate creativity, one must develop the child-like inclination for play.' Steve Jobs's personal motto was: 'Stay hungry. Stay foolish.'

This makes neurological sense. The dopamine released during games not only makes us feel good, it also helps us concentrate and learn and fires up parts of the brain that govern creative thinking and problem-solving. In a physiological sense, McGonigal is right: gaming puts us in a Slow Fix frame of mind.

Of course, not all games make the most of our brains. Many offer little more than a rollercoaster of short-term thrills where the lonely pursuit of bonuses, rewards and high scores becomes an end in itself. But many others are like a training camp for the Slow Fix. Rather than pander with instant gratification, the most compelling games demand hours of intense effort and concentration. Gamers become experts in the art of trial and error, and keeping an open mind. Around 80 per cent of the time they fail to complete tasks – collecting treasure, for instance, or slaying a dragon – but they learn from their mistakes and come back for more. Eschewing the winner-take-all ethos, many leading games strike a balance between competition and collaboration, between working alone and working together. As soon as the latest version of a game hits the market, fans flock to the Web to compare notes and help each other play better. Games like Chore Wars work because players compete within the context of a shared mission rather than a beggar-thy-neighbour free-for-all. 'Competition is a healthy part of gaming, but not when it becomes cut-throat,' says McGonigal. 'That's why I always design my games so somebody else's failure doesn't benefit you and somebody else's success can benefit you. You don't want people diminishing each other; you want everyone striving to make everyone else better.'

We have already seen a sense of play at work in many Slow Fixes. Remember how Bogotá sent cheeky mimes into the street to help change the attitudes of motorists and pedestrians. Or how aid organisations can vie for Brilliant Failure Awards. The best solutions at Odyssey of the Mind blend serious thinking with playful performance. As McGonigal puts it: 'There is a continuum from fun to the Nobel prize.'

That is certainly how many gamers see it. In 2003, when the Organisation for Economic Cooperation and Development (OECD) tested the ability of 15-year-olds across the world to solve problems beyond the confines of the school curriculum, South Korea pretty much topped the table. Why? No one seems quite sure. With its emphasis on tests, punishingly long hours and rote learning, the South Korean education system is not famous for fostering creative thinking. Could the national obsession with computer games explain the result?

South Korea is the most wired country on Earth, and gaming is a national sport, with tournaments drawing thousands of spectators and live television coverage. Top gamers are household names, revered by fans and paid huge sums for endorsements. All that electronic play has a dark side, too. Several Koreans have died during marathon gaming sessions, and the government has set up a network of counselling centres and camps to help hard-core players overcome 'internet addiction'. But the gaming community points to evidence that long hours spent in virtual dungeons and online alien worlds are making Korean kids smarter – and better at solving problems.

To find out more, I head to Chuncheon City, 75 km northeast of the capital, Seoul. Even on a gloriously sunny day the video-game parlours that line the main street are doing a brisk trade. Zone and Zone is typical. Up a scruffy staircase, past posters of iconic games such as *Starcraft*, *Lineage* and *World of Warcraft*, the playing room is a fusty cave, with dim lighting and a persistent whiff of cigarettes and trainers. A large fridge by the door is stocked with bachelor pad staples: cartons of milk and cans of pop, chilled tea and juice. There is a kettle for making instant soup and a microwave for heating up pizzas. Rows of young people, mostly men, sit in padded armchairs, playing games on screens. Each berth has an electronic pager which allows gamers to summon a waitress without taking their eyes away from the screen.

Zone and Zone is open 24/7, and many customers play for days, napping in their chairs between games. The record stay is two weeks. 'They are a bit like zombies when they leave,' says one waitress.

But there is nothing zombie-like about these gamers when they play. On the contrary, they seem to fizz with ideas and ingenuity. I settle down to watch three friends playing *Mabinogi*, a complex fantasy game that involves fighting monsters and collecting treasure. Two have samurai warriors for avatars, the third plays as a raven-haired magician in a short skirt. As they enter a richly detailed virtual dungeon, a minotaur lunges from the shadows to attack. 'Let's take him out together and then worry about the others,' cries the first boy. His two mates join in the fight until the minotaur is felled in a heap of severed limbs. Then all hell breaks loose as an army of enemies, including polar bears and ogres, closes in. The sound of battle – steel on steel, explosions, yelps of pain – rings out. 'You take the one on the left,' barks the second boy to the first. 'I'll take these two, then come back to help you.' Without conferring, the third boy retreats from the fray, lobbing small cannonballs back into the mêlée. When one of the samurai finds himself pegged back by a huge red lizard, he asks the magician, 'Do you have any healing potion?' The response, delivered in a hurried whisper: 'Yes, but let's save it for a bigger enemy. Let's kill this one now together.' As he starts conjuring spells to help his wounded mate, he calls out, with a smile: 'And why are you such a wimp, anyway?'

The trio spend about 25 hours a week playing *Mabinogi* together at Zone and Zone. They have reached level 53 and hope to reach the top level of 70 within six months. It is how they unwind and have fun. Yet all three are convinced gaming is teaching them to solve problems better in the real world.

Dressed in the universal gamer uniform of jeans, T-shirt and trainers, Cho Hyun Tae has been gaming at least 20 hours a week since he was 12. Now 19, he controls the magician avatar, and seems the most reflective of the *Mabinogi* trio. 'From the moment you start playing any game, you can feel your brain going into problem-solving mode,' he tells me. 'Everything else goes quiet and you are totally focused. You have to figure out how the game works, how everything fits together, how to deal with the effects of your own actions, how to balance short-term wins with your long-term strategy. You forget about the clock and are completely in the moment. It's almost like a Zen thing.'

The boys are especially keen on the teamwork that drives so many Slow Fixes. They all study video production at a local university, and feel the hours spent playing together help them collaborate more creatively on their homework projects. 'In the game we're not really competing against each other, we're working together as a team because collaboration is key in problem-solving,' says Cho. 'Each member of the team has his own role, strengths, weaknesses, ideas and experience. Playing together teaches you to get along, and how to bring all those different talents together.'

One of the samurai, Ji Park, chimes in. 'In gaming, you also learn to put aside your ego,' he says. 'You speak up if you're in trouble, you admit your mistakes, you are always trying to learn and help your team-mates learn. The best gamer is a humble gamer.'

265

Cho nods vigorously in agreement. He takes a swig of milk from a carton, before returning to the theme. 'That is why it is never as easy or as comfortable playing with strangers,' he says. 'That's when you realise how well you know your team-mates and how shared experience and instant communication are key to your success.' Just like a Formula One pit crew.

Gaming can even help solve tricky scientific problems. *Foldit* is an online game where anyone can come up with new ways to bend complex strings of proteins into chemically stable three-dimensional shapes, the first step to developing new drugs. It has many of the standard accoutrements of gaming, including colourful graphics, zippy music, an ever-changing leader-board and plenty of collaboration. Though most of the 250,000 players have no previous experience of folding proteins, many have, through the game, discovered a knack for it, outperforming even the best algorithms. When researchers challenged gamers to solve 10 protein puzzles in direct competition with the finest Rosetta software, the gamers won five and drew three, with neither side coming close to cracking the remaining two. Scientists are now looking into ways to incorporate problem-solving techniques used by amateur *Foldit* players – such as assembling interim structures that are chemically unstable – into the Rosetta algorithms.

In 2011 *Foldit* fans made their first medical breakthrough by unlocking the structure of a protein essential for the replication of the HIV virus. Modelling the retroviral protease had stumped mainstream scientists for years; the *Foldit* gamers cracked the code within 10 days. Writing in *Nature Structural and Molecular Biology*, the scientists behind the game hailed the breakthrough as a landmark moment: 'Although much attention has recently been given to the potential of crowd-sourcing and game playing, this is the first instance we are aware of in which online gamers solved a longstanding scientific problem.' A few months later *Foldit* players scored another epic win by designing an entirely new protein from scratch.

Some now talk of a new Scientific Revolution powered by gaming. Nodding in that direction, *Nature* magazine bent its rules to include players in the list of authors for an article on the problem-solving virtues of *Foldit*. 'Our ultimate goal is to have ordinary people play the game and eventually be candidates for winning the Nobel Prize in biology, chemistry or medicine,' says Zoran Popovic, a professor of computer science and engineering at the University of Washington and one of the lead researchers on the *Foldit* project. 'We're hopefully going to change the way science is done, and who it's done by.'

McGonigal thinks science is just the beginning. In 2010, together with the World Bank Institute, she launched EVOKE, a game that encourages players to tackle social problems in the developing world. One week the mission might be to find a source of renewable energy for a village, the next to improve one person's access to food or clean water. Though it uses the same tropes that keep *Mabinogi* players glued to their seats for days on end – cool graphics, missions, rewards, levels, feedback – EVOKE is designed to minimise time on the keyboard. On average, its players spend five to six hours pursuing missions in the real world for every hour spent in front of a screen. 'We're trying to take ordinary people who feel like they don't have a positive role to play in big planetary-scale efforts and give them the sense that they can as individuals contribute to changing the world for the better,' says McGonigal.

But EVOKE is also an exercise in unearthing the diamonds in the rough, the John Harrisons of social enterprise. The best players are rewarded with grant money and mentorships with social innovators. 'We want to find the most gifted, brightest, most motivated people,' says McGonigal, 'and invest in their social capital, development and optimism because some of them could be Nobel prize winners one day.'

Though few us will ever design our own online games, we can all tap the gaming instinct. Make more time for playful activities in your private life. Take an improvisational comedy class, say, or hold a regular games night with friends or family. The next time a child asks you to join in some make-believe, get down on the floor and let your imagination run wild. If you cannot hire someone like McGonigal to turn your problem into a game, look for other ways to inject gaming tropes – humour, fun, competition, feedback – into your Slow Fix.

As a tool for tackling problems in the real world, games still have a long way to go. Yet designers are steadily refining their knowledge of what works and what does not. When it comes to graphics, narrative, user experience, colour palettes and community-management, each new game builds on the last. 'We are still in the Dark Ages in terms of what games can do, but we're getting better all the time,' says McGonigal. 'There's constant evolution.'

CHAPTER FOURTEEN

EVOLVE: Are We There Yet?

I have yet to see any problem, however complicated,
which, when you looked at it in the right way,
did not become still more complicated.

Poul Anderson

Marco Segovia first spotted the bug in his front room. It scurried out from under a sofa, traced a small arc on the mud floor, then darted back into hiding again. It looked like a cockroach or a beetle with yellow stripes.

Segovia is a farmer in San Felipe de Aconcagua, a hard-scrabble region nestled at the foot of the snowcapped Andean mountains in Chile. The landscape here is straight out of a spaghetti western – arid, rocky, studded with cacti and stubby trees. Overhead, condors float lazily across a Technicolor blue sky. Segovia raises chickens and goats and lives with his wife and two children in a small tin-roofed shack. Insects are common here, but that sighting in his front room set alarm bells ringing. 'Right away we knew we had a problem,' he says.

The bug he saw that day was a vinchuca, which transmits the most lethal parasite in the Americas. *Trypanosoma cruzi* was discovered in 1909 by the Brazilian doctor who gave his name to the disease it causes: Chagas. The parasite is of unknown provenance. Some say it first appeared in Bolivia and was later spread around the continent by the Incas or by European settlers. Others believe it has always existed throughout Latin America. What is clear is that the vinchuca is a stealthy assassin. It scampers up onto the face of its sleeping prey, perforates the skin with stylets and then sucks out enough blood to swell to several times its original size. This vampire-like gorging takes more than 20 minutes, causes no pain and seldom wakes the victim. Some refer to the vinchuca as the 'kissing bug', but it can be the kiss of death. As it feeds, the vinchuca expels faeces that sometimes carry *Trypanosoma cruzi*, which then worms its way into the victim's internal tissues and organs. About 10 per cent of people infected go on to develop full-blown Chagas Disease. Apart from swelling around the bite, early symptoms range from fever, vomiting and convulsions to shortness of breath and locking of the neck muscles. Sometimes the next stage is death by organ failure. But Chagas has a second, more sinister *modus operandi*. In many cases victims develop an unidentified swelling and then go on to lead an apparently healthy life – before dying of organ failure years later. Before I moved to South America in the 1990s my doctor gave me every vaccination in the book and a single piece of advice: never fall asleep on the floor of an adobe hut, the favoured hunting ground of the vinchuca. Some postulate that Charles Darwin was infected with Chagas during his seminal trip to South America in the early 19th century. Throughout his life he suffered from a cornucopia of symptoms, including muscle spasms, vomiting, eczema, tinnitus and colic, among others. He eventually died of cardiac failure. In a journal entry from 1835 he wrote of an incident that occurred in Argentina, on the other side of the Andes from the Segovias' farm: 'At night, I experienced an attack (for it deserves no less a name) of the Benchuca [sic], ... the great black bug of the Pampas. It is most disgusting to feel soft wingless insects, about an inch long, crawling over one's body. Before sucking they are quite thin but afterwards they become round and bloated with blood.'

Luckily, the Segovia family knew just how to dodge that bullet. They killed the vinchuca, put it in a small jar and sent it to be analysed in a lab in the capital, Santiago. Even though the bug was found to be free of the Chagas parasite, local health authorities sent a team to fumigate their house three times. 'We haven't seen another vinchuca around here since then,' says Segovia, who has a wiry frame and a wary smile. 'It's a big relief knowing we are safe in our beds now.'

Combating infectious diseases is one of the most pressing, and complex, problems facing mankind. Every year, malaria, tuberculosis, diarrhoea, HIV/AIDS and others kill 11 million people and ruin the health of millions more. Given those numbers, the temptation is to look for a quick fix, a wonder drug that will eradicate the disease in a flash, a pharmacological magic bullet. But if our journey so far has taught us anything, it is that solving the toughest problems takes time, patience and a lot of effort.

271

Chile has had more success than most in the battle against Chagas. At the start of the 1990s vinchucas were living in up to 18 per cent of the nation's homes, with the figure hitting 40 per cent in the worst-affected areas. Today, the average is nearer 0.1 per cent. The last confirmed case of a human infected with Chagas by a vinchuca there was in 1999.

Chile pulled this off by deploying many ingredients of the Slow Fix. Taking the holistic approach, it anchored the battle against Chagas in a broader effort to improve living standards. The vinchuca thrives in the dark corners of poor, rural homes. Building better housing, with electric lighting, drove many of the bugs away. Today most of the traditional adobe huts, whose cracked mud walls the vinchuca favour, are inhabited by livestock rather than by humans.

Everyone in Chile points to one charismatic engineer who for 22 years played a catalytic role in the battle against Chagas, but there has also been plenty of teamwork and collaboration. In 1991 the country joined with Brazil, Argentina, Bolivia, Paraguay, Peru and Uruguay in a joint effort across the Southern Cone to get rid of Chagas Disease. The seven nations have worked together to fumigate millions of homes and stop cross-border infestation. They created expert commissions that have developed a formidable database of knowledge, a robust culture of feedback and self-evaluation and a strong *esprit de corps*. These so-called *vinchuqueros* know their foe as well as Peter Hodgman knows his way round a Formula One car.

Chile also taps the crowd beyond the world of medicine. In remote regions, border police and mining companies spread the word about the vinchuca, and bring back bugs for testing. Chile also worked hard to sell its Slow Fix to the public. In infected regions medical officials speak regularly about Chagas on local TV and radio and hand out T-shirts, key rings and brochures at public events. Campaigning in schools turned children into a small army of bug-hunters.

Chile could teach the Burton boys a thing or two about sweating the small stuff. All donated blood in the country is screened for Chagas, as is every newborn in high-risk areas. Chile also takes a zero tolerance approach to the vinchuca. The sighting of a single bug causes the full apparatus of pest control to swing into action. A team arrives to spray the home three times, then returns three years later to spray again. Eduardo Astudillo, who has been fumigating residences in San Felipe de Aconcagua for two decades, sees the pay-off every day at work. 'We used to go into houses for routine inspections, peel back the walls, and find entire colonies of vinchuca living there,' he says. 'Now we never find the bugs during inspections. Instead, we get called out by a home-owner who has spotted maybe one bug on the floor. The threat now is very, very small.'

So, on arriving in Chile, I expect air-punching triumphal-ism from the health minister down. What I find is something altogether more sober: a steely pride in the progress made, teamed with grim warnings that the battle is not won, and maybe never will be.

There is still no vaccine against Chagas, and treatment remains expensive, unreliable and prone to side effects. Around 14,000 Latin Americans continue to die of the disease every year, and the vinchuca has proved a more resil-ient foe than expected. With detection rates now rising in

273

parts of Brazil and Bolivia, the yellow-striped bugs have started appearing in the homes of the well-to-do on the outskirts of Cancún, Mexico. Tourism and international migration have spread Chagas Disease so that 10 million people may now be infected worldwide, with more than 10,000 of those dying every year.

Back in Chile, the campaign against Chagas has lost some of its momentum. These days children in infected areas are more likely to hunt for friends on Facebook than for insects in the dark corners of their homes. Chilean politicians would rather talk about obesity, which draws more media attention and health funding. Twenty years after the Southern Cone initiative began, many people in Santiago have only a vague idea that Chagas remains a threat in the more far-flung corners of their country.

The net effect is lowered expectations. The original dream of completely eradicating both the vinchuca and Chagas has been shelved. Even eliminating the bugs completely from homes is starting to look over-ambitious. These days, health officials in Chile talk of 'controlling' infection by keeping vinchucas and humans as far apart as possible.

The shift is not surprising. The only disease mankind has ever eradicated is smallpox, which now exists only in test-tubes secreted away in Russia and the United States. Guinea worm disease and polio may one day follow, but eradication campaigns for four other infectious diseases – yellow fever, malaria, hookworm and yaws – have all fizzled out.

Dr Loreto Caldera, who oversees the fight against Chagas Disease in San Felipe, is not surprised by the resilience of the vinchuca. 'Insects are very good at surviving, and you cannot

274

make them disappear from nature,' she says. 'We have learned that we will never solve the problem of Chagas through eradication. Instead, we have to work out how to live with the problem, how to cohabit with the vinchucas and adopt behaviours that minimise their presence in our homes.'

This underlines perhaps the most vexing truth about the search for the Slow Fix: no matter how much planning, thinking, collaborating, crowdsourcing and testing you do, no matter how strenuously you empower, inspire and connect emotionally with the people around you, no matter how humbly you learn from your mistakes and near misses, no matter how much you sweat the small stuff or have fun along the way, the truth is that some problems can never be solved. At least not completely. They may demand sacrifices we are unwilling or unable to make.

Sixty-nine per cent of conflicts between couples stem from 'perpetual problems' that can never be fixed, according to Dr John Gottman, a leading researcher on the mechanics of relationships. You know the sort of thing: he finds it hard to express his feelings; she finds it hard to rein hers in; they don't see eye-to-eye on personal finances. When it comes to building a lasting marriage, Gottman's secret sauce is learning to live with those unsolvable differences, like Chile seeking a *modus vivendi* with the vinchuca.

Many of the big problems we face today may simply be too complex to fix. Can we ever really solve poverty? Or will the poor always be with us? Fixing a problem is also in the eye of the beholder. Can we all agree on what an end to poverty even looks like? Or what it would mean to 'solve' climate change? 'The greatest and most important problems

275

in life are all in a certain sense insoluble,' said Carl Jung. 'They can never be solved, but only outgrown.'

This is not a gospel of doom. It is just common sense. Solving complex problems permanently and to everyone's satisfaction is a herculean task, maybe even a fool's errand. Such problems are often messy, fluid and ill-defined. You can never control every variable or predict every outcome. Often, the mere act of tackling a problem, of putting your fix into action, can cause the parameters to shift, throwing up unintended consequences. When Bogotá barred a proportion of motorists from its downtown during rush hour, its streets were suddenly quieter, cleaner and less congested. And then the goalposts moved. Local drivers began circumventing the new regime by buying second or even third cars. Net result: Bogotá remains plagued by epic traffic jams. Even science, which trades in the hard currency of data and empirical truths, is an ever-shifting landscape of uncertainty. We are a long way from understanding, let alone solving, every scientific problem, and even our most cherished shibboleths can wobble. Ever since Einstein unveiled his Theory of Relativity, all of physics has rested on the idea that nothing can travel faster than the speed of light. And then along came the neutrino.

This does not mean we should give up trying to solve problems. On the contrary, the strides Chile has made against Chagas are a reminder that a partial solution is often much better than no solution at all. What's more, most fixes do not face a make-or-break deadline like the World Finals of Odyssey of the Mind. Instead, they muddle along in the real world. Like science itself, most of the Slow Fixes we have encountered are works in progress, subject to constant tweaking, refining and reinvention. Norsafe has set up a management team to monitor its transformation. 'The world is constantly changing, so our solution must adapt to keep up,' says owner Geir Skaala. You see the same spirit of evolution at Locke High School in Los Angeles. When it became clear some pupils were falling through the cracks, Green Dot created the Advanced Path academy. When the academy stumbled, it placed the less motivated children in a separate stream. 'We pride ourselves on being extremely on top of things, so when something isn't right, we don't wait, we go straight back in to start making changes,' says Marco Petruzzi, 'We are tinkering with the model all the time.'

To survive over the long term, even well-established solutions need to adapt. Take the organ transplant model in Spain. Twenty years ago 80 per cent of donors were victims of traffic accidents under the age of 30. Today, thanks to a revolution in road safety, 80 per cent of donors are over 40 and many enter hospital with a gamut of health problems, which means lower-calibre organs that are harder to harvest. At the same time, economic stagnation has pushed Spain's already high rate of youth unemployment over 40 per cent, turning many young Spaniards against the state. 'We are seeing more and more younger relatives saying "Don't come asking me for anything because I'm not going to donate the organs of my mum, my dad, my sister, of anyone",' says Dr Robles. 'Our economic problems have led to a loss of solidarity and an angry reaction against the entire system.' To keep pace with these shifting sands, Spain has stepped up efforts to have hospitals share tips on how to harvest organs and cope with recalcitrant relatives. An official Best Practices Guide for the transplant system is in the works. Health authorities have also ratcheted up publicity campaigns that target the young. 'No matter how much success you have, no solution is ever perfect or complete,' says Dr Robles. 'You have to keep on looking for ways to improve and adapt.'

That is why the final ingredient of the Slow Fix is evolution. That, of course, is the *modus operandi* of the best problem-solver in town: Mother Nature. In the natural world each mutation that occurs in a species is given just enough time to prove itself. Those that fail are swiftly discarded; those that represent a smart, long-term solution are quickly rolled out species-wide. The whole ecosystem then adjusts to absorb the knock-on effect of the change. And even then the adapting and tweaking carries on.

Almost every product we use in daily life is evolving. Think of how each new iteration of the MacBook or Xbox builds on the last, how every operating system, from Linux to Apple OS to Microsoft Windows, is a work in progress, how the content on Wikipedia is constantly scrutinised and massaged by an army of volunteers. Science itself advances in a similar fashion, constantly making, testing and reformulating hypotheses. With each experiment we gather some wheat and throw away the chaff. Even the humble toothbrush is in constant evolution. More than 5,000 years ago the Egyptians and Babylonians got the ball rolling by chewing on sticks to make the ends fibrous. The Chinese came up with a new, improved version in the 16th century by pasting the hairs of cold-climate pigs onto the ends of bamboo shoots and animal bones. The nylon bristles of the plastic brushes that hit the market in the 1930s have given way to complex cross-thatching designed to reach even the most awkward corners of the mouth. Last year I upgraded to an electric toothbrush, which no doubt will be superseded by something already taking shape in a laboratory somewhere.

The cornerstone of evolution is trial and error, which comes naturally to us. Think of how we learn to tie our shoes. Instructions from mum and dad are usually no more than the starting point. We really learn by folding the laces over and over, tying and unpicking knots, enduring days when our shoes are too loose or too tight, until we finally crack it. Practice trumps theory. How do we learn to play video games? Not by reading the rulebook or mapping out strategies in advance. We jump right into the game, testing, probing, learning from our mistakes, figuring out the rules and inventing solutions on the fly.

Of course, no one likes to think of surgeons, firefighters or airline pilots experimenting on the job. But the road to expertise is always paved with years of trial and error. You learn from mistakes in training so that you do not later make them on the job.

Smart businesses are certainly fluent in trial and error. From software to pharmacology to banking, the mantra of the best problem-solvers is 'Fail early and fail fast.' Venture capitalists expect many of the companies they invest in to crash and burn. When developing a new gadget, Apple makes multiple prototypes for every feature, which then compete in a marathon of survival-of-the-fittest tests. The last prototype standing is the one that makes it into your iPhone or iPad.

Others do their trial and error on end users. Governments, aid agencies and hospitals all test programmes in small-scale pilot projects. Every year, Capital One, a leading credit card company in the United States, conducts thousands of randomised tests on ideas for everything from marketing and product design to collection and cross-selling policies. Most of the experiments fail, but the net effect is plenty of useful learning. Whether redesigning a hospital wing or a marketing strategy, IDEO also favours testing ideas as a stepping stone to the best solution. 'We don't stay abstract for very long before sharing ideas to invite a response, reaction and learning,' says Jane Fulton Suri. 'We know we are going to build multiple prototypes and be wrong, but making things tangible and experiential early on in the process shapes our thinking and approach to the problem.' One of the five guiding principles of OpenIDEO is 'Always in Beta.' Always evolving, in other words.

What this implies is that tackling complex problems involves moments of not knowing for sure what you are doing, why you are doing it or what comes next. John Keats, the Romantic poet, said a man is on the road to achievement when he is 'capable of being in uncertainties, mysteries, doubts without any irritable reaching after fact and reason'. This is something you hear across the disciplines. Though scientists reach after fact and reason, they also pass through blurry patches in pursuit of empirical clarity. 'The most beautiful thing we can experience is the mysterious. It is the source of all true art and all science,' said Einstein. 'He to whom this emotion is a stranger, who can no longer pause to wonder and stand rapt in awe, is a good as dead: his eyes are closed.'

That is why our most innovative problem-solvers revel in those moments when the way forward is foggy and confused. At the start of an IDEO project, everyone tosses out ideas, and every idea, however outlandish, is turned into a sketch or a note that stays on the wall of the project room. 'There is always a great deal of divergence early on because we are having ideas, and those ideas are being collected but not judged right away or obsessed over,' says Fulton Suri. 'That means there is a lot of uncertainty, of "it could be this" or "it could be that".' IDEO also uses stories as a way to explore and assess ideas. 'People appreciate narrative on multiple levels, so it provides one way to resolve the tension between the desire for order and process and the need to preserve an important amount of woolliness and imprecision.'

Pausing in wonder and awe is also part of the job at Le Laboratoire in Paris. 'Sometimes you're surprised by what you come up with when you surrender to the uncertainty and just play with things,' says François Azambourg, the lead designer on the WikiCells project. 'You find a solution works that you weren't expecting to work. Or you stumble on another solution you had never thought of.' Let's put that another way: sometimes the process matters more than the final result, and the journey yields richer treasure than the destination. If that sounds a little airy-fairy, David Edwards would not have it any other way. 'Creators love it when nothing is sure, all is fluid, every idea has its own legitimacy and there is space to dream,' he says. 'When we tackle a problem at Le Labo, we don't know what the end will be, let alone exactly how to get there. We learn that along the way. The day our methodology is understood and clear is the day we lose our *raison d'être* and cease to exist because there are no easy recipes or magic formulae. Mystery is essential.'

Even the most data-driven companies understand that. Google famously encouraged its engineers to devote a fifth of their working hours to personal projects. No targets, no deadlines, no penalties for failure. On the contrary, this so-called '20 per cent time' was all about pursuing hunches, taking risks, making mistakes and learning from them – and often not quite knowing where you would end up. It was also about giving staff the autonomy that could unleash their problem-solving mojo. Though most projects came to nothing, many Google products, including home runs such as Gmail and Google News, were minted during that '20 per cent time'.

Let's be honest, though. Surrendering control, letting things happen, focusing on the process rather than the outcome – none of this comes easily in a culture in thrall to targets, timetables and test results. We like to line up our ducks and reduce everything to a flowchart or a PowerPoint slide. Show me the numbers, we cry. Even Google has been accused of curbing the freedom afforded by its '20 per cent time' programme. Yet the numbers seldom tell the whole story and are usually open to interpretation. Can you really reduce a child's learning to a test score? Or the economic health of a nation to the rating from a credit agency? Is 42 really the answer to the ultimate questions of life, the universe and everything? Of course not. The most sophisticated algorithm will never capture all the subjective and emotional dimensions of problem-solving. Even after a problem is fixed, we struggle to prove exactly why. Take the sharp fall in crime in New York over the last generation. Even after years of mining the data, academics still cannot agree on precisely why it happened. Was it caused by changes in policing techniques? Zero tolerance? Higher incarceration rates? Better race relations? Rising prosperity? A canny use of the broken window theory? Falling numbers of unwanted children after the legalisation of abortion in 1973? Was it some combination of all of these, or were there other, deeper trends or triggers that we have yet to spot? We will never know for sure. In a complex world, the only certainty is uncertainty.

That is why the best fixers seldom bet the farm on a single epic win. The way to navigate through a scenario of ever-changing parameters and possibilities, according to complexity theorists at the Santa Fe Institute in New Mexico, is to blend lots of baby steps with the occasional great leap forward. In other words, most problem-solving involves grinding out a lot of small victories over the long haul. As Henry T. Ford said: 'There are no big problems; there are just a lot of little problems.'

After spending years investigating how some companies make the jump to lasting success, Jim Collins reached the same conclusion. 'No matter how dramatic the end result, the good-to-great transformations never happened in one fell swoop,' he wrote. 'There was no single defining action, no grand programme, no one killer innovation, no solitary lucky break, no miracle moment. Rather, the process resembled relentlessly pushing a giant heavy flywheel in one direction, turn upon turn, building momentum until a point of breakthrough, and beyond.'

283

Advancing step by step is certainly the goal at Locke. In one staff room, teachers scrawl ideas and *aperçus* across several blackboards. One says: 'Don't look for the quick, big improvement.' Another reads: 'What small steps can I take to motivate?'

That is sage counsel for all of us. When tackling any complex problem, it pays to take an evolutionary approach. Test, test and test lots of ideas from the start, refining, recycling and reinventing them at every turn. Take copious notes but do not file them too neatly – ideas that seem unconnected now may later spark a creative breakthrough when serendipitously spotted side by side on a messy desk. Instead of promising the earth, make it clear that your Slow Fix may always be a work in progress. Above all, resist the pressure to declare victory and scale up too soon.

In our impatient world, everyone – governments, businesses, organisations – is on the hunt for a killer solution that can be copied and rolled out right now. But a fix that works wonders in one place may not fly in another, or may need adapting to make the leap. As a city with wide streets, dense population and a strong tradition of bus travel, Bogotá is the natural home for a bus rapid transit system like the TransMilenio. The same cannot be said for the old cities of Europe, which simply do not have the road space to accommodate enough dedicated bus lanes. In North America populations are spread too thinly to make BRT the backbone of local transport. Los Angeles has built a version of the TransMilenio, but one that complements its traditional rail network, eschewing enclosed stations and other hallmarks of the Bogotá system.

That is why Petruzzi resists pressure to roll out a Locke-style revolution across the US. He wants to get a couple more turnarounds working really well before scaling up nationwide. Another charter school group, Knowledge Is Power Program, spent six years fine-tuning its model in New York and Houston before rolling out across the United States. Today, KIPP runs over 100 schools and is still tinkering with its recipe.

'I'm not timid at all, I'm super growth-oriented, and I believe we can take what we're doing at Locke to a national level,' says Petruzzi. 'But it would be stupid to jump into that too soon. We will scale up when there is really good momentum and we're ready.'

Translation: never rush a Slow Fix.

CONCLUSION

Slow Fixing the Future

It's not that I'm so smart,
it's just that I stay with problems longer.
Albert Einstein

Japan had a problem in 1941. To continue its conquest of East Asia it needed to seize control of the oil and rubber reserves in British Malaya and the Dutch East Indies, yet feared that invading either would provoke Washington to declare war. Solution: a surprise attack on Pearl Harbor that would cripple the US naval fleet and scare the Americans away from further conflict. The Japanese were so sure of erasing the US military threat in one fell swoop that they did not even bother to bomb the oil-tank farms, navy yard or other war-making infrastructure at the port.

The raid on Pearl Harbor lives in infamy not only because it was a savage and sneaky attack on a nation not at war. It also failed spectacularly. Instead of retreating to lick its wounds, the US declared war on Japan the next day and Pearl Harbor became a staple of American propaganda. The war-making infrastructure left intact by the Japanese eventually proved vital in defeating them. As one of Japan's admirals noted later: 'We won a great tactical victory at Pearl Harbor and thereby lost the war.'

Falling for the quick fix, and paying the price, is nothing new. What has changed since Japan's historic blunder in 1941 is that the pressure and appetite for speedy solutions has grown exponentially. When it comes to tackling problems in any walk of life, we all yearn to score epic wins with a single blow. Yet despite scoring some tactical victories, we end up losing a lot of wars. Look at the damage wrought by half-baked fixes in our companies, schools and private lives, in politics, diplomacy and medicine. Or look at the state of the planet.

It need not be so. Even in our hurry-up culture, the quick fix is not mandatory. We can all choose to tackle problems thoroughly.

The good news is that the world is evolving in ways that bode well for the Slow Fix. We are now better educated than ever before. Technology has given us a formidable new toolbox for solving problems. Globalisation has shrunk the planet, making it easier to work together and share ideas. Even the way we entertain ourselves is moving in the right direction. Many hours once spent in front of the television are now poured into blogging, gaming or other online pursuits that work our cognitive muscles in ways that watching re-runs of *Friends* never could. The fierce urgency of the problems now facing mankind also helps focus minds. Even the economic

288

crisis that erupted in 2008 might turn out to have a silver lining: without the cash to splurge on the latest quick fix *du jour*, we have to be more critical and creative. Or as Ernest Rutherford, the father of nuclear physics, put it during a burst of austerity in the 1920s: 'We've got no money, so we've got to think.'

We are even starting to rewrite the capitalist rule-book. Britain and a half-dozen US states have changed corporate law to make it possible to create companies that put social goals ahead of profits, and several European countries are toying with similar legislation. Cooperatives are also infusing capitalism with the spirit of the Slow Fix by stressing collaboration and putting the long-term welfare of their members, the community and the environment ahead of making a fast buck. With global membership nearing 1 billion, co-ops now own half the renewable energy in Germany and are driving the push towards solar panels and other green initiatives in parts of the United States.

Soon we will even have a monument to the wisdom of thinking beyond the here and now. Inside a remote mountain in western Texas, activists are building a huge clock that is designed to tick for 10,000 years. Every so often its chimes will ring out a completely new melody. Jeff Bezos, the founder of Amazon, is helping bankroll the project to give the world what he calls 'an icon for long-term thinking'.

Against that backdrop, a Slow Movement is gaining momentum as more and more people challenge the canard that faster is always better. To take part, you don't have to ditch your career, toss the iPhone and join a commune. Living Slow is not about living like a snail. It means doing everything at the right speed – fast, slow or whatever pace delivers the best results. Many micro-movements are already thriving under the Slow umbrella: Slow Food, Slow Cities, Slow Work, Slow Sex, Slow Technology, Slow Education, Slow Parenting, Slow Design, Slow Travel, Slow Fashion, Slow Science, Slow Art.

Bottom line: even if it feels like everything is getting faster, we are, at the start of the 21st century, exquisitely placed to embed the Slow Fix at the core of our culture. To do so, however, we must tame our addiction to the quick fix. Given human biology, and the world we inhabit, this will not be easy, but there are ways to inoculate against the virus of hurry. Let's start by overhauling education so that children learn from the earliest years how to tackle problems patiently and thoroughly. Let's shake organisations out of their comfort zones by encouraging staff to take on fresh challenges.

Remember those pesky biases that steer us towards the quick fix? Even if we can never root them out, we may be able to curb their pernicious effect by calling attention to design flaws in the human brain. Daniel Kahneman believes that adding terms such as status-quo bias, legacy problem and Einstellung effect to our everyday vocabulary can make it easier to stop them warping our judgement. Studies show that simply highlighting the problem of racial bias in medicine can spur some doctors to treat black patients more equitably. Forewarned is forearmed.

When it comes to solving problems, there are things we can all do to short-circuit the quick-fix reflex. Emulate Toyota by asking why, why and why until the root cause of the problem is revealed. Cultivate what T.S. Eliot called the 'wisdom of humility' by forcing yourself to examine points of view that clash with your own. To make sure this happens daily, engineer a Clintonian moment when you open up a fresh line of enquiry by saying 'I was wrong' or 'I didn't know that'. Compile a list of your own quick fixes gone wrong and whisper it to yourself whenever you feel the temptation to reach for the duct tape. Ring-fence time in your schedule for slow thinking.

Use the people and stories in this book as touchstones, inspiration or cautionary tales. Remember how pilot Dicky Patounas makes flying Typhoon jets safer by airing his mistakes in public. How Geir Berthelsen rescued Norsafe by taking the time to analyse and understand the roots of its dysfunction. How Green Dot put Locke High School on the road to recovery by addressing its many failings holistically. How focusing on the long-term goal of rehabilitating prisoners delivers enviably low recidivism rates in Norway. How the rockers of Van Halen used M&Ms to focus minds on the small stuff. How David Edwards pulled together a multidisciplinary team to invent a new drinking vessel at Le Laboratoire. How Iceland is using crowdsourcing to reboot democracy. How Enrique Peñalosa played a catalytic role in the transformation of Bogotá. How Ricardo Pérez became a better coffee farmer by taking charge of his own business. How Dr Juan Carlos Robles uses his heart as well as his head to persuade Spanish families to donate the organs of their loved ones. How Chile tackled Chagas Disease by adjusting its campaign to fit changing circumstances. How games like *Chore Wars* and *Foldit* and designers like Jane McGonigal are harnessing the play instinct to solve problems.

Remind the critics – and yourself – that the Slow Fix is always a smart investment. Put in the effort now, and save time and money later. Recall how Green Dot is now running Locke more cheaply than before. How dedication to their craft allows Formula One engineers to solve problems with breathtaking speed. How mathematicians collaborating in the Polymath Project found a new proof for the Hales-Jewett theorem in just six weeks.

Yet the best way to beat the quick-fix addiction is with a deeper, seismic change. What is the point of solving problems better if our lives remain a never-ending dash to the finishing line? To master the Slow Fix we need to live at a more reasonable pace. That means giving every moment the time and attention it deserves. Instead of fretting over the trivial concerns that loom so large in a life of hurry – Where are my keys? When will this traffic start moving? Why is this lift taking so long? – we can begin to confront the genuinely Big Questions: What is my purpose? What sort of world do I want to leave behind? And how can we all change course to get there? If the Earth is going to sustain 8, 9 or even 10 billion people, we need a revolution in the way we live, work, travel, consume – and think. Making that happen will be the biggest Slow Fix of all.

Time for a confession. When I began this journey, part of me hoped that putting lots of smart solutions under the microscope would yield a skeleton key to unlock every problem. Follow the recipe, do this, do that, do the other, and a Slow Fix will be yours. That did not happen for one obvious reason: a universal, step-by-step formula runs counter to the spirit of the Slow Fix. If we have learned anything over the preceding pages, it is that solving complex problems is a messy business – and mindlessly ticking boxes is a sure sign of falling into the quick fix. As IDEO's Jane Fulton Suri says, 'You don't arrive at a solution by just following steps on a checklist.'

That does not mean it hurts to have a recipe – as long as you use it in the right spirit. Think of baking bread. Following a recipe to the very last gram and fluid ounce never guarantees the best loaf. Flour, water, yeast, salt, sugar, ovens and atmospheric conditions vary, so the best bakers adapt and tweak as they go, adding a little more of this here, a bit less of that there. The same goes for tackling complex problems such as global poverty, a failing marriage or the Middle East peace process. The secret lies in finding the right blend of ingredients from the Slow Fix recipe.

Let's recap those ingredients. When taking on any complex problem, take the time to: admit mistakes; work out what is really going wrong; sweat the small stuff, think long and join the dots to build holistic solutions; seek ideas from everywhere, work with others and share the credit; build up expertise while remaining sceptical of experts; think alone and together; tap emotions; enlist a catalytic figure; consult and even recruit those closest to the problem; turn the search for a fix into a game; have fun, follow hunches, adapt, use trial and error, embrace uncertainty. When circumstances demand a quick fix, by all means deliver a quick fix, but never let it stand untested. Come back later, when time permits, to forge a more lasting solution. And whatever the time constraints, always distrust fixes that look too good to be true, because they usually are. H.L. Mencken hit the nail on the head when he warned: 'There is always an easy solution to every human problem – neat, plausible, and wrong.'

Yet the Slow Fix does get easier with experience. What you learn forging one solution can often be applied to similar problems elsewhere. All those years studying urban renewal and shaping the transformation of Bogotá have turned Enrique Peñalosa into a globetrotting Florence Nightingale for failing cities. 'I'm now like a doctor who can just look at the patient's colour and know what he's suffering from,' he says. 'I can drive through a city and just looking out the window I can tell you what is going wrong with it and what you have to do to make it right.'

Slow Fix know-how can also travel from one sphere to another. Having used *Foldit* to transform novices into experts in manipulating proteins, Zoran Popovic now builds games that can conjure similar magic beyond the laboratory. 'What excites us the most is that we can apply the same expertise development in society at large,' he says. 'We are currently working on expert-developing games to solve the key problems in education, health, and even in climate change and politics.'

Applying the Slow Fix at work can also change how you tackle problems at home. Are Hoeidal describes himself as a 'slow thinker' away from Halden prison. 'In my private life, I set goals in the long term, and then work slowly to reach them,' he says. '"One brick at a time" – that's my way to do things.' One manager at Norsafe now uses Geir Berthelsen's pause-to-think approach at home. When a feud between her daughter and partner came to a head recently, everyone in the household gathered round the kitchen table to thrash out what was going wrong. 'As a family, we needed to have a big argument with tears, but we also needed to pull the Andon rope and take time to understand why we were yelling and crying and to work out a solution,' she says. They did just that, and harmony was restored. 'It was quite cool to see this work-to-home connection for the Slow Fix.'

Following a similar vector, Ashley Good felt emboldened to take more risks in her personal life after setting up the *AdmittingFailure.com* website. She took up rock-climbing, triathlons and painting. She also became a little more humble. 'The real personal change is more subtle and day-to-day in nature,' she says. 'It is now somehow so much easier to admit my mistakes and weaknesses and take responsibility even when 100 per cent honesty presents a risk. Now I find myself accepting the limits of my own knowledge and assumptions, and in doing so build the possibility that I am wrong in to whatever opinion I present.'

Each of us will come to the Slow Fix in our own way. You might start by using the lessons in this book to tackle a problem at work or in your community. You may begin thinking differently about renewable energy or urban poverty, and lean on your elected representatives to do the same. Or you might begin closer to home, by applying a Slow Fix to your health or relationships. My guess is that once you start taking the time to solve problems well in one sphere, the same spirit will begin to percolate through everything you do.

How about me? After years of undercooked, half-arsed efforts, I have finally brought the Slow Fix to bear on my lifelong battle with back pain. The starting point was admitting that the get-well-fast approach was never going to work.

Facing up to all the time, money and effort I have wasted over the years was harder than it sounds but it helped clear the slate. Once the *mea culpa* was out of the way, I was able to think long and hard about what treatment would suit me best, which involved reading the scientific papers behind the headlines and canvassing opinion from experts and fellow sufferers. After weighing up the evidence, I decided that regular yoga was my best bet. I had dabbled in yoga before, but buying classes in advance helped solidify my commitment. Now, even on mornings when saluting the sun is the last thing on my wish-list, I make myself go. I also find time to attend drop-in classes when travelling.

Taking the holistic approach, I let yoga seep into the rest of my life. I now do hatha stretches before and after sports, and monitor my posture throughout the day, bending my body into asanas whenever the muscles feel tight or clenched, and sometimes even when they don't. That does not mean busting out the downward dog on the tube. It does, however, mean bringing more awareness to how I stand, sit and walk.

Is it working? Like every Slow Fix, mending my back with yoga is a work in progress. There have been mishaps along the way. After three months, I pushed too hard into a stretch and strained my groin so much I could hardly walk for a week. The quick fix habit dies hard.

Yet there is real progress. The next time the teacher asked us to perform the same groin stretch, I sank into it with caution, limbering up the muscles without injuring them. My back feels better than it has in years. I am more flexible, can sit comfortably for longer and have not felt any pain in my legs for over a year. My back is still a long way from perfect, and maybe it will never get there. Perhaps, like Chile with Chagas or those couples with 'perpetual problems', the best I can hope for is to find a *modus vivendi* with lumbar pain. But for now the prognosis is good: for the first time since my late teens I feel like I'm on the road to recovery.

Even the demanding Dr Woo is pleased. When I return to the clinic for a shiatsu massage, he is sitting at Reception, waiting for his next acupuncture patient. 'Where have you been?' he asks. 'It is a long time since you were last here.'

I tell him about the yoga, and how my back is improving. He nods slowly, and smiles.

'Yoga is very good for the body,' he says. 'I can see you are moving more freely now.'

A nervy silence descends. By not giving acupuncture a real chance, I feel I have let Dr Woo down. He senses my discomfort and tosses me a lifeline.

'It's OK, I am happy your back is getting better,' he says, placing an avuncular hand on my shoulder. 'But please promise me one thing: this time, you will not lose patience and give up too soon.'

His words contain a gentle admonishment, but they no longer sting – and that speaks volumes. When it comes to mending my back, the quick fix is now a fading memory. After years of piss-poor performance, I now have a long-term plan for healing, and I am sticking to it. No longer an impatient patient, I can finally look Dr Woo in the eye.

'Don't worry, I've learned my lesson,' I tell him. 'You were right: there are some things you can't fix in a hurry.'

And this time, at long last, I actually mean it.

Notes

Introduction: Pulling the Andon Rope

Average Briton pops 40,000 pills in lifetime: From research
carried out by Pharmacopoeia for its 2003 exhibition, 'Cradle
to Grave', at the British Museum.

Dieters usually regain weight: Traci Mann, Janet A. Tomiyama and
others, 'Medicare's Search for Effective Obesity Treatments:
Diets Are Not the Answer', *American Psychologist*, Volume 62,
Number 3 (April 2007), pp. 220–23.

Fat returns after liposuction: Teri L. Hernandez, John M. Kittelson
and others, 'Fat Redistribution Following Suction Lipectomy:
Defense of Body Fat and Patterns of Restoration', *Obesity*,
Volume 19 (2011), pp. 1388–95.

Nearly two million Americans abuse prescription drugs: From the
2010 National Survey on Drug Use and Health from the
Office of Applied Studies.

More than a million hospitalised every year: From a 2009 report
by the National Institute on Drug Abuse (NIDA).

New York City linked teacher pay to pupil performance: From *A Big Apple for Educators*, a 2011 report from Rand Corporation.

Downsizing is negative: Franco Gandolfi, 'Unravelling Downsizing – What Do We Know about the Phenomenon?', *Review of International Comparative Management*, Volume 10, Issue 3 (July 2009).

Football management as a revolving door: Annual figures compiled in 2012 by Sue Bridgewater of Warwick Business School for the League Managers Association.

Inside 40 hours: From the Apollo Lunar Service Journal at http://www.hq.nasa.gov/alsj/a13/a13.summary.html.

NASA spent thousands of man-hours: From the *Apollo 13 Mission Review, Hearing Before the Committee on Aeronautical and Space Sciences*, United States Senate, Ninety-First Congress, Second Session, 30 June 1970.

Chapter 1 – Why the Quick Fix?

Side salad illusion: Alexander Chernev, 'The Dieter's Paradox', *Journal of Consumer Psychology*, Volume 21, Number 2 (2011), pp. 178–83.

Many deny terminal illness: Paul Rousseau, 'Death Denial', *Journal of Clinical Oncology*, Volume 21, Number 9S (1 May 2003), pp. 52–3.

Thabo Mbeki AIDS link to HIV: Pride Chigwedere, George R. Seag, Sofia Gruskin, Tun-Hou Lee and M. Essex, 'Estimating the Lost Benefits of Antiretroviral Drug Use in South Africa', *Journal of Acquired Immune Deficiency Syndromes*, Volume 49, Issue 4 (December 2008), pp. 410–15.

Average tenure for a global CEO has fallen: Booz & Company's annual study of turnover of among chief executives, Issue 63, Summer 2011.

Half workday spent managing email and social media: Adrian Ott, 'How Social Media Has Changed the Workplace', *Fast Company*, 11 November 2010.

Public likes fast decision: Interview with Daniel Kahneman on BBC radio's *The Forum*, broadcast 20 November 2011.

11-year-olds building 'personal brand': From a 2011 study by AXA.

Chapter 2 – Confess: The Magic of Mistakes and the *Mea Culpa*

Typical air accident seven errors: From 'A Review of Flightcrew-Involved Major Accidents of US Air Carriers, 1978 Through 1990', a Safety Study published in 1994 by the US National Transportation Safety Board.

Nearly half of financial services firms do not rescue floundering projects: From a 2011 report by the Economist Intelligence Unit entitled 'Proactive response – How mature financial services firms deal with troubled projects'.

Climbing corporate ladder by concealing bad news: James Surowiecki, *The Wisdom of Crowds* (New York: Anchor, 2004), p. 205.

Four of every five products perish in first year: James Surowiecki, *The Wisdom of Crowds* (New York: Anchor, 2004), p. 218.

Domino's television commercials: Full details of the campaign available at http://www.pizzaturnaround.com/.

Fedex apologises: Blog post and video apology at http://blog.fedex.designcdt.com/absolutely-positively-unacceptable

Soothing effect of apology: M.C. Whited, A.L. Wheat *et al*, 'The Influence of Forgiveness and Apology on Cardiovascular Reactivity and Recovery in Response to Mental Stress', *Journal*

of Behavioral Medicine, Volume 33, Number 4 (August 2010), pp. 293–304.

Apology would stop nearly 40 per cent of malpractice patients from filing lawsuit: Virgil Van Dusen and Alan Spies, 'Professional Apology: Dilemma or Opportunity?' *American Journal of Pharmaceutical Education*, Volume 67, Issue 4, Article 114 (2003).

Barry Manilow T-shirt experiment: Thomas and Gilovich, Victoria Medvec Husted, 'The Spotlight Effect in Social Judgment: An Egocentric Bias in Estimates of the Salience of One's Own Actions and Appearance', *Journal of Personality and Social Psychology*, Volume 78, Number 2 (2000), pp. 211–22.

Chapter 3 – Think Hard: Reculer Pour Mieux Sauter

Doctors interrupt after 23 seconds: John M. Travaline, Robert Ruchinskas, Gilbert E. D'Alonzo Jr, 'Patient–Physician Communication: Why and How', *Journal of the American Osteopathic Association*, Volume 105, Number 1 (1 January 2005).

Slashed accident rate by 47 per cent: From 'Councils urged to cut street clutter', a press release from the UK Department of Transport, 26 August 2010.

Richer thinking when calm and free from stress: Guy Claxton, *Hare Brain, Tortoise Mind: Why Intelligence Increases When You Think Less* (London: Fourth Estate, 1997), pp. 76–7.

Lone police officers more cautious: Scott H. Decker and Allen E. Wagner, 'The Impact of Patrol Staffing on Police–Citizen Injuries and Dispositions', *Journal of Criminal Justice*, Volume 10, Issue 5 (1982), pp. 375–82. And also Carlene Wilson, 'Research on One- and Two-Person Patrols: Distinguishing Fact from

Fiction', Australian National Police Research Unit Report
Number 94 (July 1990).

Slight pause makes us more ethical: Brian Gunia, L. Wang *et al*,
'Contemplation and Conversation: Subtle Influences on Moral
Decision Making', *Academy of Management Journal*, Volume 55,
Number 1 (2012), pp. 13–33.

Chapter 4 – Think Holistic: Joining the Dots

10 per cent of US high schools produce nearly half the dropouts:
'Turning Around the Dropout Factories: Increasing the High
School Graduation Rate,' a 2012 report from the US
Department of Education.

For every dollar spent on new technology: Based on research by
Erik Brynjolfsson, a productivity expert at the Massachusetts
Institute of Technology's Sloan School of Management.

Chapter 5 – Think Long: Tackling Tomorrow Today

Recidivism rates in Norway, etc: William Lee Adams, 'Sentenced to
Serving the Good Life in Norway', *Time*, 12 July 2010; Bouke
Wartna and Laura Nijssen, 'National Reconviction Rates:
Making International Comparisons', *Criminology in Europe*,
Volume 5, Number 3 (December 2006), p. 14.

Prisoners who maintain strong family bonds less likely to reoffend:
M. Berg and B.M. Huebner, 'Reentry and the Ties that Bind:
An Examination of Social Ties, Employment, and Recidivism',
Justice Quarterly, Volume 28, Issue 2 (2010).

Higher welfare spending linked to lower incarceration rates: David
Downes and Kirsten Hansen, 'Welfare and punishment: The
relationship between welfare spending and imprisonment',

report by the Crime and Society Foundation, King's College London (November 2006).

Companies obsessed with quarterly earnings grow less: Daniel Pink, *Drive: The Surprising Truth about What Motivates Us* (London: Canongate, 2010), p. 57.

Sears mechanics invented repairs: Marianne M. Jennings, *Business Ethics, Case Studies and Selected Readings*, Sixth Edition (South-Western College, 2009), p. 505.

Money like cocaine: Hans Breiter, Itzhak Aharon *et al*, 'Functional Imaging of Neural Responses to Expectancy and Experience of Monetary Gains and Losses,' *Neuron*, Volume 30 (May 2001), pp. 619–39.

Short-term financial incentives damage the long-term performance: Research published in June 2009 by Bernd Irlenbusch at the London School of Economics Department of Management.

Artists less creative on commission: Daniel Pink *Drive: The Surprising Truth about What Motivates Us* (London: Canongate, 2010), p. 45.

Chapter 6 – Think Small: Devil in the Details

Steinway built 482 pianos: From the official Steinway & Sons website: http://www.steinway.com/about/history/.

Flaubert and Madame Bovary: Brigid Grauman, 'Madame Bovary Goes Interactive', *Prospect*, 4 May 2009.

Steve Jobs burns through nurses, oxygen masks and title bars: Malcolm Gladwell, 'The Tweaker – The Real Genius of Steve Jobs', *New Yorker*, 14 November 2011.

Poor spend heavily on lighting: Robert Bacon *et al*, 'Expenditure of Low-Income Households on Energy', *Extractive Industries for Development*, Series 16, World Bank, 16 June 2010.

Women musicians sounded better behind screens: Claudia Goldin and Cecilia Rouse, 'Orchestrating Impartiality: The Impact of "Blind" Auditions on Female Musicians', *American Economic Review*, Volume 90, Number 4 (September 2000), pp. 715–41.

Broken window theory and effects of graffiti: Kees Keizer, Siegwart Lindenberg and Linda Steg, 'The Spreading of Disorder', *Science 12*, Volume 322, Number 5908 (December 2008), pp. 1681–5.

John Wooden and basketball socks: Atul Gawande, 'Top Athletes and Singers Have Coaches. Should You?', *New Yorker*, 3 October 2011.

Van Halen and the M&Ms: Jacob Ganz, 'The Truth about Van Halen and Those Brown M&Ms', NPR's *The Record* (February 2012).

Cleared for Takeoff: Based on interview with Dr J. Terrance Davis, the Associate Chief Medical Officer who launched the programme at the Nationwide Children's Hospital.

Chapter 7 – Prepare: Ready for Anything

Art experts spotted fake sculpture: Malcolm Gladwell, *Blink: The Power of Thinking without Thinking* (London: Allen Lane, 2006), pp. 4–8.

Psychologist predicted couples who would later divorce: Gladwell, *Blink*, pp. 18–23.

Thin-slicing can happen in seconds, milliseconds, or a few minutes: Frank Partnoy, *Wait: The Useful Art of Procrastination* (London: Profile, 2012), pp. 88–9.

Wall Street traders excel at war games: Gladwell, *Blink*, p. 108.

Nearly three-quarters of accidents on first flight together: From the US National Transportation Safety Board.

Grand Master chess players make right moves at high speed: Gary Klein, *Sources of Power: How People Make Decisions* (Cambridge, MA: MIT Press, 1999), p. 163.

80 per cent of fire captains decide within one minute: Klein, *Sources of Power*, p. 4.

Autopsy reports showed doctors wrong 40 per cent of time: Jessica Leavitt and Fred Leavitt, *Improving Medical Outcomes: The Psychology of Doctor-Patient Visits* (New York: Rowman & Littlefield, 2011), p. 103.

Algorithms beat 284 experts: Philip Tetlock, *Expert Political Judgement: How Good Is It? How Can We Know?* (New Jersey: Princeton University Press, 2005).

Green-lighting fewer applicants on rainy days: Donald A. Redelmeier and Simon D. Baxter, 'Rainy Weather and Medical School Admission Interviews', *Canadian Medical Association Journal*, Volume 181, Number 12 (8 December 2009).

Judges grant parole more after eating: Leva, Danziger and Avnaim-Pesso, 'Extraneous Factors in Judicial Decisions', *Proceedings of the National Academy of Sciences*, Volume 108, Number 17 (2011), pp. 6889–92.

Witnesses more accurate in police line-ups when choosing quickly: 'Unusual Suspects – How to Make Witnesses More Reliable', *Economist*, 3 March 2012.

Faster heartbeat activates biases and bad decisions: Gladwell, *Blink*, p. 225.

Chapter 8 – Collaborate: Two Heads Are Better Than One

Nobel science laureates more artistic: Michele and Robert Root-Bernstein, 'A Missing Piece in the Economic Stimulus:

Hobbling Arts Hobbles Innovation', *Psychology Today*, 11 February 2009.

Matt Ridley on connections and creativity: Matt Ridley, 'From Phoenecia to Hayek to the "Cloud"', *Wall Street Journal*, 24 September 2011.

More creative solving others' problems: Evan Polman and Kyle J. Emich, 'Decisions for Others Are More Creative than Decisions for the Self,' *Personality and Social Psychology Bulletin*, Volume 37, Number 4 (February 2011), pp. 492–501.

Talmud scholars distrust unanimous verdicts: Ivan L. Tillem, *The Jewish Directory and Almanac*, Volume 1 (New York: Pacific Press, 1984), p. 221.

Too much internal competition hurts creativity: Bill Breen, 'The 6 Myths of Creativity', *Fast Company*, 19 December 2007.

White paper from MIT: Phillip A. Sharp, Charles L. Cooney *et al.* 'The Third Revolution: The Convergence of the Life Sciences, Physical Sciences, and Engineering' (Washington: MIT, 2011).

Teamwork surged in science: Stefan Wuchty, Benjamin F. Jones and Brian Uzzi, 'The Increasing Dominance of Teams in Production of Knowledge', *Sciencexpress*, 12 April 2007.

Analysis of 35,000 papers: Lee, Kyungjoon, Isaac S. Kohane *et al*, 'Does Collocation Inform the Impact of Collaboration?', *Public Library of Science ONE*, Volume 5, Number 12 (2010).

Isaac Kohane quote: Jonah Lehrer, 'Groupthink: The Brainstorming Myth', *New Yorker*, 30 January 2012.

Chapter 9 – Crowdsource: The Wisdom of the Masses

Wutbürger as German word of the year: Full list available from German Language Society at http://www.gfds.de/aktionen/wort-des-jahres/

Guessing the weight of an ox: James Surowiecki, *The Wisdom of Crowds* (New York: Random, 2005), pp. xii–xiii.

Pinpointing vessel lost at sea: Surowiecki, *The Wisdom of Crowds*, pp. xx–xxi.

Public identifies Mars craters: Surowiecki, *The Wisdom of Crowds*, p. 276.

Diversity Trumps Ability Theorem: Based on my interview with Scott Page.

John Harrison: For the whole story check out Dava Sobel, *Longitude: The True Story of a Lone Genius Who Solved the Greatest Scientific Problem of His Time* (London: Fourth Estate, 1998).

Teenager invents method for detecting pancreatic cancer: Jake Andraka won first place at the 2012 Intel International Science and Engineering Fair (Intel ISEF), a programme of the Society for Science and the Public.

IBM idea jams: From the company website at https://www.collaborationjam.com/

Netflix offers $1 million prize: 'Innovation Prizes – And the Winner Is', *Economist*, 5 August 2010.

Fiat builds first crowdsourced car: 'The Case for Letting Customers Design Your Products', *Inc. Magazine*, 20 September 2011.

Prototype military vehicle crowdsourced: Based on interview with Ariel Ferreira of Local Motors.

Steve Jobs on designing without focus groups: From interview in *Business Week*, 25 May 1998.

Consultants compared 600 programmers across 92 companies: Based on the 'Coding War Games' study by Tom DeMarco and Timothy Lister.

Open-plan offices make us anxious, hostile, etc: Susan Cain, 'The Rise of the New Groupthink', *New York Times*, 13 January 2012.

Chapter 10 – Catalyse: First among Equals

Rising emissions from traffic: From the *Environmental Outlook to 2030 Summary* (OECD, 2008).

Bicycle use rocketed: From a case study by the Danish Architecture Centre's Sustainable Cities project.

Traffic deaths nosedived: Jon Cohen, 'Calming Traffic on Bogotá's Killing Streets', *Science*, Volume 319, Number 8 (February 2008), pp. 742–3.

Air quality along BRT corridors: Alasdair Cain, Georges Darido *et al*, 'Applicability of Bogotá's TransMilenio BRT System to the United States', Federal Transit Administration (May 2006) pp. 24–5.

Powerful people stop listening and make bad decisions: Kelly E. See, Elizabeth Wolfe Morrison, Naomi B. Rothman and Jack B. Soll, 'The Detrimental Effects of Power on Confidence, Advice Taking, and Accuracy', *Organizational Behavior and Human Decision Processes*, Volume 116, Number 2 (November 2011).

Daniel Goleman's findings on emotional intelligence: 'What Makes a Leader?', *Harvard Business Review*, January 2004.

Google study on best managers: Adam Bryant, 'Google's Quest to Build a Better Boss', *New York Times*, 12 March 2011.

Ernest Shackleton's story: Alfred Lansing, *Endurance: Shackleton's Incredible Voyage to the Antarctic* (London: Phoenix, 2000).

Chapter 11 – Devolve: Self-Help (in a Good Way)

Starbucks' Schultz accuses speculators: Debarati Roy, 'Coffee Speculation Inflates Price, Hurts Demand, Starbucks Says', *Bloomberg*, 18 March 2011.

Demes solved local problems in Ancient Greece: James Surowiecki, *The Wisdom of Crowds* (New York: Random, 2005), p. 71.

Subsidiarity and Catholicism: Don Fier, 'The Principle of Subsidiarity and the "Welfare State"', at CatholicCulture.org.

Staff-owned companies more resilient and productive: From 'Model Growth: Do Employee-Owned Businesses Deliver Sustainable Performance?', a 2010 report by Cass Business School for John Lewis Group.

Research showing people work better when they feel ownership: Surowiecki, *The Wisdom of Crowds*, p. 210.

Nurses at Georgetown University Hospital: V. Dion Haynes, 'What Nurses Want', *Washington Post*, 13 September 2008.

Empowering staff at SAS: From Jan Carlzan, *Moments of Truth, New Strategies for Today's Customer-Driven Economy* (New York: Harper & Row, 1989).

Toyota workers learn factory process from start to finish: James P. Womack, Daniel T. Jones and Daniel Roos, *The Machine That Changed the World: The Story of Lean Production* (New York: HarperCollins, 1991).

Experiment with noise-cancelling button: Surowiecki, *The Wisdom of Crowds*, p. 212.

Failed fish-freezing plant: 'Kenya's Turkana learns from Failed Fish Project', *Reuters*, April 2006.

310

Bolsa Familia: Full World Bank report at http://web.worldbank.
org/WBSITE/EXTERNAL/NEWS/0,,contentMDK:214470
54~pagePK:64257043~piPK:437376~theSitePK:4607,00.html
Cash with no conditions in An Loc: Rowena Humphreys,
'Periodical Review of the Cash Transfers for Development
Project', *Oxfam Great Britain in Viet Nam*, December 2008.
99 per cent of KIVA borrowers pay back: Figures supplied by
KIVA up to July 2012 were 98.98 per cent repayment for
$245,905,375 in ended loans.
VERSO statistics in Finland: Supplied by Maija Gellin.

Chapter 12 – Feel: Twiddling the Emotional Thermostat

Disengaging emotionally hurts productivity: James K. Harter and
Frank L. Schmidt, 'Causal Impact of Employee Work
Perceptions on the Bottom Line of Organizations', *Perspectives
on Psychological Science*, Volume 5, Number 4 (July 2010), pp.
378–89.
Image of human eyes boosts honesty: Melissa Bateson, Daniel
Nettle and Gilbert Roberts, 'Cues of being watched enhance
cooperation in a real-world setting', *Biology Letters*, Volume 2
(2006), pp. 412–14.
Band of brothers: William Darryl Henderson, *Cohesion: The
Human Element in Combat* (Washington, DC: National Defense
University Press, 1985), pp. 22–3.
Sir Richard Branson on great delivery: From column in
Entrepreneur, 20 April 2011.
Knowing names helps teams: Atul Gawande, *The Checklist
Manifesto: How to Get Things Right* (London: Profile, 2010),
p. 108.

Happy staff more creative: Bill Breen, 'The 6 Myths of Creativity', *Fast Company*, 19 December 2007.

Chapter 13 – Play: Solving Problems One Game at a Time

Spanish housework study: Salomí Goñi-Legaz, Andrea Ollo-López and Alberto Bayo-Moriones, 'The Division of Household Labour in Spanish Dual Earner Couples: Testing Three Theories', *Sex Roles*, Volume 63, Numbers 7–8 (2010), pp. 515–29.

Household chores raise blood pressure: Rebecca C. Thurston, Andrew Sherwood *et al*, 'Household Responsibilities, Income, and Ambulatory Blood Pressure Among Working Men and Women', *Psychosomatic Medicine*, Volume 73, Number 2 (February/March 2011), pp. 200–205.

Doing housework reduces men's risk of divorce: Wendy Sigle-Rushton, 'Men's Unpaid Work and Divorce: Reassessing Specialization and Trade in British Families', *Feminist Economics*, Volume 16, Number 2 (2010), pp. 1–26.

Three billion hours gaming per week: Jane McGonigal, *Reality Is Broken: Why Games Make Us Better and How They Can Transform the World* (New York: Penguin, 2011), p. 6.

Age and gender of gamers: Based on 2012 figures from Entertainment Software Association.

Guardian expenses scandal game: See latest figures at http://mps-expenses.guardian.co.uk/

Pedometer users walk more: Dena M. Bravata, Crystal Smith-Spangler *et al*, 'Using Pedometers to Increase Physical Activity and Improve Health – A Systematic Review', *Journal of the American Medical Association*, Volume 298, Number 19 (2007).

Street in Brighton cuts electricity use: Full report on the Tidy
Street project at http://www.changeproject.info/projects.html
Medical non-compliance: 'Adherence to Long-Term Therapies',
World Bank report (2003). Lars Osterberg and Terrence
Blaschke, 'Drug Therapy: Adherence to Medication',
New England Journal of Medicine, Volume 353, Number 5
(2005), p. 488.
Feedback loops improve behaviour by 10 per cent: Thomas Goetz,
'Harnessing the Power of Feedback Loops', *Wired*, 19 June
2011.
Gamers fail 80 per cent of time: McGonigal, *Reality is Broken*, p. 63.
South Korean 15-year-olds excel at problem-solving: From 2003
OECD report entitled 'Problem Solving for Tomorrow's World
– First Measures of Cross-Curricular Competencies from
PISA'.

Chapter 14 – Evolve: Are We There Yet?

Vinchucas living in 18 per cent of homes: All facts and figures
about Chagas Disease based on documents and comments
supplied by Alonso Parra Garcés, Head of Vector Control in
the Environmental Health Department at Chile's Ministry of
Health.
10 million may be infected with Chagas worldwide: All
international figures from Pedro Albajar Viñas, the expert on
Chagas at the World Health Organisation in Geneva.
69 per cent of relationship problems are perpetual: Explored by
John Gottman in *The Seven Principles for Making Marriage Work*
(London: Orion, 2007).
Constant testing by Capital One: Charles Fishman, 'This Is a
Marketing Revolution', *Fast Company*, 30 April 1999.

Google accused of curbing 20 per cent time: David Goldman, 'Ex-Google Employee says Google+ Has Ruined the Company', *CNNMoney Tech*, 14 March 2012.

Blend baby steps with great leaps: Tim Harford, 'Positive Black Swans', *Slate*, 17 May 2011.

Conclusion: Slow Fixing the Future

Cooperative membership hits 1 billion: From report by Gary Gardner for the Worldwatch Institute.

Clock will tick for 10,000 years: More details at http://longnow. org/clock/

Slow Movement gaining momentum: Explored in Carl Honoré, *In Praise of Slow* (London: Orion, 2004). Also visit www. carlhonore.com and www.slowplanet.com.

Racial bias in doctors: Frank Partnoy. *Wait: The Useful Art of Procastination* (London: Profile, 2012), pp. 99–100.

Resource List

I read many books, blogs, articles and academic papers for my research into the art of problem-solving. Here are some that stood out.

Butler-Bowdon, Tom. *Never Too Late To Be Great: The Power of Thinking Long*. London: Virgin Books, 2012.

Cain, Susan. *Quiet: The Power of Introverts in a World That Can't Stop Talking*. London: Viking, 2012.

Chang, Richard Y. and Kelly, Keith. *Step-By-Step Problem Solving: A Practical Guide to Ensure Problems Get (And Stay) Solved*. Irvine: Richard Chang Associates, 1993.

Collins, Jim. *Good to Great: Why Some Companies Make the Leap ... and Others Don't*. London: Random House, 2001.

Collins, Jim. *Good to Great and the Social Sectors*. London: Random House, 2006.

Edwards, David. *Artscience: Creativity in the Post-Google Generation*. Cambridge, MA: Harvard University Press, 2008.

Edwards, David. *The Lab: Creativity and Culture.* Cambridge, MA: Harvard University Press, 2010.

Fraenkel, Peter. *Sync Your Relationship: Save Your Marriage.* New York: Palgrave MacMillan, 2011.

Gawande, Atul. *The Checklist Manifesto: How to Get Things Right.* London: Profile, 2010.

Gladwell, Malcolm. *Blink: The Power of Thinking without Thinking.* London: Allen Lane, 2006.

Gladwell, Malcolm. *Outliers: The Story of Success.* London: Allen Lane, 2008.

Heath, Chip and Dan. *Made to Stick: Why Some Ideas Survive and Others Die.* New York: Random House, 2007.

Hewitt, Ben. *The Town That Food Saved: How One Community Found Vitality in Local Food.* New York: Rodale, 2009.

Howe, Jeff. *Crowdsourcing: How the Power of the Crowd Is Driving the Future of Business.* London: Random House, 2008.

Johnson, Steven. *Where Good Ideas Come From: The Natural History of Innovation.* London: Allen Lane, 2010.

Jones, Morgan D. *The Thinker's Toolkit: 14 Powerful Techniques for Problem Solving.* New York: Three Rivers Press, 1995.

Kay, John. *Obliquity: Why Our Goals Are Best Achieved Indirectly.* London: Profile, 2010.

Kay, John. *The Hare and The Tortoise: An Informal Guide to Business Strategy.* London: Erasmus, 2010.

Klein, Gary. *Sources of Power: How People Make Decisions.* Cambridge, MA: MIT Press, 1999.

McGonigal, Jane. *Reality Is Broken: Why Games Make Us Better and How They Can Transform the World.* New York: Penguin, 2011.

Micklus, Dr Sam. *The Spirit of Creativity.* Sewell: Creative Competitions, 2006.

Neustadt, Richard E. and May, Ernest R. *Thinking in Time: The Uses of History for Decision Makers*. New York: Free Press, 1986.

Partnoy, Frank. *Wait: The Useful Art of Procrastination*. London: Profile, 2012.

Pink, Daniel. *Drive: The Surprising Truth about What Motivates Us*. London: Canongate, 2010.

Roam, Dan. *The Back of the Napkin: Solving Problems and Selling Ideas with Pictures*. London: Marshall Cavendish, 2009.

Robertson, Ian S. *Problem Solving*. Hove: Psychology Press, 2001.

Ridley, Matt. *The Rational Optimist*. London: Fourth Estate, 2010.

Rosenberg, Tina. *Join the Club: How Peer Pressure Can Transform the World*. New York: W.W. Norton & Company, 2011.

Schulz, Kathryn. *Being Wrong: Adventures in the Margin of Error*. London: Portobello, 2010.

Shirky, Clay. *Here Comes Everybody: How Change Happens When People Come Together*. London: Allen Lane, 2008.

Silard, Anthony. *The Connection: Link Your Deepest Passion, Purpose and Actions to Make a Difference in the World*. New York: Atria Books/Beyond Words, 2012.

Steel, Dr Piers. *The Procrastination Equation: How to Stop Putting Things Off and Start Getting Things Done*. Harlow: Pearson Education, 2011.

Surowiecki, James. *The Wisdom of Crowds*. New York: Anchor, 2004.

Thaler, Richard H. and Sunstein, Carl R. *Nudge: Improving Decisions about Health, Wealth and Happiness*. London: Penguin, 2008.

Watanabe, Ken. *Problem Solving 101: A Simple Book for Smart People*. New York: Penguin, 2009.

Whybrow, Peter. *American Mania: When More Is Not Enough*. London: W.W. Norton & Company, 2005.

Acknowledgements

This was a hard book to write, and I leaned heavily on many people.

As always, my agent, Patrick Walsh, got the ball rolling with his usual blend of charm, wisdom and commercial acumen. I was blessed with a wonderful team of editors whose patience, imagination and rigour were a godsend: Jamie Joseph and Iain MacGregor at HarperCollins UK, Gideon Weil at HarperOne San Francisco and Craig Pyette at Random House Canada. A big thank you also to my copy-editors, Steve Dobell and Diana Stirpe, who helped with the fine-tuning.

I am grateful to my early readers, including Annette Kramer, Peter Spencer, Jane McGonigal, Anthony Silard, Geir Berthelsen and Benjamin Myers, whose input helped shape the book. A special thanks to my old friend Thomas Bergbusch for raking through the manuscript with a fine-toothed comb. He has a rare knack for driving me nuts while also forcing me to sharpen my thinking.

I was especially lucky to persuade Cordelia Newlin de Rojas to ride shotgun with me. She is the perfect researcher: bright, cogent, meticulous, connected, tenacious, clear-eyed, creative and quick to see the funny side of things. She was also a sharp but generous early reader. When we couldn't face talking about the Slow Fix any more, we talked about food. This book would not be the same without her.

Of course, there would be no book at all without the many people around the world who spoke to me for my research. A heartfelt thanks to each and every one of them for taking the time to share their stories and insights – and for putting up with my relentless follow-up questions and fact-checking. Even those not named in the book added vital pieces to the puzzle. I am also indebted to the many people who helped arrange interviews and visits around the world. Special gratitude to Douglas Weston, Henry Mann, María Teresa Latorre, Alonso Parra and Park Yong-Chui.

I also wish to thank my parents for helping to knock the book into shape. My mother is a sage of syntax and grammar, and it is her voice I hear every time I reach for the keyboard. As ever, though, my deepest thanks go to Miranda France, la fille qui m'accompagne.

Index

321